Phil Harrison's grasp of the Twelve Step
with a different addiction, I found eacl
insights and clear explanations were very
to *anyone* who hungers and thirsts after gr
The result will be a renewal of your pr
Christ, which will enable you to remain addiction-free.

—Joy S.

I am most impressed with this book and can really relate to it. There is something about what Phil Harrison says and how he says it that totally captivates me. I feel that this book is something the Lord wants me to know and will be of eternal value to me and my family. God bless you, Phil, for your sharing!

—B.C.

Clean Hands, Pure Heart is one of the most straightforward and truthful books I have ever read. It is deeply moving and spiritual. It is written sensitively and with great care for the tender feelings of all who may read it. Its principles can be applied to any addiction, compulsive addictive behavior or "bad habit" we may struggle with in this mortality. The same principles can help the loved ones of an addicted person just as well. I was deeply touched and changed by Phil's description of our common need for Christ's healing power. He has helped me to face the truth that my own addiction to overspending is a form of "lust," as it is based on greed, not gratitude, and leads a person into bondage, not freedom.

I've tried many therapies for my own addiction, but have found only one permanent solution—the one described so powerfully in this book. Christ is the Master Physician, therapist and healer. His miracle awaits. His gifts are only waiting for us to rejoice in them more than in the things of the world. Our gratitude will open them to us. I was most impressed by the depth of Phil's chapters on making amends, something most of us skim over.

There are many modalities of healing out there today which call "lo here, lo there," but Christ gives the only true and lasting healing as portrayed in *Clean Hands, Pure Heart*. The gospel principles in this book will lead a person not only to repent and find forgiveness but to also find a remission of their sins.

—C. D.

If you've tried and failed time and time again to overcome a sexual struggle, you may have begun to wonder whether there is a way out. Perhaps you've even begun to doubt that God could possibly still love or forgive you. Well, get ready for some really good news! In *Clean Hands, Pure Heart*, Phil Harrison describes a reliable, step-by-step route out of the hell of addiction. This is a landmark volume because Phil not only teaches the Twelve Steps, he shows us exactly how we can use them to keep relying on the Lord and thereby regain our freedom, sanity, and serenity. Thank you, Phil, for your courage, your faith, and for sharing this hard-won map with the rest of us!

—Mark Chamberlain, Ph.D., Clinical Psychologist
author of *Wanting More* and coauthor of *Willpower Is Not Enough*

Any person could learn a great deal from this book. It is more than a book about sexual addiction. It is a book that teaches all of us how to have a closer relationship with Jesus Christ. I can see it being helpful to seminary teachers as well as bishops, addicts, and parents of teens having problems. People with other addictions, such as food addictions, could also find it helpful. I was especially appreciative of Phil's use of the scriptures and quotations from General Authorities. I look forward to having this book as a source of reference that I can use with other people.

I recommend reading the Preface. It is an indispensable introduction to the author's intent, and you feel the spirit that he has. In Chapter One he briefly relates his experience and in the balance of the book explains his journey to implement the Twelve Step program as he works to "come unto Christ."

—JoAnn Hibbert Hamilton
author of *To Strengthen the Family* and founder of the organization "Citizens for Families"

To all the hundreds of men and women who have been encouraged by my Steven Cramer books, but felt the need for a more practical, step-by-step, how-do-I-make-it-happen guide, here at last is the book we have all been waiting for. If I could only recommend one book to someone struggling with addiction, this is the book I would choose. The sexual addictions I describe in *The Worth of Every Soul* would never have lasted thirty years if someone had taught me the principles and the process explained so masterfully in *Clean Hands, Pure Heart*. How I wish Phil Harrison had been born fifty years sooner!

The scriptures tell us the Lord delights in plainness. All our lives we've heard how simple the gospel is. But it doesn't seem simple or plain when an overpowering addiction has us tangled in defeat and shame and we can't seem to make the principles work for us. In my opinion, this book illustrates the path to recovery so plainly, so understandably and convincingly that one cannot wait to throw away the shackles and start anew on the road to recovery, confident that, this time, the changes will be permanent.

As one who was addicted to pornography for over thirty years, and as one who has been blessed to experience the new birth and mighty change of heart that can only come from the Savior, I've been writing about the recovery and the healing process for over twenty years. After eight books of my own, I am thrilled to share my opinion that no one has explained it better or made it more believable than Phil Harrison in this book. If you are yearning to be free of addiction, sin and guilt, if you are yearning for peace and to feel right with yourself, your loved ones and your Lord, please read, study, digest, trust and apply the principles you will discover in this book.

Beyond the scriptures, there is no book that can save you or give you freedom, victory and cleanliness, for only the Lord can do that. But *Clean Hands, Pure Heart*, better than any other book I've read, can help us set aside our doubts and fears, help us to open the door to our heart and make it possible for the Savior to enter and work his miracles within us.

—Steven A. Cramer
author of *The Worth of a Soul, Great Shall Be Your Joy, Putting On the Armor of God, Conquering Your Own Goliaths, In the Arms of His Love, In His Image, Draw Near Unto Me,* and *The Worth of Every Soul*

Philip A. Harrison, a recovering pornography addict, has produced a remarkable document entitled *Clean Hands, Pure Heart: Overcoming Addiction to Pornography through the Redeeming Power of Jesus Christ.* This is a Twelve-Step workbook which makes use of LDS scriptures and sources to guide the reader through a journey of healing. It is highly readable, doctrinally on target, and therapeutically sound. This could be very useful for group as well as individual use.

I really like the way Philip Harrison communicates and personalizes things. It makes it so easy for the reader to walk in his shoes and identify with all of the challenges that he had to face. I also liked the way he makes use of scriptures and the "word of God" to lead the reader through the Twelve Steps in a doctrinally correct way.

I have a number of areas that I feel I have some considerable competence in as I treat people with sex addiction problems. I went to each of these areas in *Clean Hands, Pure Heart* to see how he handled them, and with every one I felt that he was on solid ground therapeutically. He didn't exaggerate or go beyond what we know. I found him again and again hitting the bull's-eye with correct and useful information.

—Victor B. Cline, Ph.D., Licensed Clinical Psychologist,
Professor Emeritus, Dept. Of Psychology, University of Utah

Clean Hands, Pure Heart

Overcoming Addiction to Pornography through the Redeeming Power of Jesus Christ

Philip A. Harrison

WINDHAVEN
PUBLISHING & PRODUCTIONS
RECOVERY MATERIALS FOR THE LDS COMMUNITY
PLEASANT GROVE, UTAH

Windhaven Recovery, Inc. dba

WINDHAVEN
PUBLISHING & PRODUCTIONS
RECOVERY MATERIALS FOR THE LDS COMMUNITY

PO BOX 282
PLEASANT GROVE, UT 84062
WWW.WINDHAVENPUBLISHING.COM

Cover Art: "The Lord Is My Shepherd", ©2001 Simon Dewey. Used with permission.
Design & Typesetting: Professional Pre-Press, Pleasant Grove, Utah.

This book is designed to provide you with information on Twelve Step recovery so that you can deal more effectively with compulsive/addictive behaviors in yourself or in those you love. However, results from applying these principles will vary with the individual. As a result, this book is sold with the understanding that neither the author nor the publisher is engaged in rendering specific psychotherapy or other professional counseling services to any individual.

ACKNOWLEDGMENTS

My first acknowledgment must go to my first wife, Kathy Francis Harrison, who introduced me to the principles of the Twelve Steps, and showed me how beautifully they correspond to the principles of the gospel, especially faith and repentance. Kathy showed me through her life's example the efficacy of these principles. Furthermore, when I finally admitted my need for help with my own addiction, she graciously stood by me in spite of the pain I caused her. I wish I had the space in this book to share the tender story of how, just five months after introducing me to the recovery program that would save my life, Kathy silently laid down her own burden of mortality. After decades of bravely carrying on her struggle with a damaged heart, including two open-heart surgeries and countless doctor visits, it was finally enough. I wish I could also share with you the miracle of how, from the other side of the veil, Kathy played such a powerful role in my subsequent marriage to Colleen, who had been such a friend and mentor to us both in the months before Kathy's passing. It is a story worth telling, but it will have to wait for another time.

Next I want to thank my current wife, Colleen. She has been the most influential teacher I have known in all my life. Both through her testimony in *He Did Deliver Me from Bondage* and in person, she taught Kathy and me how to establish a closer relationship with the Lord Jesus Christ, which opened the way for my release from the addiction that had plagued me for most of my life. Colleen not only helped me learn the principles I have recorded in this book, she also stood by me as I continued learning to apply them in my own life. In addition to the help she has given me in my own recovery, she, as a most able and thorough editor, also helped me write this book. Her gift for the flow of language and ideas has made this a much more readable book than it would have otherwise been. If you enjoy reading *Clean Hands, Pure Heart*, as I sincerely hope you will, thank Colleen next time you see her.

Many others have read *Clean Hands, Pure Heart* in manuscript form and have offered helpful suggestions which have found their way into this book. I particularly want to thank Darla Isackson, Cheryl Day, Joy Stubbs and Karlene Browning for their editing assistance, as well as Karlene for her expert and beautiful typesetting.

I also want to thank the brave souls who have both preceded me and joined me in Twelve Step recovery, especially through Heart t' Heart and Sexaholics Anonymous. Their written testimonies, their example and fellowship, gave me the courage to believe recovery was possible. Their encouragement along the way has helped me stay the course. Since the quest for recovery doesn't end with attaining sobriety, I also thank these same friends for their support and love in the future as I continue to be strengthened by associating with them.

My most profound gratitude is reserved for the one individual without whom there would be nothing to write about: my Lord and Savior, Jesus Christ. He has indeed rescued me from a hell of my own making and has made me clean once more. He has done this with such love and tenderness that I am moved to tears just to think of Him. He has become more than my Savior—He has become my very best Friend. Without Him I am nothing.

TABLE OF CONTENTS

The Words I would say. By: Sidewalk Prophets

HOW TO USE THIS BOOK AS A STUDY GUIDE

I make no secret of the fact that I have patterned this book after *He Did Deliver Me from Bondage,* by Colleen C. Harrison. I hope this book can be used in the same ways her book is used, to help others come unto Christ and receive relief from addiction and other problems. If *Clean Hands, Pure Heart* reaches even a fraction of the number of people who have been blessed by *He Did Deliver Me,* I will be immensely grateful. In the same spirit that *He Did Deliver Me* has been applied, I suggest *Clean Hands, Pure Heart* may be used in the following ways:

First: In a personal recovery program by individuals seeking recovery from addiction to pornography or other sexual addictions.

Second: As a study guide for classes supervised by priesthood leaders in wards or stakes, or by professionals in a counseling setting. Covering one chapter each week, the class would run for 17 weeks.

Third: As study materials to be used in LDS Twelve Step groups. *Clean Hands, Pure Heart* has been designated as "Approved Literature" by Heart t' Heart. Specific helps for Twelve Step meetings, including a sample meeting format, are included in Appendix C.

Fourth: As a reference guide for those seeking a greater understanding of sexual addiction, including spouses and other loved ones of addicts, priesthood leaders and professional counselors.

Fifth: By anyone who wishes to develop a closer, more personal and life-changing relationship with our Lord and Savior, Jesus Christ. I pray that my experiences may help you on this same journey, whatever your personal challenges may be.

PREFACE

An epidemic of pornography and related inappropriate sexual behavior is sweeping over the earth, and sad to say, the saints are not escaping unscathed. The messages we hear with increasing regularity from our prophets are evidence of the scope of this problem. Quoting two earlier prophets, President Ezra Taft Benson wrote:

> The plaguing sin of this generation is sexual immorality. This, the Prophet Joseph said, would be the source of more temptations, more buffetings, and more difficulties for the elders of Israel than any other. (See *Journal of Discourses*, 8:55.)

> President Joseph F. Smith said that sexual impurity would be one of the three dangers that would threaten the Church within—and so it does. (See *Gospel Doctrine*, pp. 312–13.) It permeates our society...

> If we are to cleanse the inner vessel, we must forsake immorality and be clean. (Ezra Taft Benson, "Cleansing the Inner Vessel," *Ensign*, May 1986, 4–5)

In more recent years, President Gordon B. Hinckley stated:

> We can reach out to strengthen those who wallow in the mire of pornography, gross immorality, and drugs. Many have become so addicted that they have lost power to control their own destinies. They are miserable and broken. They can be salvaged and saved. (*Ensign*, Nov. 1991, 59)

I am writing this book as one who has experienced firsthand the plague of addiction to pornography. In fact, I endured thirty-five years of slavery to this vile degradation before I found the right combination of true principles that taught me how to come unto Christ and receive a remission of these sins. In overwhelming gratitude, I feel an intense desire to share with others my story and the principles that helped me.

As I prayed and pondered about what to include in *Clean Hands, Pure Heart*, I knew I wanted to emphasize the miracle of my recovery rather than the details of the addiction itself. I also knew there were enough books expounding the evils of pornography. Having read many of them myself, I felt acutely aware of the potential of engendering more evil by dwelling on it too explicitly. As Elder Boyd K. Packer has said:

> The study of the doctrines of the gospel will improve behavior quicker than a study of behavior will improve behavior. Preoccupation with unworthy behavior can lead to unworthy behavior. That is why we stress so forcefully the study of the doctrines of the gospel. (*Ensign*, Nov. 1986, 17)

If you are reading this book as a loved one of a sex addict, let me reassure you that I am keenly aware of your sorrow and your sensitivity toward these things. Like Jacob, I do not wish to **"enlarge the wounds of those who are already wounded" (Jacob 2:9),** yet I fear I may have to run that risk. Addiction hides and thrives in the darkness of denial, rationalization, and minimization. If this book is to be of use to those suffering from this malady, I feel I must speak with plainness. Though I will not discuss in detail the behaviors that constitute sexual addiction, I will mention pornography and masturbation as I discuss the recovery process.

I recognize that I am taking a step into relatively uncharted territory within the Latter-day Saint community by revealing my own identity as one who has struggled with these demoralizing and degrading practices. Naturally, I wonder how my story will be received, but I feel reassured that my offering of total honesty will have a positive effect on many of my brothers and sisters who are seeking a way out of this trap. It is time that we all realize that it is Satan who revels in keeping sin a secret and isolating the sinner in shame. It is time that we share the glorious good news of Christ's power to deliver us from addiction—even *sexual* addiction. I also trust that the Saints will be charitable toward my family members—parents, siblings, spouse, and children—and recognize, as I now do, that they do not deserve any blame or shame for my choices.

Ultimately, I am willing to disclose my own life story because I have felt the Savior invite me to do so. Like Paul and Alma the Younger, who also spent a portion of their lives in serious darkness and were delivered from it by Christ Himself, I am willing to allow my life to be an example of someone the Lord has rescued from "the darkest abyss." Alma's words ring out from the depths of my own heart:

> **My soul hath been redeemed from the gall of bitterness and bonds of iniquity. I was in the darkest abyss; but now I behold the marvelous light of God. My soul was racked with eternal torment; but I am snatched, and my soul is pained no more. (Mosiah 27:29)**

If there are any who may think poorly of me for the mistakes I have made or for being so open in writing about them, I bear no ill will toward them. I will bear their disapproval for His name's sake. He has truly changed my life. I owe Him everything. I am reborn and have no more disposition to indulge in sexual misbehavior. In other words, I need to thank the Lord publicly, in *my* own name, for in *His* own name He has redeemed my soul from hell. Together with Nephi, I declare:

> **I glory in plainness; I glory in truth; I glory in my Jesus, for he hath redeemed my soul from hell. (2 Nephi 33:6)**

I share this witness with you in humble gratitude for the incomparable grace and love that has been extended to me by my Savior and Friend, in His holy name, even the name of Jesus Christ, amen.

— *Philip A. Harrison*

Who shall ascend into the hill of the Lord?
or who shall stand in his holy place?
He that hath clean hands, and a pure heart.

Psalm 24:3–4

1 *My Story*

Hi. My name's Phil—and I'm in recovery from sexual addiction.

Since you are reading this book, I assume you are concerned about sexual addiction, either for your own sake or for the sake of someone you love. Perhaps you are concerned because you have a priesthood stewardship over someone struggling with a sexual addiction. Maybe this is the first book you have read on this subject, or maybe you've read several. Maybe you're beginning to feel desperate for a solution, rather than yet another rehearsal of the severity of the problem.

Pornography addiction and the practices which generally accompany it are difficult subjects to think about, much less write about. It causes embarrassment to those who haven't experienced it and shame to those who have. This is especially true in a society as dedicated to high moral and ethical standards and values as the Latter-day Saint community.

A Latter-day Saint who indulges in pornography knows, by the light of Christ and by the loss of the Holy Ghost, that he is doing wrong. Already in a state of inner spiritual hell, he can't face the thought of sharing his terrible secret with anyone else. If he mentions it at all, he minimizes it to priesthood leaders, who are as perplexed as he is about his total lack of self-control and his chronic return to the habit, requiring yet another confession. Eventually, he may give up telling anyone. Unfortunately, this slide into withdrawal and isolation cuts him off from any possible help. So it was with me for many years.

Today, I am able to rejoice in abstinence from any deliberate exposure to pornography since November of 1999. Believe me, after over thirty-five years of slavery, trying and failing over and over again to free myself from this horrible bondage, I know my abstinence is absolutely nothing short of a miracle. I am thrilled as I watch the progressive restoration of a state of innocence that I thought I had lost forever. I can gratefully testify that the healing influence of the Savior's forgiveness and His marvelous Atonement have brought me to a place of rejoicing in His power, finally free from my sexual addiction. With Alma, I can truly say today that I am **"harrowed up by the memory of my sins no more" (Alma 36:19)** and that:

> **There could be nothing so exquisite and so bitter as were my pains. Yea, and again I say unto you,… that on the other hand, there can be nothing so exquisite and sweet as [is] my joy. (Alma 36:21)**

I would like to share my testimony with each of you, heart to heart and soul to soul, that *there definitely is a solution,* and a blessed end to this problem. There is every reason to have hope for recovery from sexual addiction. I know, because I have lived it. In these pages I am going to offer you, step by step and concept by concept, the pathway that saved my life.

PUBERTY, LONELINESS AND INSECURITY

My sexual addiction began as I experienced the powerful feelings accompanying puberty and continued, as I said before, for over three decades, interrupted occasionally by short periods of repentance. I was a typical teenager, plagued with the normal onslaught of insecurities and anxieties that most teens experience. At the time though, I thought my plight was much worse than anyone else's. Prone to such self-pity, as well as self-doubt, I discovered masturbation. Although it drained me of all self-respect, it provided at least a temporary distraction from my fears and loneliness. Pornography was far less available at that time—in the

1960s—at least where I lived. Thus, although it was a smaller problem for me then, the seeds were planted for greater challenges later on.

As contradictory as it may sound, even while I was developing this addiction, I never doubted the truthfulness of the gospel, and I had a deep desire to serve a mission. As the time to submit my papers and receive my call approached, I made an increased effort to repent of what I thought of as a bad habit. Surely the time had come to put away childish things and I had no doubt I would be able to do so.

Just a few months before my mission call came, another reason to clean up my life became apparent. I met Kathy, the most wonderful young woman I had ever known. For a couple of months we were just good friends, but friendship eventually led to dating. Within weeks we both felt the Lord witness to us that we had each found our eternal companion. A desire to be worthy to take this precious girl to the temple as soon as I returned home from my mission sealed my resolve to forsake my unrighteous behaviors.

MISSION AND MARRIAGE—
NEW CIRCUMSTANCES, OLD PROBLEMS

My mission to Germany was so exciting! I had no idea before I went that I would love the people, the place and the Lord's work so much. And I loved the Lord, deeply, sincerely. What could be better than serving Him so totally? It was challenging, but it was worth it. Yet, before my mission was half over, I had given in to my weakness once more. What had happened? I thought my problem was entirely in the past! How could I be so weak? Still, I didn't think the offense was *that* serious. I was stunned however, when in district meeting, our district leader brought up the issue and said that anyone struggling with masturbation needed to confess the problem directly to the mission president. In spite of my embarrassment, I had a deep desire to do the right thing. I took the district leader aside immediately after the meeting and told him I needed to talk with the mission president. Within minutes I was on the phone with him, making my confession. Gratefully, that was the end of my indulgence while on my mission.

Kathy and I married soon after my return home. While I loved being married, I was dismayed to find that marriage was not a cure-all for my addiction. Contrary to what I had expected, the adjustment to a legitimate sexual relationship was very difficult for me. In fact, my wife had a much healthier attitude about sex than I did. My earlier indulgence in pornography had twisted my perception of sexuality, convincing me that it was "dirty." I began to realize that though I had abstained from the act of masturbation since my talk with my mission president, I hadn't allowed my heart and mind to be made clean. I didn't know how to become healed from those unhealthy attitudes.

Within a year or two of being married, I began to indulge in pornography again. I found it much easier to obtain than it had been in my teens. Our entire society was getting sicker, and I continued to sicken right along with it. As our family began to grow and the cares of work intensified, I found myself with more and more excuses to retreat into my secret world of sexual indulgence. Sensuality made me numb to everything else, distracting me with lust, then demoralizing me with inevitable bouts of remorse and self-loathing.

Looking back, it is plain to me that what I was practicing was nothing less than a form of insanity! Why would a person keep going back to something that made him feel like slime? Why would anyone choose to live in this secret hell? The whole situation is so ludicrous and insane that even the addict can't explain why he continues in such slavery. Of course, in those years, I had no idea I was an addict. I thought I was a lot of things—a liar, a sham, a reprobate—but "addict" hadn't dawned on me yet.

A NIGHTMARE OF TRYING AND FAILING

Over the next few decades I struggled frequently to give up what I considered to be merely a "bad habit." I talked with my bishops and stake presidents over and over again in order to "clear things up." Trying to encourage me and give me the benefit of the doubt, they always trusted I had fully repented and changed, and sometimes I even thought I had. Sooner or later though, the urge, the "need," the desire would return and I would act out again. I tried all kinds of what I have since come to realize were "half-measures" to manage and control my behavior. I rationalized so much that at one point I convinced myself that viewing pornography wasn't *that* bad, if I did it without acting out physically. I also justified my actions by rationalizing that the things I was doing weren't nearly as bad as what a lot of guys did. Eventually, all those lies numbed my conscience and I began to settle into a long, slow, downward slide.

As video rental stores opened and the Internet became available, I was sucked into the easy access to pornography and the relative anonymity they offered. I found myself making all kinds of excuses for getting home late "from work," when the truth was I had been wandering video aisles trying to find explicit movies with innocent sounding titles (in case my wife saw them). Later, after the family had gone to bed, I would stay up late so I would be "free" to pursue my addiction. Free? *Free to become enslaved.* Addiction is such madness!

Every once in a while, I would hear the amazing transformation recorded in **Mosiah 5:2** and would feel a heart-wrenching longing to experience the same change of heart the people of King Benjamin did. Their hearts were so changed that these people literally had **"no more disposition to do evil, but to do good continually."** Finally in a moment of overwhelming despair, I went to the Lord and pled with Him to relieve me of the "disposition" or desire to sin, begging Him to take it away. Much to my surprise and relief, I found the compulsion was lifted. A week went by, then another, without any craving to act out! Unaware of the truth that one must continue to exercise faith in Christ in order to *retain* this changed heart, I became complacent, assuming that everything was "taken care of." Soon, however, the tensions and insecurities of everyday life began to build up again—and having no idea that I could take *those* feelings to the Lord also, my need for escape began to reassert itself, and I fell again. How could I do that after the Lord had made me clean? My shame and discouragement were even worse than before.

Having never considered the word "addict" in connection to my situation, I had no way of recognizing that I was caught in the classic cycle of addiction, with its characteristic build-up of tension, acting out, remorse, repentance and eventual relapse. As I mentioned earlier, I would often go to my current bishop when I reached the repentance phase of the cycle and confess again...and again...and again. Little did any of us know that addiction could not be overcome by the level of repentance I was practicing. It wasn't that my repentance wasn't sincere; it was sincere as far as it went. It just didn't go far enough. It would be years before I learned there must be a complete *remission* of sin administered by the Lord Himself if I was to have a changed heart. Trying to change my habits simply wasn't enough.

In this spiritually sloppy way, I was able to justify holding a temple recommend most of the time. Still, my conscience often led me to put restrictions on myself. For months at a time I would not attend the temple because I did not feel worthy. I avoided opportunities to give blessings to my family and others, and occasionally outright declined when asked. Curiously, my opportunities to serve in church callings also diminished. I had no comprehension of how my addiction was draining every bit of spirituality out of my life. Living the half-truth, half-lie of my life was nothing short of a nightmare, but one from which I couldn't wake up. Even at 40, when I was offered the blessing and privilege of being ordained a high priest, I was still juggling reality and had more to confess. Hoping to motivate me to abandon my weakness once and for all, the stake president delayed my ordination. He wanted me to have a few months to *really* repent. Embarrassed and ashamed, I readily complied and was eventually "worthy" to be ordained. Unfortunately, my repentance was still not "recovery." After my ordination, the pressure to stay clean was off, and I let down my guard again—and once more began to act out. The fact that I was now a high priest only added to my shame.

THE BEGINNING OF THE END OF MY SLAVERY

It is always marvelous to me to look back from my vantage point of today, and recognize the hand of the Lord preparing my rescue from the clutches of addiction years before I was ready to allow myself to be rescued. I can see how He mercifully led me, step by step, to recovery through the instrumentality of my sweetheart, Kathy.

You see, Kathy knew something of addictive behavior herself, though she, too, didn't know to call it that at first. As a young girl she had developed a dependency on overeating as a means to get through her life's stresses. Needless to say, with several babies in quick succession, little money, and supporting me while I finished graduate school, Kathy lived with intense stress during the early years of our marriage. Her overeating and subsequent weight gain troubled both of us. Then one day she told me about a new group she had learned about, Overeaters Anonymous (OA). It was a support group that applied the Twelve Steps of Alcoholics Anonymous (AA) to the challenges of compulsive overeating.

I'd never heard of OA before and was unfamiliar with AA and the Twelve Steps. Besides, I was still hard pressed to finish graduate school and reluctant to commit to babysit so Kathy could attend meetings. But on the other hand, it was free, and I knew how desperate she was to find some kind of help, so I finally agreed. As the first weeks passed, I was gratified that she actually began to find relief from her compulsive behavior. Line upon line, she shared with me what she was learning about the Twelve Steps. It was obvious to us both that each step represented a true gospel principle—faith, repentance, rebirth. Still, as insane as it seems to me now, I could not see any need for such a program in my own life. The thought that my problem with pornography could also be defined as an addictive or compulsive behavior never crossed my mind. It's truly amazing how deeply into denial addiction can drag us. I was so ready to admit my wife's weakness and her need, but I could not (or *would* not) see the shrinking of my own soul, as year after year I persisted in my own degradation.

By the spring of 1998, at the age of fifty, I could no longer deny the spiritual death into which my sins were plunging me. The voice of the liar, the enemy of my soul, had become almost audible. When the Lord's Spirit would invite me to participate in some spiritual activity, such as praying or reading the scriptures, the adversary's tempting, taunting voice would cry, "Oh, don't do *that*. That will spoil our fun! If you do that, you won't feel like *playing* anymore." Finally, there came a day when I felt the negative influence I was harboring inside of me recoil at the very mention of the Savior's name! Instantly, I knew it was not *me* having such a reaction to the Savior. It was then I realized that something or someone who *hated* Him was taking possession of my mind, of my soul. I knew I had never been in such spiritual danger. If something dramatic didn't happen soon, I would be lost! In despair, I began to picture the certain result of continuing in my present course. Unlike drugs or alcohol, this secret destroyer wouldn't kill me early. I imagined what it would be like to be an old man, maybe in my eighties or nineties, robbed of all integrity and dignity, still a slave to my lust for unrighteous sex. I had heard of men like that. Furthermore, I began to conclude it was only a matter of time before my behavior finally crossed the line into adultery, and I would be excommunicated. Hope for anything better was all but dead in me.

Mercifully however, the Lord was about to give me another chance to grab hold of the true principles that had saved Kathy from her overeating. Once again, just as she had years before, Kathy began to share her excitement with me about yet another Twelve Step program she had recently learned about. She said it was called Heart t' Heart, and it was designed especially for Latter-day Saints. It coordinated the principles in the Twelve Steps with the teachings of the prophets and the Book of Mormon. There was even a support meeting just 15 minutes away in a neighboring community.

Despite my discouraged state, there awoke a tiny flicker of belief in me that I might still receive a remission of my sins and escape this terrible disease of the soul. After Kathy attended her first Heart t' Heart meeting, I tentatively asked her if I could go to the next meeting with her. Perplexed, she replied, "It's fine for you to go with me, but I don't know why you would want to." In her desire to believe the best about me over the years, she had apparently repressed any fear of my "problem." Though she had caught me watching a sleazy movie once, she had willingly accepted my excuses and remained oblivious to the extent of my degradation. Suddenly, then and there, I was faced with the first step on my journey of recovery. I had to take the terrifying risk of getting honest with this special woman whom I so deeply loved and admired, but whom I had so deeply wronged. Somehow, by the grace of God, I found the courage to tell her why I needed to attend the Heart t' Heart meetings. She listened quietly and although I could tell she was saddened and hurt, she expressed her hope and faith that these principles would help me, and that my life could be turned around and healed. After my confession to her, I noticed she was nervous whenever I was on the computer, but even so, she resisted the impulse to step in and assume responsibility for my recovery. She gave me room to grow. She knew the power of these principles and was willing to give them time to work in my life as they had in hers. Whether it was her Twelve Step recovery or her basic Christ-like nature that let her respond to me with such patience and compassion, I don't know, but I continually thank the Lord for it. My tutoring in the Twelve Steps began with her merciful example.

Together, Kathy and I attended Heart t' Heart meetings and began to read the study guide, *He Did Deliver Me from Bondage.* We often stayed after the weekly meetings for long discussions with its author, Colleen. Through a combination of those meetings and our personal study and prayer, our appreciation of these gospel principles and their power to open our hearts to the Savior's atoning power grew rapidly. We also eagerly listened to audio tapes of Heart t' Heart's previous annual conferences. I cannot express the extent of my amazement as I heard the testimonies of other Latter-day Saint men and women who were recovering from a number of addictions, *including sexual addiction.* A feeling began to stir within me that I almost didn't recognize, I had been so long without it. It was hope!

COMING TO LOVE THE PROCESS OF RECOVERY

Today, I recall those first experiences as the equivalent of being brought back from the brink of spiritual death. One meeting at a time, I felt my life slowly beginning to change. Week by week, month by month, as one false belief after another began to fade from my heart and mind, I began to feel alive again. I started feeling a willingness to participate in spiritual activities once more. I began to pray sincerely, with real intent. I started to enjoy the uplifting feeling I found while reading the scriptures.

Though total abstinence did not come immediately, the episodes of acting out began to happen less and less often, until I finally realized that the Lord had blessed me with the miracle I had sought for over thirty long years. I began experiencing an abstinence that was lasting, and with it, an overwhelming feeling of freedom and peace.

I'd like to finish my story with a verse of scripture that years ago used to depress me, because I had no idea *how* to come unto Christ. Today, the words of this verse have become a part of my own personal reality. I have lived to see these words fulfilled in my own life:

> **And if men come unto me I will show unto them their weakness. I give unto men weakness that they may be humble; and my grace is sufficient for all men that humble themselves before me; for if they humble themselves before me, and have faith in me, then will I make weak things become strong unto them. (Ether 12:27)**

Thank you for letting me share my story with you. There are many people with similar stories, but this one is mine. Let me now invite you to continue with me in the following chapters to consider some of the principles that have helped me along this journey. I fervently pray that they may bless your life as well.

MAKING THE MOST OF THIS CHAPTER

At the end of each chapter in this book, you will find a section called "Making the Most of This Chapter." In these sections, I will invite you to do some personal reflecting and writing about what you have read. Please pay close attention to these invitations, as the reflection and writing will make a huge difference in how much you get out of this book. Change is an internal process, one that is not reached by merely taking in information by reading. In order for that information to have the power to change us, it has to be assimilated into our innermost selves. That is the goal of these short writing assignments.

I suggest you get a special journal for recovery writing. Call it a "recovery journal" if you like. Use it to record the insights that come to you as the Lord **"shows [you your] weakness" (Ether 12:27)**. The questions at the end of each chapter will stimulate your thinking and give you things to write about. Space for writing is not provided here because people will vary in how much space they need. Even so, please consider this a workbook and do the writing exercises in your recovery journal. If you decide the writing is just too much, too soon—that you are not ready for this level of introspection and honesty—please read through *Clean Hands, Pure Heart* to the end. Then come back and go through it a second time, doing the writing. You will find you gain much more when you write about your thoughts and feelings.

Those of you who do not struggle with sexual addiction, but are reading this book out of concern for a loved one, can still benefit from answering these questions. All of us struggle with something, whether it's an actual addiction, a bad habit, or just life in general. Feel free to insert any problem in place of the references to sexual addiction and answer the questions accordingly.

Now for some questions relating to this chapter:

1. Write about your response to my story. If there were things to which you related, what were they? In what ways is your story different from mine?

2. Write a brief outline of your own story. When did you become aware of sex? Did you learn more from your parents or from your peers? How much of what you "learned" later turned out to be wrong? Have you adopted any sexual behaviors you might consider to be addictions?

3. Did your parents talk to you about sex? Did you feel you could ask them questions? (If the answer is "No," don't feel bad. You have lots and lots of company!) Write about your communications with your

parents (or other adults, such as teachers or church leaders) about sex.

4. If you could picture your Heavenly Parents sitting down with you to tell you about sex, how do you imagine it? Write down some of the things you think they might say.

5. Write about what you would like to get out of this book. What understanding would you like to gain? What changes in your life would you like to see happen?

Chapter 2 | *Undoing the Lies About God*

Once I was willing to face the truth, admit I was addicted to pornography and let go of the lie that it was only a bad habit, I also had to admit that acquiring "clean hands" (a change in my actions) would require me to confront a lot of other lies with which I had become infected over my lifetime. The process of cleansing my heart would involve changing my beliefs as well.

CHAINS MADE OF LIES

Addiction is a terrible condition of spiritual bondage that undermines our agency and gradually enslaves us by dragging us deeper and deeper into a way of life based on lies. We who have experienced addiction of any kind know the feeling of suddenly realizing we are trapped, caught, enslaved. We can no longer picture life without our addiction. What we usually don't perceive is that our bondage to evil began one subtle justification or rationalization at a time, one little lie at a time. Nephi clearly understood the connection between believing lies and becoming enslaved:

> And others will he pacify, and lull them away into carnal security, that they will say: All is well in Zion; yea, Zion prospereth, all is well—and thus the devil cheateth their souls, and leadeth them away carefully down to hell. And behold, others he flattereth away,

and telleth them there is no hell; and he saith unto them: I am no devil, for there is none—and thus he whispereth in their ears, until he grasps them with his awful chains, from whence there is no deliverance. (2 Nephi 28:21–22)

From Nephi's chilling warning, we see how subtly we can be bound by chains woven of the lies we hold onto—lies about life, about God, about ourselves and about others. Thus Satan, "the father of lies," lays the groundwork for our addiction, and in fact, for all sin. Satan doesn't want us to turn to God and find healing. He wants us to continue to stumble around, looking for happiness in all the wrong places. Thus, sin does not begin with behaviors, but with *beliefs*.

LIES THAT HAVE KEPT ME FROM TURNING TO GOD

President James E. Faust spoke about the importance of having a close, personal relationship with the Lord:

> Some time ago in South America, a seasoned group of outstanding missionaries was asked, "What is the greatest need in the world?" One wisely responded, "Is not the greatest need in all of the world for every person to have a personal, ongoing, daily, continuing relationship with Deity?" Having such a relationship can unchain the divinity within us, and nothing can make a greater difference in our lives as we come to know and understand our divine relationship with God and His Beloved Son, our Master. (*Ensign*, Jan. 1999, 2)

As I look back at my relationship with God during my youth and most of my adulthood, I see that most of my interactions with Him—or should I say, my *avoidance* of interaction with Him—was firmly rooted in the negative beliefs Satan had planted in my heart and mind concerning the nature of God. The most powerful way the adversary influenced me to avoid God was to lie to me about who God is and what He is like. Erroneous beliefs about the nature of God served to keep me in my addicted state, afraid to turn to the only true source of help. How could I have a relationship with a God I feared? It is only in undoing these lies that I have been able to finally come to God and be healed, first from the lies, then from the addiction those lies nurtured.

I have heard it said in Twelve Step circles, "If your picture of God is not helping you get sober, you may have to fire your old God and get a new one." Said another way, "If your understanding of God is not helping you, you may need to come to a new understanding." My recovery began when my understanding of God came to coincide more closely with the whole truth about Him—that He is a being of both perfect justice *and* of infinite mercy. The following are some of the *false* ideas about God that kept me running and hiding from Him for years. I am so grateful to be free of them today.

The Distant God

As a scientist, my academic training emphasized the operation of natural laws. At church I was taught that God also obeys and uses natural laws to accomplish His purposes. As I embarked upon the study of science, I enjoyed thinking of God as the greatest of all scientists. This picture of God gave legitimacy to my own choice of profession and I found it personally reassuring to think that life unfolded by rules one could count on.

This "logical" view of God can be taken too far, however. While many of my professors were faithful men who believed in God, some of them subscribed to the idea that God set up the world, then let it go. He didn't interfere in the daily affairs of men, instead letting them get along the best they could. This is often referred to as the "watchmaker" concept of God—as if the world were a watch God made, set in motion, and then left to run by itself. The idea was that everything we need is already here, and that beyond a few general guidelines—like the Ten Commandments—we don't need God's interference or help in our lives. This philosophy gives rise to the lie:

> *God created the earth, but does not get involved in our personal lives. We are pretty much on our own here in mortality.*

The Angry, Vengeful God

Even when I finally began to believe that God might sometimes get involved in our lives, I still wondered just what form that involvement would take. I often agonized: "What does He expect of me, and how upset with me will He be when I fall short?" It was not until I got into recovery that I began to admit how powerfully my assumptions about my Heavenly Father's character were colored by my earthly father's attitude toward me. For example, there were occasions when, as a child, I stopped off at this or that friend's house instead of coming straight home after school as my parents expected me to. When I finally did get home, my mother would express her disappointment with me, but would leave me to wait for my father to come home and discipline me for my offense. Needless to say, I spent those afternoons filled with anxiety and dread of Dad's arrival and the spanking I would often receive. Somewhere along the way, I began to feel the same way about God as I felt about my father. I was sure that "coming home" to God would also result in being punished. After all, I had certainly been a "bad boy" in my adult indiscretions. Thus, I came to believe this lie:

> God is a stern disciplinarian who is angry with me because of
> my sins and weaknesses.

This seems to be a common belief among those who have become entangled in Satan's traps. When we sin we naturally suffer the pangs of conscience that sin brings. Then Satan jumps in to exploit and exaggerate our fears and tell us lies about God that keep us from turning to Him for help. I think of Alma the Younger and how he dreaded coming into the presence of God because of the memory of his sins:

> **The very thought of coming into the presence of my**
> **God did rack my soul with inexpressible horror. Oh,**
> **thought I, that I could be banished and become**
> **extinct both soul and body, that I might not be**
> **brought to stand in the presence of my God, to be**
> **judged of my deeds. (Alma 36:14–15)**

What a trap Satan has constructed for keeping us in sin! First he entices us to commit the sin. Then he slams us with the greatest lie he can tell: That our only possible helper—the Lord—is an ogre! If we believe that, then Satan really has us, for he has cut us off from our only source of redemption.

I am sure the adversary is 100% responsible for this distorted picture of an angry God who delights in wrath. This concept has been handed down for centuries, even within our Christian culture. For example, I remember a sermon written by a Puritan preacher, Jonathan Edwards (1703–1758), which I was required to read in high school, entitled "Sinners in the Hands of an Angry God."

> The God that holds you over the pit of hell, much as one holds a spider, or some loathsome insect over the fire, abhors you, and is dreadfully provoked: his wrath towards you burns like fire; he looks upon you as worthy of nothing else, but to be cast into the fire; he is of purer eyes than to bear to have you in his sight; you are ten thousand times more abominable in his eyes, than the most hateful venomous serpent is in ours. You have offended him infinitely more than ever a stubborn rebel did his prince; and yet it is nothing but his hand that holds you from falling into the fire every moment.

Having already developed a number of faults, including a chronic problem with sexual self-gratification, I was understandably unsettled by that terrible description, and was very grateful that I belonged to a church that taught that God was merciful and kind. For some reason though, I was still persuaded by Satan's lie that while God might be merciful and kind *to others*, when it came to me and my sins He felt more like the God Jonathan Edwards described. I was convinced that if God was not outright angry with me, He was at least very disappointed and probably outright disgusted. As a result, I avoided any consistent personal effort to approach God. I was sure I would only be met with rebuke. I once saw a bumper sticker that said: "Jesus is coming—and boy is He ticked!" I laughed, but inside I cringed. I was afraid that at least where His feelings toward me were concerned, that bumper sticker wasn't far off the mark.

Under the influence of this lie, even my reading of the scriptures was twisted and confused. It seemed I couldn't open them without finding a verse that portrayed God as angry and fearsome:

> **Remember, and forget not, how thou provokedst the Lord thy God to wrath in the wilderness: from the day that thou didst depart out of the land of Egypt, until ye came unto this place, ye have been rebellious against the Lord. Also in Horeb ye provoked the Lord to wrath, so that the Lord was angry with you to have destroyed you. (Deuteronomy 9:7–8)**

> **For this ye know, that no whoremonger, nor unclean person, nor covetous man, who is an idolater, hath any inheritance in the kingdom of Christ and of God. Let no man deceive you with vain words: for because of these things cometh the wrath of God upon the children of disobedience. (Ephesians 5:5–6)**

> **And [the wicked] said to the mountains and rocks, Fall on us, and hide us from the face of him that sitteth on the throne, and from the wrath of the Lamb: For the great day of his wrath is come; and who shall be able to stand? (Revelation 6:16–17)**

Verses like these totally eclipsed in my guilt-ridden mind the far more frequent verses that testify of God's goodness, patience, and long-suffering nature.

A NEW UNDERSTANDING OF GOD

After years of avoiding this indifferent or disgusted God I had imagined, and hiding in the den of addiction, I finally reached a point where, as Alma described, I too was racked with the torment of a damned soul. And like Alma, though I was afraid to face God, I finally accepted the truth that I had to turn to Him and seek the Savior's direct intervention in my behalf if I was to ever find relief:

> And it came to pass that as I was thus racked with
> torment, while I was harrowed up by the memory of
> my many sins, behold, I remembered also to have
> heard my father prophesy unto the people concerning
> the coming of one Jesus Christ, a Son of God, to atone
> for the sins of the world. Now, as my mind caught
> hold upon this thought, I cried within my heart: O
> *Jesus, thou Son of God, have mercy on me, who am in*
> *the gall of bitterness, and am encircled about by the ever-*
> *lasting chains of death.* And now, behold, when I
> thought this, I could remember my pains no more;
> yea, I was harrowed up by the memory of my sins no
> more. (Alma 36:17–19, emphasis added)

Like Alma, I had finally become desperate enough to reach out to
the Lord. Even though I was not sure what would happen to me, I knew
that anything He might do could not possibly be worse than the slow
soul-rot of my addiction. I had to have help! My own strength was
failing me miserably. Somehow I, too, came to understand that Jesus was
the only One who could save me. Trembling, but resolute, I confessed
to Him my utter helplessness and my total dependence on Him. To my
great astonishment and relief, He did not reject me as I feared. Instead,
He welcomed me with open arms. The lies I had believed immediately
began to fall away and I saw Him with new eyes. He was indeed a God
of love and tenderness!

As I studied the scriptures with this new heart, softened toward
God, I began to realize the phrase "the wrath of God" can be viewed
differently than I had ever seen it before. I think of that phrase now, not
as a description of His feelings toward us, but as the inevitable consequences of disobeying the eternal principles God Himself lives and is
trying to teach us through the commandments He gives us:

> Therefore, they have drunk out of the cup of the
> wrath of God, *which justice could no more deny unto*
> *them than it could deny that Adam should fall because*
> *of his partaking of the forbidden fruit;* therefore, mercy

> **could have claim on them no more forever. (Mosiah
> 3:26, emphasis added)**

I was amazed at this new perspective! My heart was even more
tender toward God when I realized that He had no choice but to allow
Adam to experience the Fall as a consequence of his eating the
forbidden fruit! I had always thought of God as "all-powerful," and I still
believe He most certainly does have all the power it is possible for any
being to retain in righteousness. Today, though, I believe that because of
His strict obedience to eternal laws, including the interplay of agency,
justice, and mercy, there are some things God cannot do. He cannot
save us in our sins. He cannot bless us for keeping commandments we
have not kept. These are just other ways of saying He cannot "lie" or
pretend that something is true that isn't, for He is a God of truth in all
things. In a similar way, He cannot keep us from the consequences of
our sins if we refuse to repent **(Helaman 3:29, D&C 19:16–17).**

Today I realize my old images of God were not consistent with the
teachings of the Book of Mormon. God is not indifferent to my life. He
is very much involved in all our lives, but He must respect the same
eternal principles He requires us to respect. God is bound by eternal
laws, laws which God Himself must obey or He would cease to be God
(2 Nephi 2:13). Justice demands payment for laws that are broken.
Jesus was willing to suffer *for* us, so we ourselves would not have to suffer
the penalty required by justice. But that substitution of His suffering for
ours is only possible if we turn to Him and consciously and deliberately
accept His gift. If we refuse to do so, God cannot interfere with the
eternal law of justice, which demands the automatic implementation of
the penalty. Our repentance, coupled with Jesus' willingness to meet the
demands of justice is the only way mercy can *satisfy* justice without
robbing or negating it **(Alma 42:14–26).**

Thus, since God is the embodiment of these principles, He becomes
a representation of them, and the punishment exacted by these laws is
expressed as the "wrath of God." This expression does not mean that He
is *personally* angry with us or that He *personally* has to execute the
punishments. His reaction is rather one of sorrow at our disobedience—
not because He needs our obedience, but because of the sorrow and

suffering we bring upon ourselves when we disobey. Like any loving parent, He suffers *with us*:

> And it came to pass that the God of heaven looked upon the residue of the people, and he wept; and Enoch bore record of it, saying: How is it that the heavens weep, and shed forth their tears as the rain upon the mountains? And Enoch said unto the Lord: How is it that thou canst weep, seeing thou art holy, and from all eternity to all eternity? (Moses 7:28–29)

And God explained to Enoch:

> Unto thy brethren have I said, and also given commandment, that they should love one another, and that they should choose me, their Father; but behold, they are without affection, and they hate their own blood;…and among all the workmanship of mine hands there has not been so great wickedness as among thy brethren…Satan shall be their father, and misery shall be their doom; and the whole heavens shall weep over them, even all the workmanship of mine hands; *wherefore should not the heavens weep, seeing these shall suffer?* (Moses 7:33, 36–37; emphasis added)

Notice the heavens weep when we sin because sinning causes *us* to suffer. And as Enoch began to share God's perspective, he too, wept:

> And it came to pass that the Lord spake unto Enoch, and told Enoch all the doings of the children of men; wherefore Enoch knew, and looked upon their wickedness, and their misery, and wept and stretched forth his arms, and his heart swelled wide as eternity; and his bowels yearned; and all eternity shook…And as Enoch saw [those who would be destroyed in the flood], he had bitterness of soul, and wept over his brethren, and said unto the heavens: I will refuse to be comforted; but the Lord said unto Enoch: Lift up your

> **heart, and be glad; and look…And behold, Enoch saw the day of the coming of the Son of Man, even in the flesh; and his soul rejoiced. (Moses 7:41, 44, 47)**

All sorrows can be erased in the Atonement of our Beloved Savior, if we will but repent. It all depends on our willingness to come to Him. This new perspective not only colors the way I hear the scriptures, it also colors my prayers, and opens to my understanding a new relationship with my Savior. Like Alma, I no longer fear Him but instead rejoice in His reality in my life. I never knew it was possible to love anyone the way I love Jesus and the way I now understand He loves me and has always loved me. With Alma, I no longer fear the coming of the Lord, but rejoice in it and long for that great day to come. Alma testified:

> **And now we only wait to hear the joyful news declared unto us by the mouth of angels, of his coming; for the time cometh, we know not how soon. Would to God that it might be in my day; but let it be sooner or later, in it I will rejoice. (Alma 13:25)**

What an amazing change of heart Alma had experienced! He had come to know and trust the goodness of God, which enabled him to repent and be reborn. I am humbled to be able to add my testimony to his that such changes are possible. A life out of tune can be put right again. A soul tortured with guilt can once more know peace. The Savior only waits for our decision to come unto Him.

FINDING HEALING IN UNDERSTANDING GOD AS JOSEPH SMITH KNEW HIM

And so it was that, just as the old Twelve Step adage said, I had to "fire" my old beliefs about God and "hire" some new ones. To put it more literally, I had to finally make the effort to come to *know* the Lord as He is revealed in the fullness of the restored gospel. I had to admit that all my church activity and "busyness" in the service of others over my lifetime had not amounted to coming to *know* Him **(Matthew 7:23).**

As I studied more deeply and sincerely, I was led to the *Lectures on Faith*. There I "joined" the School of the Prophets, as the Prophet Joseph revealed several things about the true character of God.

> First, that He was God before the world was created, and the same God that He was after it was created.
>
> Secondly, that He is merciful and gracious, slow to anger, abundant in goodness, and that He was so from everlasting and will be to everlasting.
>
> Thirdly, that He changes not, neither is there variableness with Him; but that He is the same from everlasting to everlasting, being the same yesterday, today, and forever; and that His course is one eternal round, without variation.
>
> Fourthly, that He is a God of truth and cannot lie.
>
> Fifthly, that He is no respecter of persons: but in every nation he that fears God and works righteousness is accepted of Him.
>
> Sixthly, that He is love. (*Lectures on Faith*, 35)

Prayerfully, I sought to understand how knowing these characteristics of God could help me in overcoming my addiction. Let me share some insights I feel He gave me:

1. *God was God before the world was made, and he is the same God today.* He knows what is going on. You might say, He has been around the proverbial "block" a few times. He totally understands not only the way the *worlds* work, but also the way *people* work. In other words, he knows the principles of happiness just as well as the principles of astronomy and physics. When God gives us a commandment, He isn't doing it arbitrarily. He's actually trying to share with us what works to bring lasting satisfaction and joy in life. After all, He's the expert. He's seen it before. He has lived it Himself. I began to realize that if I would trust these true principles, I could be led by a *perfected*

human who has experienced a thousand times more than I will ever be required to endure in mortality.

2. *God is merciful and gracious, slow to anger, and abundant in goodness.*
This means He wants to help me. He is not sitting on the judgment throne waiting for a chance to condemn me, as I had previously thought. Instead, He wants to do all that He can to redeem me from the suffering I have thus far brought upon myself. As I accepted these truths, I began to realize I can trust that if I go to Him, I will find help, not criticism or condemnation. The Prophet Joseph wrote:

> Unless He was merciful and gracious, slow to anger, long-suffering and full of goodness, such is the weakness of human nature, and so great the frailties and imperfections of men, that unless they believed that these excellencies existed in the divine character, the faith necessary to salvation could not exist; for doubt would take the place of faith, *and those who know their weakness and liability to sin would be in constant doubt of salvation if it were not for the idea which they have of the excellency of the character of God, that He is slow to anger and long-suffering, and of a forgiving disposition, and does forgive iniquity, transgression, and sin.* An idea of these facts does away with doubt, and makes faith exceedingly strong. (Joseph Smith, *Lectures on Faith*, 35–36, emphasis added)

If you weren't really impressed by that paragraph, you might want to read it again. Read it as if Joseph were talking, one-on-one and heart-to-heart with us addicts. He is saying that we need to know God is loving so we can trust Him and take our addictive behaviors to Him. From my own experiences I can testify that the Lord does welcome us home and does not condemn us.

3. *The nature of God does not change.*
This means I can *always* trust Him. He is not going to be good to me one day and cruel the next. We need to be told this because we don't see that same steadiness in the people around us. None of us in

mortality is perfectly consistent, but as hard as it may be to imagine, God *is*. Sometimes we excuse ourselves when we are irritable or uncooperative by saying we are "having a bad day." God never has "bad days."

4. *God cannot lie.*

All the promises God has made to me will be fulfilled. I can count on Him. I may have been let down and disappointed by others in my life, but God will not let me down. It may take time for us to fully believe this, but we need to give Him the chance to prove it to us.

5. *He is no respecter of persons.*

If He has helped *any* other person recover from addiction or any other challenge, He will also help me. God's promises don't just apply to others; they apply to *all* of us, without exception!

6. *God is love.*

The characteristic of love so permeates the nature of God that it can be said of Him that He *is* love. Every action He takes toward us is based in love. I can trust that whatever His response to my petitions to Him, *it will be loving and benevolent.*

When I started to gain a more accurate understanding of the true nature of the Savior as "the Eternal God" (title page of the Book of Mormon), I started to let go of my fear of Him. I started to gain hope and confidence that motivated me to come to Him for help. As I came to Him, I found that He reciprocated! I felt Him draw near to me, as he has promised:

> **Draw near unto me and I will draw near unto you; seek me diligently and ye shall find me; ask, and ye shall receive; knock, and it shall be opened unto you. (D&C 88:63)**

What joy I experienced when I found that promise applied to me— to sinful, slothful, weak, backsliding, unhappy me! What a miracle! What a revelation!

As I approached the Lord and felt Him welcome me, I began to feel I knew Him, not just as a concept or a historical figure, but as a Person,

cont'.

as a Man—the most glorious and exalted Man I have ever known in this life. I began to get a sense of His personality, His goodness, His kindness and patience. As I reflected on this "new-found" relationship, I began to realize that it was really one of the longest standing relationships I have. Suddenly the gospel teaching that Jesus was my older brother since I first came into being as a spirit child of our Heavenly Father was more than just a pretty story to me. I *knew* it was true! He has known me and been my example, my teacher and my friend for eons. The recovery of this "memory," of this sure witness, has been the central meaning of the word "recovery" for me as I've continued to work my program. I find myself continuing to recover from my addiction in direct proportion to how much of my former relationship with the Lord I allow myself to believe and receive. In the course of this recovery process I have come to know that He still loves me, despite my sins. I know that although He abhors my *sins*, He still loves and accepts *me*.

As this very personal testimony of Christ's love for me began to enlighten my mind and heart, I saw that none of the angry, impatient sentiments I had felt toward myself all these years had come from Him. They were a fabrication, woven of my own shame and the lies I had believed about how God felt about me, lies whispered to me by the enemy of my soul.

AWAKENING TO THE LOVE OF GOD

As I have come to know the goodness of God and to believe I could be a recipient of this goodness, I have started to rejoice in the scriptures that tell me of His true, tender and loving nature. I now identify with the prophets who have written of Him, because I now know the same God they knew. Their testimony resonates in my soul in a way it never did before. Let me share some favorite passages with you:

> And the angel said unto me: Behold the Lamb of God, yea, even the Son of the Eternal Father! Knowest thou the meaning of the tree which thy father saw? And I answered him, saying: Yea, it is the love of God, which sheddeth itself abroad in the hearts of the children of

men; wherefore, it is the most desirable above all things. And he spake unto me, saying: Yea, and the most joyous to the soul. (1 Nephi 11:21–23)

Behold, I say unto you, that the good shepherd doth call you; yea, and in his own name he doth call you, which is the name of Christ. (Alma 5:38)

O Jerusalem, Jerusalem...how often would I have gathered thy children together, even as a hen gathereth her chickens under her wings, and ye would not! (Matthew 23:37)

The Lord repeated the same lament to those who survived the destruction at the time of His death (3 Nephi 10:4–6), saying how readily He would have gathered those who had fallen if they had come unto Him. He has renewed that promise in our own day:

For, behold, I will gather them as a hen gathereth her chickens under her wings, if they will not harden their hearts; Yea, if they will come, they may, and partake of the waters of life freely. (D&C 10:65–66)

The scriptures are also full of the promise the Lord makes to us, that if we will repent, He will forgive us and help us out of the bondage to which we have subjected ourselves. In these scriptures I again see the loving nature of God and the hope for healing and forgiveness:

In a little wrath I hid my face from thee for a moment [I let you experience the consequences of your own actions]; but with everlasting kindness will I have mercy on thee, saith the Lord thy Redeemer. (Isaiah 54:8)

O Israel, thou hast destroyed thyself; but in me is thine help. (Hosea 13:9)

Yea, and as often as my people repent will I forgive them their trespasses against me. (Mosiah 26:30)

I am so grateful for this understanding of the true nature of God that has been given us through the revelations of the restoration. While these truths have been restored to us *as a people*, we must each allow them to be restored to us *individually* and to take effect in our own hearts and lives. In this restored understanding, let us come unto Christ and not be afraid of Him.

> **Let us therefore come boldly unto the throne of grace,**
> **that we may obtain mercy, and find grace to help in**
> **time of need. (Hebrews 4:16)**

A NEW RELATIONSHIP WITH GOD

It is hard to describe the difference it makes to have this reawakened relationship with my Savior. Some have described having the Spirit in their lives as walking in the light compared to walking in shadows. To me it is a feeling of peace instead of a feeling of fear. Fear is a natural consequence of sin, and I think the adversary takes great delight in playing upon this fear. The Lord, on the other hand, desires for us to have peace.

> **Peace I leave with you, my peace I give unto you: not**
> **as the world giveth, give I unto you. Let not your heart**
> **be troubled, neither let it be afraid. (John 14:27)**

Peace comes into our lives as we come to know Christ's goodness and mercy. It comes as we understand that while mercy cannot rob justice, it can *satisfy* justice. An even deeper peace settles upon our hearts when we come to know the Lord Himself, and realize that He knows us and either will, or already has, forgiven us for our sins as we continue to repent. If we trust Him and continue to come to Him, He will help us with each and every step of our mortal journey. The Prophet Joseph Smith taught:

> When we begin to learn this way, we begin to learn the
> only true God, and what kind of a being we have got to
> worship. Having a knowledge of God, we begin to know
> how to approach Him, and how to ask so as to receive an

answer. When we understand the character of God, and know how to come to Him, he begins to unfold the heavens to us, and to tell us all about it. When we are ready to come to him, he is ready to come to us. (*Teachings of the Prophet Joseph Smith,* 349–350)

What a glorious promise! If we only knew what amazing blessings were in store for us, none of us would hold back. We would all rush quickly into His arms!

MAKING THE MOST OF THIS CHAPTER

Capturing is one of the most helpful practices I have found for making the scriptures and other written materials come alive for me. This tool has been of immeasurable value in helping me come to know myself and the Savior. I recommend it to each of you with all my heart. I am sure you will find it of great benefit, not only while working through this book, but for the rest of your life.

ASSIGNMENT: Before continuing, please turn to Appendix A and read the section called "Capturing" starting on page 251.

For years I had heard the counsel that I should keep a journal. I made a few feeble attempts at journal writing through the years, but I didn't really catch the vision until I started working on a serious recovery program. I found that writing was not just for the purpose of keeping a record. As I wrote about my recovery experiences and feelings, I began to see things I had not previously been able or willing to see. As I wrote about things I was reading in the scriptures, I was amazed and delighted to see what new insights were opened to me. Above all, I came to understand that the Lord was mindful of me. He was willing to counsel with me personally as I used the tool of writing to slow down my thoughts and listen for His thoughts and impressions. Recently, I became aware of Elder Richard G. Scott's testimony of the appropriateness of writing down our personal revelation:

> The Savior said, 'I will tell you in your *mind* and in your *heart*, by the Holy Ghost' (D&C 8:2, emphasis added)... An impression to the *mind* is very specific. Detailed words can be heard or felt and written as though the instruction were being dictated. (*"Helping Others to Be Spiritually Led,"* Doctrine and Covenants and Church History Symposium, August 11, 1998, Brigham Young University, 2, emphasis added)

It is my testimony that He will do the same for you, and that writing will be a vehicle for receiving much guidance and healing. This is true even if you haven't written much before. It will work even if you don't like writing. I strongly encourage you to try. It will bring you great rewards. *Please take the time to write about these questions; the process of writing will make a big difference in how much you gain from this book.*

We behave as we believe, and in order to change our actions, we need to change some of our beliefs. In order to see which beliefs may be holding us back, we need to know what our beliefs are. The following questions will help you examine your beliefs. You may want to write about one each day for the next five days.

1. Joseph Smith said, "It is the first principle of the Gospel to know for a certainty the character of God" (*Teachings of the Prophet Joseph Smith*, 345). What has your concept of God been until now? Write about three men you know who have some characteristics that seem to you to be like God's.

2. Alma wrote that at death, **"The spirits of all men, whether they be good or evil, are taken home to that God who gave them life"** **(Alma 40:11).** Write about why a loving Father would want to visit with all His children, even the wayward ones. What might He want to say to them before they go to their assigned place in the spirit world? How do you picture Him expressing His love for them?

3. A proverb in Ezekiel's time said, **"The fathers have eaten sour grapes, and the children's teeth are set on edge" (Ezekiel 18:2).**

We may have acquired beliefs about God, from our parents or others, that either hinder us or help us in coming to Him. Write about where you think most of your *feelings* about God (not just facts) came from. How appropriate do you think they are now?

4. Describe in writing how you feel about your relationship with the Lord, and about your hopes for your future relationship with Him.

5. The quote from Joseph Smith cited in question 1 continues: "And to know that we may converse with him as one man converses with another." Prayerfully ponder and write about what you imagine your conversation with the Lord would be if you could have a private priesthood interview with Him.

Chapter 3

Undoing the Lies About Us

When the prophets tell us we need "clean hands," they mean, of course, in the spiritual sense, but a comparison with the physical can help us understand the spiritual. For example, suppose you have been working on your car's engine. Your hands are really grimy with ground-in oil and dirt. You wash with soap and water, but that's not enough. What do you do? You use a stronger cleaner, maybe a solvent. You'd never consider cutting your hands off because they're dirty. After all, it's only the dirt that's undesirable. Underneath the dirt, you know you still have a really good pair of hands, even if it takes strong measures to get them clean. So it is with our spiritual "hands," our spiritual selves. God doesn't want to cut *us* off, he wants to make us clean again.

Differentiating between who we are (our hands) and what we have done (the dirt on our hands) is an important step in learning to see the truth about ourselves. How *we* see *ourselves* is an integral part of everything we do. The way we behave is strongly influenced by the picture we have of ourselves. That is why the adversary conducts such a vicious campaign against our self-image. One avenue of attack comes through the messages from our society. Sexual transgression has been part of every age, and the times we live in are particularly permissive. Even so, there still exists a definite disdain or contempt for those who let their sexual urges get out of hand. Those of us who have been caught in these out-of-control sexual behaviors have felt this contempt. We have even joined in our own condemnation, shaming and blaming ourselves more than anyone else could. This shame leads us to isolate ourselves from others, from society, and especially from God, thus cutting ourselves off from all sources of help and healing.

THE TRUTH ABOUT OUR BASIC CHARACTER

In the process of becoming trapped in addiction, we believe and accept a number of lies which make our enslavement possible. Recovery can be defined as a process of recognizing these lies and replacing them with truth. The sweet joy recovery brings comes from being reunited with the truth about God's character (as we covered in the last chapter) and also from reawakening to a knowledge of our own true character.

Joseph Smith taught a powerful lesson about understanding God and ourselves:

> There are but a very few beings in the world who under-
> stand rightly the character of God...If men do not
> comprehend the character of God, they do not compre-
> hend themselves. (*Teachings of the Prophet Joseph Smith*,
> 343)

If men do not comprehend God's character, they do not comprehend their own! Why would Joseph say that? I believe he was trying to tell us that we are—in our truest and deepest selves—more like our Heavenly Father than we can even imagine. It is not just symbolic or poetic language to call us children of God. As the apostle Paul said, **"We are also his offspring" (Acts 17:28).** We are of the same family—the same species, the same race. We are the same kind of being. We are not just His creations, His puppets or His creatures. We are His *children.* Just as our physical bodies reflect characteristics of our earthly parents, our spirits have inherited many traits of our heavenly parents. Our Father and Mother in Heaven are immortal human beings, and although they are much farther along in their eternal progression, there are still many ways we are more *like* them than we are *different* from them. I imagine that those among us who have progressed the farthest, in their best moments are not very different in character from God. I believe that God has many of the same feelings, sentiments, and instincts we do.

> **For we have not an high priest which cannot be touched with the feeling of our infirmities; but was in all points tempted like as we are, yet without sin. (Hebrews 4:15)**

Jesus, our great High Priest, understands us far better than we understand ourselves. He remembers us as we once were, before the fall. He believes in us, even when we don't believe in ourselves. He believes in us, *even when we don't believe in Him.*

Paul talked about our relationship to God, and how we become more and more like our Father as we grow spiritually:

> **And because ye are sons, God hath sent forth the Spirit of his Son into your hearts, crying, Abba, Father. Wherefore thou art no more a servant, but a son; and if a son, then an heir of God through Christ. (Galatians 4:6–7)**

The title "Abba" is an interesting one. In Aramaic, the language Jesus spoke, Abba is not the formal term for "Father." Rather, it is the type of endearing term a small child might use, such as "Papa" or "Daddy" (Hugh Nibley, *BYU Studies*, vol. 19, 50). Jesus also used this term in the Lord's Prayer, which, if we heard it as He spoke it, might sound something like "Our Daddy, who art in heaven." The tenderness of this sweet relationship that the Spirit tells me I enjoyed with my "Daddy" in Heaven before my birth into mortality melts my heart and brings tears to my eyes.

SATAN TWISTS THE GIFT OF CONSCIENCE

One mission of both the Holy Ghost and the Light of Christ is to testify to us of the truth, even when the truth is that we have done something wrong. This is the gift of conscience. Sometimes, instead of taking courage in the promise of forgiveness for repentance, we allow Satan to twist this gift of conscience, using it to keep us in sin rather than to turn us back to God. Responding to the urging of the adversary, we give in to blame and shame. We take those thoughts of correction and run with them down the field in the wrong direction—toward our opponent's goal. We turn the Lord's invitation to repent into a reason to demoralize ourselves and set ourselves up to be even more vulnerable to sin.

Thus, Satan uses the enticings of our own conscience to defeat us. Unlike the Lord, he doesn't respect us and is totally devoid of integrity. He doesn't fight fair. He entices us to sin, saying "Hey, this will be fun, this will be great—come and try this out! It's not that bad. It won't do any harm." Then when we give in, he turns on us and sneers in our face, in a cruel, sadistic imitation of our conscience: "You sinner! You scum! You are the biggest slimeball in history. No one could possibly tolerate you (let alone love you) if they knew what you are *really* like." On and on it goes. Is it any wonder the adversary is referred to as **"the accuser of our brethren" (Revelation 12:10).** The really sad part is that after a while, we take up the cry ourselves, becoming our own accusers. Our enemy has convinced us to join his side *against ourselves,* exactly as he intended. He knows if he can confuse our perception of our conscience enough, if he can get us to *identify ourselves* as sinners, we are that much easier to coax into sin. We act as we believe, and if we believe ourselves to be bad, we are much more likely to act badly. We say to ourselves: "Why shouldn't I do (whatever)? That's just the sort of person I am. There's no point in expecting anything better from me." Thus our negative beliefs contribute to our own defeat. As the scriptures tell us, **"For as he thinketh in his heart, so is he" (Proverbs 23:7).**

When the Light of Christ, one function of which is our conscience, speaks to our hearts, we must learn to react in a balanced way. We cannot take our sins too lightly, minimizing their severity and short-changing our repentance. On the other hand, we must not be demoralized over our mistakes. We need to take courage and move forward, realizing the Lord has confidence in us, and that correction from Him is truly an evidence of His love:

> **My son, despise not thou the chastening of the Lord, nor faint when thou art rebuked of him: For whom the Lord loveth he chasteneth, and scourgeth every son whom he receiveth. If ye endure chastening, God**

> **dealeth with you as with sons; for what son is he whom
> the father chasteneth not?...but he [chasteneth us] for
> our profit, that we might be partakers of his holiness.
> Now no chastening for the present seemeth to be
> joyous, but grievous: nevertheless afterward it yieldeth
> the peaceable fruit of righteousness unto them which
> are exercised thereby. (Hebrews 12:5–7, 10–11)**

Not only is the Lord's correction done with love, but it arises from His desire to bring us peace, righteousness, and exaltation. While it is never a comfortable feeling to have our conscience witness to us that we have made a mistake and therefore need to repent, the corrections we receive are a reminder of the Lord's confidence in us and His invitation to us to become something better. Elder Neal A. Maxwell cautions:

> What can we do to manage these vexing feelings of inad-
> equacy?...We can distinguish more clearly between
> divine discontent and the devil's dissonance, between
> dissatisfaction with self and disdain for self. We need the
> first and must shun the second, remembering that when
> conscience calls to us from the next ridge, it is not solely
> to scold but also to beckon. (*Ensign*, November 1976,
> 14)

ASSAILED BY LIES

If I am truly the son of a divine, loving Father in Heaven, how did I come to see myself so negatively? How did I become convinced of the worst about myself? The apostle Paul gave us at least part of the answer:

> **For we wrestle not against flesh and blood, but against
> principalities, against powers, against the rulers of the
> darkness of this world, against spiritual wickedness in
> high places. (Ephesians 6:12)**

We are not alone on this earth. Nor are all those who share this earth with us friendly. Satan and his followers have determined to destroy us, and they will continue that campaign until they are finally bound and stopped. In the meantime, we have a battle on our hands. Even so, we should always keep in mind, as the Prophet Joseph put it:

> All beings who have bodies have power over those who have not. The devil has no power over us only as we permit him. (*Teachings of the Prophet Joseph Smith*, p. 181)

As long as we resist the adversary, the only power he has is to lie to us. Yet this is still a formidable power. Lies are the basis of all the evil in the world. Every person who indulges in sin has accepted the lie that happiness can be found in sin.

Satan is also leading a major campaign to rob us of our knowledge of God. One of the most damaging lies Satan has perpetrated is that we cannot know our Heavenly Father. Some churches have been deceived into accepting this lie, teaching that God is "unknowable." This lie robs us of the knowledge of our kinship with God, isolating us and making us easier to deceive and enslave.

In the midst of addiction, I wandered in a fog of lies—lies I believed, as well as lies I told. Before I could get free from addiction, I needed to become free from these damaging falsehoods that I both believed and acted upon. One of the most detrimental lies was this:

> *I am fundamentally a bad person because of my sins and my addiction. The fact that all my attempts at repentance have not freed me from these despicable behaviors must mean that my basic nature is really evil.*

If you have never experienced firsthand the devastation of addiction, you may think this statement is an exaggeration. If you have struggled as I have, however, I think you will recognize these feelings. Sometimes I was so consumed with guilt that it was hard for me to see *anything* good about myself. It is one thing to feel remorse for a particular behavior, but I went in for wholesale condemnation. Today I realize that these self-judging thoughts didn't come entirely from myself. The forces of evil are continually at work, striving to tear down every positive feeling we have toward ourselves.

THE LIE OF LABELING

Years ago I saw the movie "Dr. Zhivago." I was struck by a scene where a middle-aged man was deviously carrying out an attack on a young woman's basic character by saying: "There are two kinds of women in the world—and we both know which kind you are." By trying to get the girl to define herself in a negative way, he hoped to convince her to behave according to that definition. Satan used the same sort of manipulation on me, and for many years, I believed his lies. "There are good men and there are those who give in to temptation. There are men who are above it all, and there are men who slip and fall. We both know which kind of man you are." And so I came to believe another lie:

> *There are men who have never made mistakes anything like the mistakes I have made. They are practically perfect. I am fundamentally different from them and always will be. I am made of lesser stuff.*

I have often looked at the prophets and other General Authorities, even my bishops and stake presidents, and thought what wonderfully spiritual men they are. I said to myself, "Surely these men have never been tempted by the sins I have participated in. They would never understand me or my challenges." I thought these men were not only *better* than I was, but a better *kind* of man than I was. This sort of thinking kept me from seeking the friendship of those whom I considered to be truly good men, thinking "They wouldn't want to be around someone like me." I thought of these good men of the Church being like the priesthood holders Alma described, as **"pure and spotless before God, [who] could not look upon sin save it were with abhorrence"** **(Alma 13:12).** These men were certainly on a higher plane than I was. They didn't even seem to have the same reaction to temptation that I did. In other words, sin wasn't even appealing to them.

Well, I knew that surely wasn't me. I didn't look upon sin with abhorrence. I looked upon sin, first with curiosity, then with tolerance, then eventually with longing. I lived out Alexander Pope's poem:

> Vice is a monster of so frightful mien,
> As to be hated needs but to be seen;

> Yet seen too oft, familiar with her face,
> We first endure, then pity, then embrace.
> (Alexander Pope, *Essay on Man*. Epistle ii. Line 217)

I didn't start out with this blatant acceptance of sin. There was a time, years and years ago, when I was repulsed by the world of sin which pornography represented. But years of toying with temptation eventually brought me to believe that sexual indulgence could be my cure-all. I used sex to comfort my feelings of uneasiness. Nevertheless, each time I acted on the temptation, the knowledge that I had been deceived, *yet again*, pierced my heart with inevitable clarity. Sin promised relief but only delivered sorrow and despair. I came to hate the *consequences* of sin, but unfortunately, this wasn't the "abhorrence" Alma spoke of. As I became increasingly trapped, it wasn't so much the sin I looked upon with abhorrence, it was me! Although I suffered the pain of having sinned, after a while the pain would lessen and I would again become enticed, entranced by the lures of lust. I was so weak and so different from these good men described by Alma, I felt I must have been born without some critical element which they had in abundance. What I lacked was the ability to find sin abhorrent *before* I sinned, not *after!*

SEEING THE SCRIPTURES WITH NEW EYES

Just as I shared in Chapter Two that the lies I believed about God affected my ability to interpret the scriptures, so had the lies I believed about myself. For example, because I believed the lie that I was an inferior sort of person, I was blinded to an important lesson taught in the passage from **Alma 13** referred to above. One day, after I started working a Twelve Step program, I read this passage again and saw things I hadn't noticed before. As my brain cleared and my spiritual eyes opened, I saw that these wonderful, righteous brethren, described in the scriptures, *hadn't always been like that.* They had needed repentance too. Alma recorded:

> **There were many who were ordained and became high priests of God; and it was on account of their exceeding faith *and repentance...choosing* to repent**

**and work righteousness rather than to perish. (Alma
13:10; emphasis added)**

These men, who were so righteous they could not look upon sin
except with abhorrence, *were once guilty of sins that put them in danger of
perishing!*

As I read further, I realized these verses told a story of purification,
not perfection. These men were not simply *born* pure, but rather,
through their repentance and the Lord's sanctifying influence in their
lives, they *became* pure:

> **Therefore they were called after this holy order, *and
> were sanctified, and their garments were washed white
> through the blood of the Lamb.***
> **Now they, *after* being sanctified by the Holy Ghost,
> having their garments *made* white, being [*after* their
> repentance] pure and spotless before God, could not
> look upon sin save it were with abhorrence; and there
> were many, exceedingly great many, who were *made*
> pure and entered into the rest of the Lord their God.
> (Alma 13:11–12, emphasis added)**

Alma was describing the *process* of repentance these men had gone
through, and the miracle of their having been made pure and clean by
the Savior through the ministering of the Holy Ghost. And then this
wonderful invitation in the next verse:

> **And now, my brethren, I would that ye should
> humble yourselves before God, and bring forth fruit
> meet for repentance, *that ye may also enter into that
> rest.* (Alma 13:13, emphasis added)**

This time I read these words with real understanding. What hope
and encouragement they contained! *I* could be made clean and become
sanctified, or holy, and enter into this same rest. I *wasn't* a different *kind*
of person, after all. I had the same potential as these righteous brethren,
whom I had respected all these years. If I chose to repent, I could have
the same blessings they received. What a liberating thought! What

freedom! What love and goodness our Lord extends to all of His children, even to me! No one is ever excluded from the promises of God.

THE SAVIOR'S INVITATION TO US ALL

As I began to turn away from the lies I had believed, and started accepting the truths the Lord was revealing to me about myself, I saw how deceived I had been to think there was anyone the Savior didn't love enough to die for—including me! After all, I knew men and women right here on earth who made a genuine (and usually successful) attempt to be sympathetic and gracious toward everyone. If they could do that as well as they did, why did I ever imagine that God, the greatest of all, couldn't and wouldn't feel even more kindhearted and patient?

While it is true, according to the scriptures, that at some future time, commonly referred to as "the end of the world," the Savior will take up His role as the judge of mankind, that time has not yet arrived. In the Gospel of John, which is often referred to as "the gospel of love," we read this statement by Jesus to his disciples: **"I came not to judge the world, but to save the world" (John 12:47).** I believe with all my heart that this is still a true description of the Savior's mission. He is still pleading with us to repent, hoping to save us rather than to judge us. Someone once said that when the time finally comes that the Savior must put on the robes of judgment, it will be with tears streaming down His face. I believe that. I think it is impossible for us to fully comprehend the depth of His compassion for us, even in our sins. Consider the story of the woman taken in adultery:

> **When Jesus had lifted up himself, and saw none but the woman, he said unto her, Woman, where are those thine accusers? hath no man condemned thee? She said, No man, Lord. And Jesus said unto her, Neither do I condemn thee: go, and sin no more. (John 8:10–11)**

How kind, how loving was our Savior's response to this woman. Can you imagine a more gentle way than this to counsel someone who had committed the sin that has been called **"most abominable above all**

sins save it be the shedding of innocent blood or denying the Holy Ghost" (Alma 39:5)? The kindness of His reply is profoundly moving to me. It touches me even more to realize that this is the *same* Savior who watches over *me* today. His nature has not changed, and His disposition toward me is no different from His disposition toward this unfortunate woman. He does not minimize the importance of repentance and keeping the commandments, but *He respects the person He corrects.*

On the other hand, we must not assume that because of God's great love for us, He will or even *could* save us in our sins **(Alma 11:37).** We must not rationalize or minimize our poor choices. We must realize that unless we repent, our sins will bring terrible heartache and pain to ourselves and to others. Why? Because **"wickedness never was [nor ever will be] happiness" (Alma 41:10).** It might bring numbness for awhile, or maybe distraction, but it can never bring us genuine happiness or joy. *That's a fact, not a judgment.* As we learned in Chapter Two, even God has to live by such eternal truths.

SEEING OURSELVES AS GOD SEES US: WITH MERCY, HOPE AND LOVE

Psychologists tell us a child does not have the ability to see himself except in the "mirror" others hold up to him. Parents, of course, have a tremendous influence on their children. If the parents express confidence in the child, the child develops confidence in himself. If the parents are critical and demeaning, the child sees himself as deserving criticism and becomes hesitant and insecure. If the parents are forgiving, the child learns he can try new things, even risking mistakes. On the other hand, if the parents are quick to condemn mistakes, the child will fear attempting new things. In time, a parent's disapproval of a child becomes the child's own disapproval of himself.

How do any of us mortals, with our limited view of ourselves, come to know who we *really* are? How do we come to accurately assess our own behavior, to trust that we see ourselves correctly? The apostle Paul said:

> **When I was a child, I spake as a child, I understood as a child, I thought as a child: but when I became a man, I put away childish things. For now we see through a glass, darkly; but then face to face: now I know in part; but then shall I know even as also I am known. (1 Corinthians 13:11–12)**

What a revelation it would be to know ourselves as God knows us. We might be surprised. I certainly was.

As I let go of the lies Satan told me and began to listen to the truth as it was spoken to my heart by the Spirit of the Lord, I found a great sense of joy and even relief. As I continue to trust the Lord, actively seeking and accepting His guidance in my life, I hear His voice reassuring me of His great love for me. We are told **"the testimony of Jesus is the spirit of prophecy [or revelation]" (Revelation 19:10).** Perhaps the most important "testimony of Jesus" we need to receive is *His* testimony concerning *us* and our worth to Him.

MAKING THE MOST OF THIS CHAPTER

Please take time to answer the following questions in your recovery journal.

1. At this point in your life, how do you see yourself? Get a piece of paper and as fast as you can, fire off a list of adjectives describing yourself. Try to include at least ten—twenty, if you can. (Do this now, before reading the rest of the question.) Now, number them, beginning with the ones that ring the truest to you. What source— negative (the adversary) or positive (the Lord)—do you feel or sense has prompted each of the descriptions on your list?

2. Have you ever felt you were "more powerful to mess up than God is to heal?" Does God think of you differently than He does His other children? Write about how you feel regarding your personal chances for forgiveness.

3. Read of the Savior's kindness toward the woman taken in adultery
    (John 8:1–11). Suppose you were "caught in the act" of practicing
    your addiction and were taken to Jesus. How would you feel? What
    do you imagine He would say to you? Can you imagine Him
    speaking to you as gently as He spoke to this woman? Write some
    gentle words you feel He might speak to you.

4. Who is the most Christlike person you know? (Pick someone you
    know well.) Does this person know about your addiction? If yes, how
    did he or she respond to you when they learned about it? If this
    person doesn't know yet, how do you imagine they would respond if
    you told them? Write about what they said or what you can picture
    them saying to you.

5. If someone came to you and told you they were struggling as you
    have struggled, would you condemn them? Write a response you
    might share with this person. Next write about how you have
    treated yourself. Do you deserve to be treated any worse than you
    would treat someone else with your problem?

Chapter 4

Step One

We admitted we were powerless over
compulsive addictive behaviors—that
our lives had become unmanageable.
(Heart t' Heart traditional version, adapted from A.A.)

Admitted that we of ourselves are powerless, nothing
without God. (Mosiah 4:5; Alma 26:12)
(Heart t' Heart scriptural version)

How do I interpret Step One for myself? How do I apply it to my own life? The painful tutoring of my own experience has taught me I am powerless over sexual addiction. I cannot quit by myself. I cannot abstain from sexual actions or thoughts without the intervention and grace of Christ. I simply don't have the power to do it. All I can bring to the problem is my willingness to be helped, to be cleansed from the addiction by a Power greater than my own.

PERFECTIONISM, POWERLESSNESS AND ME

From my earliest years I had an intense concern with doing things right. I wanted to make others happy with me and not disappoint them. The specter of failure loomed large, and I feared it immensely. Being called a "failure" was one of the most devastating insults I knew. In short, I was a perfectionist. I used to think it was ludicrous to call myself that because I consistently fell short in so many areas. I have since learned that perfectionism is not the same thing as *doing* everything correctly, it is the *obsession* with doing everything correctly. It is not the admirable virtue I used to think, but rather a debilitating frame of mind that constantly drained me of motivation.

When I became entangled in sinful sexual behaviors, my inability to free myself presented a near death blow to my self-esteem. Nevertheless, I still hoped that maybe somewhere inside I had the power to succeed— if I could only find it. The idea that I might be powerless over this behavior was too hard for me to accept. Stubbornly, I continued to struggle, sure that my own strength would eventually prove sufficient. The thought that I might *not* have the power to master my weaknesses was repulsive to me. Thoughts like, "Be a man, not a weakling," and "You can do anything you put your mind to" kept going through my head. I had attended a number of classes on motivation, on being my best self, on overcoming my self-defeating behaviors. I knew if I just found the right approach to this problem, it would yield to "the invincible power of the human spirit" in me. Hadn't all these men I read about overcome *their* challenges and gone on to become great, self-sufficient, even wealthy? Surely I could at least overcome this one bad habit!

These thoughts of "You can do it!" were so comforting, so encouraging, so enticing, so *seductive* to my ego (my pride) that I kept on trying to overcome not just my sexual problems on my own, but all my other problems as well—procrastination, being habitually late, starting projects and not finishing them, even my perpetually disorganized way of living. I was sure I could conquer all these weaknesses if I just read the right book, took the right class, or found the right inspirational person to follow and to emulate.

MY "UNCONQUERABLE" SOUL

Puffed up on all this learning of men, I had great confidence that all my challenges and limitations would soon yield to the "positive mental attitude" I was always just *about* to acquire. Sentiments like these, expressed in the poem "Invictus" by William Ernest Henley, inspired me:

Out of the night that covers me,
Black as the Pit from pole to pole,
I thank whatever gods may be
For my unconquerable soul.

In the fell clutch of circumstance
I have not winced nor cried aloud.
Under the bludgeonings of chance
My head is bloody, but unbowed…

It matters not how strait the gate,
How charged with punishments the scroll,
I am the master of my fate:
I am the captain of my soul.

(*Best Loved Poems of the American People,* Hazel Felleman)

Irrationally, I took comfort in thinking of myself as "the master of my fate," and "the captain of my soul," even though my helplessness over sexual actions continually proved otherwise. Convinced that my eventual success or failure was entirely in my hands, I increased my efforts to overcome all my problems, including my growing sexual indulgence, through my own insufficient strength. I was determined to win by sheer persistence.

When I was in graduate school, I ran across another quote that affected me strongly. I couldn't decide, however, whether I was more encouraged or discouraged by it. On the one hand, it was very inspiring, but on the other hand, it was also faintly disturbing:

Nothing in the world can take the place of persistence. Talent will not; nothing is more common than unsuccessful men with talent. Genius will not; unrewarded genius is almost a proverb. Education will not; the world is full of educated derelicts. Persistence and determination alone are omnipotent. (Calvin Coolidge)

What was it about this thought that bothered me? After all, it was touting persistence, the very quality I clung to as my one last hope for freedom from my sin. Still, I couldn't find any reassurance in President

Coolidge's words. Why? After considerable reflection, I recognized an old familiar threat in this quote: *the threat of failure.* It rang too close to what I had heard all my life: "Philip, you could do so much better if you would just apply yourself and live up to your potential!" So instead of inspiring me to more consistent effort, as I am sure Coolidge intended, his words seemed to condemn me to a fate I already feared: "It doesn't matter if you *do* have talent. You are going to fail anyway, because you can't be persistent enough!"

In my desperation to believe in myself, I turned a blind eye to certain scriptures that suggested more humility was in order. Verses like these troubled me:

> **O how great is the *nothingness* of the children of men; yea, even they are *less than the dust of the earth.* (Helaman 12:7, emphasis added)**

> **I would that ye should remember, and always retain in remembrance, the greatness of God, *and your own nothingness,* and his goodness and long-suffering towards you, *unworthy creatures,* and humble yourselves even in the depths of humility. (Mosiah 4:11, emphasis added)**

> **Yea, I know that I *am nothing;* as to my strength I am weak; therefore I will not boast of myself. (Alma 26:12, emphasis added)**

Even though I thought I believed the Book of Mormon to be true, I found these verses impossible to comprehend or accept. For one thing, they didn't square with what I desperately wanted and *needed* to believe about myself so that I could continue in my illusion of self-sufficiency. After all, wasn't I a child of God, made in the image of the Creator of the Universe? Wasn't I a "god in embryo?" That must mean I had *something* going for me. I might have a few problems, but I wasn't "nothing" (regardless of what these prophets had said).

Year after year passed, and in my own way I kept trying, and trying, and trying. I prayed (but not too hard, nor too consistently) and I read the scriptures (but not too often, nor too deeply). I fasted and asked the Lord to give me the strength to overcome (but not too wholeheartedly). I confessed to my bishops and to my stake presidents. I repented, over and over again. It seemed that my every prayer began, "Heavenly Father, please forgive me for my sins..." but invariably, as soon as the stresses in my life built up again, I would seek comfort or relief by returning to my behaviors. How well I came to identify with the disgusting and pitiful image in **3 Nephi 7:8,** of returning **"like the dog to his vomit, or like the sow to her wallowing in the mire."**

SLIDING INTO THE DEPTHS OF DESPAIR

As the years passed and none of my intentions to change had any lasting effect on my slavery to lust, my indomitable spirit began to crumble, like the façade it was. I was starting to accept the adversary's continually whispered lie that I was already beaten. The "dream" of one day overcoming these habits started to fade, and I found myself coming to the conclusion that I would *never* be free of these behaviors, that I would die still enslaved to the power of this degrading life of sin and sensuality. I found myself sliding deeper and deeper into despair. Hadn't I tried as hard as I could to quit? Hadn't I wept bitter tears over my endlessly repeated failures? Bludgeoned with discouragement, I eventually came to the point where I had practically lost all hope. I began to reason that if I had not been able to free myself with the effort I had put forth year after year, then the amount of willpower required to ever *really* succeed was beyond me.

As my hope faded, I began to be tormented with an awful specter. I had so far escaped what I had always considered to be the ultimate disaster, adultery, but the way I was going, I wasn't sure how long I would hold out. I frequently wondered what it would feel like to stand in front of the Stake High Council, in front of brethren I had known and respected for years, and be confronted with sins serious enough to strip me of my priesthood and my Church membership! I started to picture the scene, not realizing that Satan was subtly, carefully preparing my mind to accept the inevitability of just such an outcome. I didn't recognize that this true principle was operating—that all things are created spiritually before they are created physically, *even our destruction.*

I eventually came across some literature on sexual addiction and even though I was startled to see myself in those pages over and over, that awakening still didn't give me the power to change. I considered the possibility that I might actually be an "addict." I knew an addict was someone who could not shake off his habit, no matter how hard he tried, and whether I liked it or not, that description fit me perfectly!

Terrified by the nightmarish future that each indulgence in my addiction made more likely, I found myself asking a question every addict must eventually face: Had I had enough? Had I given away enough of my soul; had I lost enough integrity? Had I finally fallen far enough? In short, was I humbled enough yet to be willing to offer the Lord whatever might be required to put myself within the saving influence of His mercy and grace?

I have since come to realize that this whole process of admitting powerlessness is the same "tutoring" experienced by the Prodigal Son **(Luke 15:11–32).** In other words it is a process of becoming humble— truly humble. I had never before identified with this poor, lost prodigal. After all, I had never left the Church. I believed in its teachings. I was faithful in so many ways. It was only in what I thought of as "just this one area" that I was stalled out. In my perverse pride, I ignored my desperate need for humility, insisting that life teach me the hard way. On the one hand, I prayed for help from God, while on the other, I clung insanely to the very poison that was destroying me spiritually, and which I *knew* would eventually wreck my whole life. Just as I had turned a deaf ear to the prophets' insistence that I was "nothing," and that in my own strength I was weak, I also ignored Alma's invitation to become humble without having to be compelled:

> **Therefore, blessed are they who humble themselves without being compelled to be humble; or rather, in other words, blessed is he that believeth in the word of God...without stubbornness of heart, yea, without**

> being brought to know the word, or even compelled to
> know, before they will believe. (Alma 32:16)

In my stubbornness of heart, insisting on finding the way out of my dilemma without coming down into the depths of humility, I was setting myself up to be compelled, or as Alma puts it, "blessed."

> **And now, because ye are compelled to be humble
> blessed are ye; for a man sometimes, if he is compelled
> to be humble, seeketh repentance; and now surely,
> whosoever repenteth shall find mercy; and he that
> findeth mercy and endureth to the end the same shall
> be saved. (Alma 32:13)**

HITTING BOTTOM—THE DEPTHS OF HUMILITY

> **And save they shall cast these things away, and
> consider themselves fools before God, and come down
> in the depths of humility, he will not open unto them.
> (2 Nephi 9:42)**

"Hitting bottom" is an expression that's been used in recovery work ever since the beginning of Alcoholics Anonymous. It refers to the devastating emotional bankruptcy most of us have to reach before we are finally ready to seek divine help in a state of total surrender. When we fall, we *keep* falling until we hit something that stops us—the bottom. Hitting bottom is the inevitable end to a fall.

Most of us hit a few jarring bumps before we hit that final "bottom." Said another way, we get several wake up calls, inviting us to see ourselves as the fools we are before we finally *do* wake up. Looking back at my own life, I am now amazed to see the depths of foolishness and degradation I fell into but could not (or would not) see.

One "wake-up call" happened after I moved to the east coast to attend graduate school. I had just graduated from BYU in Provo, Utah, and the culture shock of my new environment was enormous. The year was 1974. The "women's movement" was in full swing, and the university I was attending was in the forefront of the "bra-burning" crusade.

As a result, a number of the young women on campus dressed very immodestly. In this temptation-laden environment, my addiction kicked into high gear. I graduated from noticing things I couldn't avoid to actively seeking out opportunities to lust. One day I was in an elevator with a fellow graduate student. A girl got on the elevator and stood opposite, facing us. After a moment she nervously crossed her arms. When she got off the elevator, my companion spoke up: "Did you notice how we both looked at that girl just now, you know, to see what we could see?"

I was mortified! I knew *I* had noticed her, and I wasn't surprised that he had too, but I had no idea he had noticed *me* noticing her! I felt like such a fool! My friend wasn't a member of the Church, *but he knew I was.* What kind of example was I setting for others about the morals of Latter-day Saints? I made some lame excuse about how sad it was that some girls dressed in such a provocative way that we guys had become conditioned to looking at *all* women that way. But my excuses didn't make it any better. They never have.

Did this wake-up call turn me around and motivate me sufficiently to change my behavior? Sadly, it didn't. I went on like this for another twenty-five years, and all along the way I had experiences that could have become turning points, but I never let them.

Another wake-up call came when I turned forty and the stake president interviewed me about being ordained a high priest. I confessed to him some things I had not previously cleared up. He listened intently, counseled me about my mistakes, and then set a date for my ordination. I went home, relieved the confession had gone so well, and called my father to invite him to ordain me. He gladly agreed and I told him the day and time. He said he and my mother would be happy to make the trip and were looking forward to the experience. Moments after I hung up, the phone rang. It was the stake president calling to say he was sorry, but after thinking it over, he had come to the conclusion that we needed to wait awhile for my ordination. I protested that I had already told my parents, and explained how embarrassing it would be for me to call them back and postpone it. He kindly, but firmly, reminded me he was a "judge in Israel," and he had the responsibility to see that things were done properly. He also apologized for not realizing earlier what needed to be done. With no other recourse, I called my parents back and told them the ordination had been postponed, but even then I was still light years away from being able to explain why. Did this incident wake me up? Again, sadly, no. I was able to "white knuckle" it (abstain through sheer willpower) long enough to be ordained, but no "heart-deep" change had happened, and, for the umpteenth time, my repentance didn't last.

I have heard stories from other men about things they have gone through before they finally hit bottom. More than one brother has been fired from his job for viewing Internet pornography on his computer at work. One said: "I knew it wouldn't happen to me," and he took the chance—and got caught. Others have been disfellowshipped or excommunicated for serious sins. Some have lost their families. The devastation can take on terrible proportions if that is what is required to wake us up. When I hear these stories, I think, "There, but for the grace of God, go I," and I thank God my addiction didn't take me any further down than it did.

THE SUPREME PRINCIPLE OF AGENCY

It seems it is the Lord's will to let us learn from our own experience to distinguish good from evil, to learn what works and what doesn't work. The Lord loves us and wants us to repent so we don't have to suffer, but agency is a sacred principle, and He will never violate our agency by forcing us to do what is right:

> I ought not to harrow up in my desires, the firm decree of a just God, for I know that he granteth unto men according to their desire, whether it be unto death or unto life; yea, I know that he allotteth unto men, yea, decreeth unto them decrees which are unalterable, *according to their wills*, whether they be unto salvation or unto destruction. (Alma 29:4, emphasis added)

God allows us to experience the natural consequences of our actions until we finally learn that **"wickedness never was happiness" (Alma 41:10).** Elder Neal A. Maxwell described this painful teaching process:

> If we have grown soft, hard times may be necessary. If we are too contented, a dose of divine discontent may come. A relevant insight may be contained in reproof... *One may be scorched by humiliation, so pride can be melted away. Whatever we lack will get attention, one way or another.* (*Ensign*, Nov. 1995, 25; emphasis added)

Those of us who have been compelled by addiction to be humble face a great opportunity. We can respond to the humbling events we have already experienced and thus not require still more serious and painful humbling. In some educational programs, you can take a test part way through the course, and if your test results show you understand the current topic, you can move on to the next principle. I think the Lord teaches us that way. If we haven't learned the lesson yet, it keeps coming back until we "get it," but if we can show Him we have learned the lesson already, we can "graduate" and we won't have to go through the sting of further "learning experiences." When the course is as painful as addiction, graduating as quickly as possible makes a lot of sense. If I could have one wish, it would be that the testimony of my own experiences might help others to turn around where they are, rather than have to experience the full pain of devastation that continuing in addiction will surely bring. AA refers to this as "bringing the bottom up," or in other words, "getting" the message without having to experience the worst consequences addiction can bring.

POWERLESSNESS TURNS TO HOPE

I have gained so much through attending Twelve Step meetings in the Heart t' Heart program. In Heart t' Heart, each of the original Twelve Steps of AA is paraphrased in a "scriptural version." The scriptural version of Step One reads: "(We) admitted that we of ourselves are powerless, nothing without God." Here was that principle of "nothingness" that I had so long resisted. Now, somehow, life had taught me the truth of it in an irrefutable manner. I could not deny that when I weighed the years of effort I had put into trying to quit against the results my efforts got me, "nothing" was a perfect description. The facts of my life bore witness to me of my powerlessness so plainly that I could not deny the truth in Step One when I heard it. As Alma had promised, by being compelled to be humble, I had finally been brought to a **"preparation [willingness] to hear the word" (Alma 32:6).**

Paradoxically, admitting my powerlessness did not make me feel hopeless. I started studying the Twelve Steps in earnest when I began attending Heart t' Heart meetings. There I met people who were being freed from a variety of destructive behaviors. Hope was everywhere. I began to think: "If they can quit, maybe *I* can, too." I have heard it said that the first thing a person experiences when they start attending Twelve Step meetings is a rebirth of hope. That began happening for me as soon as I got out of isolation and started going to meetings.

Hope continued to dawn on me as I started to turn to the Lord **"with full purpose of heart" (Mosiah 7:33),** willing to see myself as a fool and admit my **"nothingness," (Mosiah 4:5, 11** or in other words my total need for Him. With this new perspective, the scriptures started to take on deeper and *more hopeful* meanings. Truly, just as was promised in **2 Nephi 9:42,** the Lord was opening the scriptures unto me!

For example, when I went back and looked at those verses I mentioned earlier that had bothered me, I found I had not been hearing the whole message. I had only heard that part of the message I thought condemned me. What I was missing was the realization that in each of these passages there was also the promise of help, of success, of joy! These inspired writers weren't condemning me for *not* using my own power—they were testifying to me of *God's* power and inviting me to take advantage of it. Listen to what Ammon said:

> **My brothers and my brethren, behold I say unto you, how great reason have we to rejoice; for could we have supposed when we started from the land of Zarahemla that God would have granted unto us such great blessings?**

> **And this is the blessing which hath been bestowed upon us, that we have been made instruments in the hands of God to bring about this great work...**
> **Blessed be the name of our God; let us sing to his praise, yea, let us give thanks to his holy name, for he doth work righteousness forever. (Alma 26:1, 3, 8)**

Does this sound like someone who is beaten down and discouraged over being "nothing?" Quite the opposite. Ammon is bubbling over with enthusiasm in his rejoicing. His exuberance even evokes a reprimand from his brother.

> **And it came to pass that when Ammon had said these words, his brother Aaron rebuked him, saying: Ammon, I fear that thy joy doth carry thee away unto boasting. (Alma 26:10)**

But Ammon could not be deterred from his rejoicing *in the Lord.*

> **Behold, my joy is full, yea, my heart is brim with joy, and I will rejoice in my God. Yea, *I know that I am nothing;* as to my strength I am weak; therefore I will not boast of myself, but I will boast of my God, for in his strength I can do all things. (Alma 26:11–12, emphasis added.)**

Ammon confesses his own nothingness and his own weakness, and in the same breath gives glory to God for being the One who has brought about these mighty miracles. His admission of powerlessness is far from discouraging; it is exalting! It's all right that I am nothing, because Christ is *everything!* I do not have to be able to do all things, to move mountains and change the course of rivers, because I have a Friend who can, and who *does* do these things. He has moved the mountain in my life that I could not move! He has wrought an amazing change in me, one I thought would never happen!

Step One is an exercise in letting go of the notion that recovery is going to happen through our own strength. We will need to take action, to take certain steps, but the power to do so comes from God. The amazing result is marvelous peace and joy!

MAKING THE MOST OF THIS CHAPTER

Please take time to answer the following questions in your recovery journal.

1. Let's revisit the truth we read in **2 Nephi 9:42**—**"Save they shall cast these things away [pride in their learning, wisdom and riches], and consider themselves fools before God, and come down in the depths of humility, he will not open unto them."** I'd like to invite you to walk head-on into the miraculous process of entering the depths of humility by honestly reviewing your own history of sex-related behaviors. I recommend that you write your history down—even if it's for your own eyes only. Start with your earliest awareness of sexuality and each experience since. At what point did you begin to feel these thoughts or activities were "getting out of control"? What have you tried in your efforts to stop? Do you feel truly powerless over this behavior yet? Do you accept that it is actually an addiction?

2. When we are trapped in addiction, we are not only doing things we wish we weren't, we're also letting a lot of good things that we wish we were doing slip out of our lives. We are even as the apostle Paul wrote: **"For the good that I would I do not: but the evil which I would not, that I do" (Romans 7:19).** Write about how this applies in your life. Make a list of the things you once enjoyed, or hoped to enjoy, that have either slipped out of your life or haven't materialized because of your addiction.

3. In **Mosiah 27:29**, Alma the Younger, uses words like **"gall of bitterness," "bonds of iniquity," "darkest abyss,"** and **"racked with eternal torment"** to describe his depths of despair and humiliation. Write about whether you can relate to any of these expressions.

Write about the hardest moments you've experienced so far—or have seen someone else experience, and know in your heart that you're headed for yourself.

4. In **Alma 38:11 and 14,** Alma reminds his son, Shiblon, to not be lifted up in pride, but to **"acknowledge your unworthiness before God at all times."** Write a list of people, places, and circumstances you have used as excuses to turn to sexual addiction. How has using them for excuses been a way of avoiding admitting your own **"unworthiness,"** or bondage to addiction?

5. Read the "Psalm of Nephi" **(2 Nephi 4:16–35)** in its entirety. Note the "I am..." statements Nephi makes about himself: **"I am encompassed about, ...wretched."** Nephi doesn't seem to be afraid to tell the straight truth about his human frailties. Write about how you feel about being "encompassed about" by addiction. Write about how you feel when you finally say, "I am *addicted*," or even "I am an *addict*." How can facing this truth set you free?

Chapter 5

Step Two

Came to believe that a Power greater
than ourselves could restore us to sanity.
(A.A. and Heart t' Heart versions)

*Came to believe that God has all power and
all wisdom and that in His strength we can do all things.*
(Mosiah 4:9; Alma 26:12)
(Heart t' Heart scriptural version)

God has all power, both in heaven and on earth. He has the power to touch my soul; He can change my heart. I cannot of myself change my behavior, my heart, my will, or my desires. I can only turn to God, who has the power to change me from the inside out. He can change my desires so that I no longer want to sin, so that in my heart of hearts, I want God more than I want any earthly pleasure. But before I am willing to make this surrender, I must *believe* He *can* and *will* perform this great miracle in me.

Step One left me sobered with the realization of my powerlessness. In Step Two, my hope is rekindled. There is a way out of the morass of addiction—through Jesus Christ, my Savior.

VOLUNTARY INSANITY

In the original AA wording of Step Two, we read: "[We] Came to believe that a Power greater than ourselves *could restore us to sanity.*" In the Heart t' Heart version of Step Two, the wording softens the focus, placing emphasis on the miracle that in God's strength we can do all things—*including* overcome our addiction. I found, though, that I needed to honestly face the indictment of insanity found in the original version of the step.

I have heard insanity defined as *"doing the same thing over and over again, hoping for a different result."* What better description could be found for the endlessly repeating cycle I was caught in for most of my life—acting out, then suffering inevitable demoralization? Over and over I asked, "Why do I keep hurting myself this way? It just doesn't make sense to keep doing something that, in the end, always brings such sorrow and despair!" However, my thinking *was* "insane," because I just kept saying to myself, "Maybe this time I can get away with it. Maybe this time I will only have the rush and not the guilt. Maybe this time, wickedness *will* be happiness!" I might just as well have jumped off a building and hoped I would fall *up*. Need I say, in this area of my life, I have been a very slow learner. Actually, my downfall wasn't a matter of needing to *learn* something. I knew *intellectually* that **wickedness never was happiness" (Alma 41:10),** I just didn't *believe* it. I wasn't really a "slow learner" as much as I was a "slow *believer*." Thus, my need—as ridiculous as it may seem, since I was a lifelong active member of the Church—was to take Step Two and *come to believe*.

BECOMING A BELIEVER

I began my recovery work by attending Heart t' Heart meetings and studying the LDS version of the Twelve Step program outlined in *He Did Deliver Me from Bondage;* both of these activities helped me immensely. Once the basic principles for overcoming addiction began to sink into my understanding, I was eager to find Twelve Step literature specifically addressing *sexual* addiction. I obtained a copy of *Sexaholics Anonymous* (The White Book), and was amazed and delighted with the insights I found on almost every page. On page 89, I found the process of Step Two broken into three separate parts that all of us who have come to this type of fellowship can recognize:

We *came*
We *came to*
We *came to believe*

First of all, *we came*. We came to a meeting. We came to a book or a website or some other vehicle that allowed us to participate in the fellowship of recovery. Like the early disciples of Jesus, heeding his call to "Come follow me," we became willing to listen. Maybe we didn't believe yet, but we were willing to sit still and hear and consider these new ideas.

We came to. It was as if our addiction had knocked us unconscious. We were in a trance and needed to be awakened. As we heard the words, the thoughts and experiences of those who were ahead of us on the path to recovery, a light dawned: there might be an answer here for us as well! We also came to admit that happiness could never come the way we had sought it. We had tried to force happiness from life instead of obeying the principles of Life itself.

We came to believe. The more we listened, the more the Spirit worked on us, teaching us that the Savior's love applied to us as well. Our newly awakened belief gave us the courage to try concrete actions in our attempts at recovery. We gained the faith to test the promises of the Lord. We began to truly look to Him to restore us to sanity—to sane living.

I knew there was truth in these ideas. I knew there had to be a way back. I knew I had not always been "like this." I remembered a time in my life when I was innocent, when I didn't automatically cave in when temptations came along. Perhaps the Lord could help me get back to that place.

DEALING WITH DOUBTS

Facing these issues of just *how much* I believed and just *what* I believed brought me face to face with three questions that had been lurking in the shadows of my unexamined thoughts for years.

1. **Could God really take this addiction away from me?** Could He really free me from the control of this terrible disease? I had already prayed for relief, but it hadn't helped much. Was the deficit in the level of my belief?

2. **Why *would* God take my addiction from me?** While I believed God had helped others to overcome addictions to things such as tobacco and alcohol and even sex, could I believe He would help me—specifically, me—overcome my own loathsome weakness?

3. **Why *should* God help me, if I haven't yet done all I can do on my own?** My own punitive belief about what God should do for someone like me hampered my faith. I interpreted the words "all that I can do" (see **2 Nephi 25:23**) to mean that only by working until the day I died would I have done all I could do on my own, and that was what was required before His grace was available to me.

Each of these unacknowledged doubts about whether God could, would or even should help me acted as invisible barriers that kept me from turning to Him. Perhaps I was like Laman and Lemuel who told Nephi that they did not ask for revelation because **"the Lord maketh no such thing known unto us" (1 Nephi 15:9).** It seems that, like them, I was judging God, attributing limits to His willingness to help me long before I gave Him the chance. In order to get past the barriers these doubts represented, I had to examine them one by one.

1. **Could God really take this addiction away from me?**

From the vantage point of recovery, considering all the miracles God *has* done in my life and in the lives of others, it seems almost blasphemous that I ever entertained this idea, yet it was truly one that haunted me. I had struggled with my addiction to pornography for years and had asked the Lord repeatedly for relief, but none had come—at least, not permanently. In my weakened faith, perhaps the easiest, natural-man explanation for my continuing plight was to doubt God. As ridiculous as it sounds, I was in effect saying, "I know God can move mountains, and even *make* mountains, but this addiction thing is really hard! I'm not sure He can fix *this*."

If you want to indulge in this kind of foolish thinking, you'd better stay away from the scriptures, because they won't let you get away with it. For example, consider the people of King Benjamin. They responded to the invitation of their prophet king to repent, and they experienced a marvelous change as a result:

> **And they all cried with one voice, saying: Yea, we believe all the words which thou hast spoken unto us; and also, we know of their surety and truth, because of the Spirit of the Lord Omnipotent, which has wrought a mighty change in us, or in our hearts, that we have no more disposition to do evil, but to do good continually. (Mosiah 5:2)**

For years I read this verse with a combination of amazement and envy. I thought how wonderful it would be to be free of the ravages of temptation simply because I didn't have the desire to act out any more. On the other hand, I thought this blessing was somehow beyond my reach. I was so easily attracted to sin that I felt if it was possible at all for me to get to the point where I had no more disposition to do evil, it would take me the equivalent of several lifetimes.

Now, in recovery, I have experienced the truth that **"the things which are impossible with men are possible with God" (Luke 18:27).** My testimony today is that God can, and does, work miracles in our lives when we come to Him. I know this because He has now taken this obsession from me. I no longer have the desire to look at pornography. I have learned that this blessing given to the Nephites in King Benjamin's day is just as available to us today. I know. I am living it! As Colleen wrote:

> Part of the process of coming unto Christ and truly applying His atonement to our own lives and the lives of others is to lose our fear that there is some power or effect of evil the Savior can't overcome. (*He Did Deliver Me from Bondage*, 48)

In a similar way, Nephi had to remind his brothers of the power of the Lord in their lives:

> Yea, and how is it that ye have forgotten that the Lord
> is able to do all things according to his will, for the
> children of men, if it so be that they exercise faith in
> him? Wherefore, let us be faithful to him. (1 Nephi
> 7:12)

2. Why *would* God take my addiction from me?

Addiction is so devastating. It gives us such feelings of unworthiness
and even worthlessness. As I was caught in this swamp of self-loathing
and self-disgust, someone said to me, "Do you realize that if you were
the only person who needed the Savior's Atonement, He would have
willingly gone through it all, just for you?" That thought just blew me
away. Why would the Lord love me that much? Why would He value
me when I had turned my back on Him so many times and refused His
invitation to turn away from my despicable practices? I think the answer
can be found in these thoughts expressed by Elder Hartman Rector Jr.:

> God doesn't love us because we are good. God loves us
> because he is good. God is good and so he loves us, and
> those who are the best love the best. (*Conference Report*,
> Oct., 1969, 76)

God's love is based on His character—not mine! What an amazing
thought this was to me. It meant I did not have to *earn* the Savior's love
through my behavior. He has always loved me, even knowing He would
have to suffer for me. Unfortunately, the many years I spent in addiction
clouded my mind to this truth. Only after I began to open myself to Step
Two was I able to feel the Savior's love confirmed to my soul once again.

Since opening my mind and heart to His goodness, I now see it
everywhere in the scriptures. There are so many stories of men who
have been rescued from a life of sin—the apostle Paul, Alma the Elder
and Alma the Younger, the sons of Mosiah and Zeezrom, to mention
only a few. Right there in the testimony of the scriptures was example
after example that the Lord would save those with chronic tendencies
to sin, if and when they finally surrendered their lives to Him. None of
these men were living exemplary lives when the Lord reached out His
hand and touched them. In fact, most of these men were actively

opposing the Lord's work. It didn't seem they had done anything (at least, in *this* life) to "earn" any particular privileges—and yet, the Lord saved them. That gave me hope. If, as Elder Rector said, God loves us because He is good, maybe He would help *me* change, too.

3. Why *should* God help me, if I haven't yet done all I can do on my own?

One of the strongest traditions in my cultural heritage as a Latter-day Saint is the tradition of self-sufficiency. In addition, I was raised by parents who had inherited a powerful work ethic, reinforced by the experience of marrying and starting a family during the Great Depression. I was raised to be proud of working for what I received, paying my own way, and not relying on others to supply my wants or needs. Simultaneously, I was taught that "faith without works is dead," and that anyone who thinks grace is a free gift is sorely mistaken. Needless to say, when combined with the frightening concept of God I explained in Chapter Two, these ideas painted a pretty bleak picture. Small wonder that my interpretation of the following verse had made me feel hopeless:

> **For we labor diligently to write, to persuade our children, and also our brethren, to believe in Christ, and to be reconciled to God; for we know that it is by grace that we are saved, *after all we can do.* (2 Nephi 25:23, emphasis added)**

Today I realize that I totally misunderstood this verse. I read it with hardly more than a passing thought for the faint and distant hope of "grace." To me, grace represented God's help given *after* this life. I read the word "after" in the sequential sense, as in this sentence, "*After* I finish mowing the lawn, then I will go to the store." In this interpretation, I heard the verse was saying to me: "Philip, even though some grace may be extended to you at the end of your life, don't forget that you have to do absolutely everything you possibly can until the day you die, and then *maybe* you will qualify for enough grace to be saved." What a discouraging message that was!

It dawned on me one day that "after" could be seen as part of the phrase "after *all*," which gives it a very different meaning. "After all" can be used in discussing which of two contributing factors carries the most weight, or it can mean "in spite of." For example, *"After all* I tried to do to cheer her up, *your* letter really made the difference." In other words, I may have done all I could, but your letter was what really did the job. In a similar sense, I may do all I can toward my own salvation, but that is almost negligible compared to the Savior's marvelous contribution of grace. To me, that principle is echoed in the words later spoken by King Benjamin: **"I say, if ye should serve him with all your whole souls yet ye would be unprofitable servants" (Mosiah 2:21).** We are not enough, but the Savior is, and that is a great comfort!

Today, when I read this passage in 2 Nephi, the emphasis in my heart and mind is not on *me*, but rather on Jesus Christ and His power to redeem me. This is because I have taken Step Two and have come to believe that a Power greater than myself (my beloved Savior) can, and will, *and has* restored me to sanity. As I write this book **"to persuade...[my] brethren, to believe in Christ, and to be reconciled to God," (2 Nephi 25:23)** I am rejoicing that I did not have to wait until the end of my life to receive this dispensation of grace. Now it is easy for me to see and confess the truth that it was my pride and desire to "do it all myself" that blinded me to Nephi's real message. Nephi wasn't teaching the importance of self-sufficiency. He was teaching the importance of believing in Christ, and being reconciled to God! Why? Because it is only through our faith in Christ and becoming reconciled with God that we place ourselves in a position to receive the grace that is so necessary to our salvation. For even though we work as hard as we can, we will never be saved by our works alone. In spite of all we can do, we are dependent upon the grace (power) of the Savior for our salvation. Just a couple of verses earlier, Nephi testified:

> **As the Lord God liveth, there is none other name given under heaven save it be this Jesus Christ, of which I have spoken, whereby man can be saved. (2 Nephi 25:20)**

CLAIMING THE ATONEMENT FOR MYSELF

"None other name given under heaven!" I had never grasped such a powerful statement before. There is no other name whereby I can be saved than the name (and grace, or power unto salvation) of Jesus Christ. I certainly can't be saved in the name of Philip Harrison! Years of struggling in my own inadequate strength have proven that. Again, Nephi's message was *not* one of self-sufficiency in the matter of our salvation, but rather *dependence upon Christ.* Consider how this invitation is repeated throughout the scriptures:

> Wherefore we labored diligently among our people, that we might persuade them to come unto Christ, and partake of the goodness of God, that they might enter into his rest. (Jacob 1:7)

> And now, my beloved brethren, I would that ye should come unto Christ, who is the Holy One of Israel, and partake of his salvation, and the power of his redemption. Yea, come unto him, and offer your whole souls as an offering unto him, and continue in fasting and praying, and endure to the end; and as the Lord liveth ye will be saved. (Omni 1:26)

> And again I would exhort you that ye would come unto Christ, and lay hold upon every good gift, and touch not the evil gift, nor the unclean thing... Yea, come unto Christ, *and be perfected in him,* and deny yourselves of all ungodliness. (Moroni 10:30,32, emphasis added)

In *He Did Deliver Me from Bondage* (A–6), Colleen refers to the "spiritual dyslexia" we often experience in reading the scriptures. For many years I heard two of the phrases in this last verse **(Moroni 10:32)** backwards—when I heard them at all. I would have sworn it said, "Perfect yourself in order to qualify to come unto Christ." After all, the scriptures also say that **"no unclean thing can dwell...in his presence" (Moses 6:57).** I thought, "If that is true, I certainly would have to clean myself up a great deal before I could even approach Him."

A deeper understanding of the truth, however, taught me that Moroni is saying we must first "come unto Christ," and *then* "be perfected in Him," before we can deny ourselves of our ungodly tendencies. We *have* to come unto Him, give ourselves to Him, surrender our will to His before He can "perfect" us. I had it backwards. In my mind I had reversed the process, which doesn't make sense at all. Since Christ is the only one who can heal us, how can we ever be healed if only those who are well are allowed to approach Him? It's like breaking a leg, and then saying, "As soon as this broken leg heals up, I'll get myself down to the doctor's office."

Another reason that **"no unclean thing can dwell in [God's] presence"** is that when we *do* come to Him, He cleans us up. He removes from us the stains that make us unclean. Doesn't He say, **"Come unto me, all ye that labour and are heavy laden, and I will give you rest" (Matthew 11:28)?** What greater rest could I find than to finally put down the burden of temptation, sin, and addiction that had plagued me for years!

Elder Boyd K. Packer has also taught that we don't have to wait until we die for the Savior's Atonement to take effect. We can enjoy the blessings of His Atonement right now:

> The Atonement offers redemption from spiritual death and from suffering caused by sin. For some reason, we think the Atonement of Christ applies *only* at the end of mortal life to redemption from the Fall, from spiritual death. It is much more than that. It is an ever-present power to call upon in everyday life. When we are racked or harrowed up or tormented by guilt or burdened with grief, He can heal us. While we do not fully understand how the Atonement of Christ was made, we can experience "the peace of God, which passeth all understanding." (*Ensign*, May 2001, 23; emphasis original)

THE CAPTAIN OF MY SOUL

In the chapter on Step One, I cited the poem "Invictus" by William Ernest Henley as an example of determined self-sufficiency. Since in the matter of our salvation, we are *not* self-sufficient, Elder Orson F. Whitney, of the Council of the Twelve, wrote a reply to Henley's declaration of personal independence, which he entitled "The Soul's Captain." Elder Whitney responded to the phrase, "I am the master of my fate: I am the captain of my soul" this way:

> Art thou in truth? Then what of Him
> Who bought thee with his blood?
> Who plunged into devouring seas
> And snatched thee from the flood?
>
> Of what avail thy want of strength
> Apart from His vast might?
> Pray that His light may pierce the gloom
> That thou mayest see aright…
>
> Bend to the dust that head unbowed,
> Small part of life's great whole,
> And find in Him and Him alone
> The captain of thy soul.
> (Boyd K. Packer, Conference Report, October 1962, 47)

The phrase "The captain of thy soul" reminds me of President Ezra Taft Benson's statement:

> Christ changes men, and changed men can change the world. Men changed for Christ will be captained by Christ. Like Paul they will be asking, "Lord, what wilt thou have me to do?" (Acts 9:6.) Peter stated they will "follow his steps." (1 Pet. 2:21.) John said they will "walk, even as he walked." (1 John. 2:6.)
>
> Finally, men captained by Christ will be consumed in Christ…Their will is swallowed up in his will. (See John 5:30.) They do always those things that please the Lord. (See John 8:29.) Not only would they die for the Lord,

but, more important, they want to live for Him. (*Ensign,* July 1989, 4–5)

From all these new ways of looking at the Atonement, I now picture the Savior and myself working together in a mutually loving relationship. I believe His personal testimony:

> I am come a light into the world, that whosoever believeth on me should not abide in darkness. And if any man hear my words, and believe not, I judge him not: *for I came not to judge the world, but to save the world.* (John 12:46–47, emphasis added)

Instead of seeing Him as a judge, watching to see if I am "doing it right," I have come to see Him as my constant counselor and guide, willing to assist me each step of the way, and endow me with His grace, or in other words, the power to overcome my sins and be restored to innocence.

I GLORY IN MY JESUS

Before I came to understand how loving and kind the Savior is, "coming unto Christ" and submitting myself to Him was a scary proposition. When I actually did begin to come unto Christ, a miracle occurred—I lost all fear of Him, and began to see Him for who He really is. One of the testimonies that helped me the most in this process of coming to know the real Jesus was Colleen's. She wrote about this verse from the Book of Mormon:

> I glory in plainness; I glory in truth; I glory in my Jesus, for he hath redeemed my soul from hell. (2 Nephi 33:6)

Describing the impact this verse had upon her, Colleen wrote:

> "*I glory in my Jesus…*" *My Jesus… My…Mine!* I could not get past the personal intimacy of Nephi's statement. Tears welled up, spilling down my face. I burned through and through as with a fire, a passionate and yet childlike

love for God. I felt as if someone had just given me permission to approach the Lord, to actually embrace Him, at least in spirit. I felt such a burning, such a passionate and yet childlike adoration for the Lord. It felt as if I had suddenly awakened to Nephi's example of approaching the Lord and coming to know Him as my dearest friend, as *my* Jesus.

I wept in gratitude to the humble, tender Nephi who had preserved this saving truth of Christ's availability. His personal administration in our lives can be ours, as soon as we are ready to believe and receive it from Him. I mounted up in my imagination as on eagle's wings **(D&C 124:99)**, carried by the power of the love I felt for Him and from Him. I had never before comprehended how close the Savior is willing—and even desires—to be to us.

How can I possibly convey the spiritual awakening, the change, that began to dawn in my heart from that hour? As I continued to read the Book of Mormon, I found one witness after another that there did not have to be any distance between the Lord and me; that His love and power to redeem were enough to save even me. His arm was strong enough to encircle me and give me safety from my weaknesses. A few pages later I read Jacob's words:

> **Wherefore, my beloved brethren, I beseech of you in words of soberness that ye would repent, and come with full purpose of heart, and *cleave unto God as he cleaveth unto you.* And while his arm of mercy is extended towards you in the light of day, harden not your hearts. (Jacob 6:5; emphasis added)**

I knew it was true. I knew by my own experience that He lives and that He lives for me. Something had changed.

I had lived this reality with the Savior. He was my friend,
my Jesus. (*He Did Deliver Me from Bondage*, 32–33)

Colleen's testimony has since been confirmed to my own heart. I
now know, as she does, that Jesus is amazingly available to us. He is
ready to take the burdens from our hearts as soon as we will let go of
them. He loves us more than we can begin to understand, and will
respond with kindness to our efforts to reach out to Him.

MAKING THE MOST OF THIS CHAPTER

Please take time to answer the following questions in your recovery
journal.

1. In **Alma 15:8** we read this testimony, **"If thou believest in the
   redemption of Christ thou canst be healed."** To be healed is the
   equivalent of being restored to sanity. How do you feel about the
   Lord's ability to perform this miracle for you? Think of a situation in
   which you behaved "insanely" by trying to get comfort or happiness
   from addictive behaviors. Did it work? Did it last? Write about it and
   how you would have behaved if your addiction had been removed
   and you had acted sanely.

2. In **Helaman 14:13** we are told that we **"may have a remission of
   [our sins] through *his* merits."** The Lord can give you peace and
   remission. Write about any feelings you still have that you must *earn*
   or *merit* His atoning power. Do you feel there is anything you have
   to do totally on your own before you can ask the Lord's help? Where
   do you think this feeling comes from?

3. **2 Nephi 33:6—"For *he* hath redeemed my soul from hell."** Christ
   has the power to redeem us, no matter how deep or personal our
   individual hell has been—even if we got ourselves into it by our own
   deliberate choices. Write about the idea that Christ came to redeem
   you, even from a hell of your own making.

4. In **John 5:39**, the Savior Himself testifies to us of the power the scriptures have to bring us closer to Him in thought and testimony. Write about your past experiences with the scriptures, including attempts to find hope in them that have failed and attempts that have succeeded. Look back at a scripture in this chapter and write about the feelings and thoughts you have in response to it.

5. In **Mark 9:24** a man expresses in tears his less than perfect belief: **"Lord, I believe; help thou mine unbelief."** The Lord did not rebuke him for his double-mindedness, but proceeded to work the miracle he asked for. Write about how it makes you feel to realize the Lord is willing to accept your faith, even if it is imperfect and faltering. You may want to consider writing your thoughts directly to Him, as if in a letter. This exercise can open your heart to the Spirit of the Lord like few other things can.

6 *Step Three*

Made a decision to turn our will and our lives over to
the care of God as we understood Him.
(A.A. and Heart t' Heart versions)

*Made the decision to reconcile ourselves to the will of God,
offer our whole souls as an offering unto Him, and trust
Him in all things forever. (2 Nephi 10:24; Omni 1:26;
Mosiah 3:19; 2 Nephi 4:34)*
(Heart t' Heart scriptural version)

In working Step Three, I am asked to make the decision to turn my
life over to my Father in Heaven and to my Savior, Jesus Christ. I am
asked to realize that the Savior not only *will* save me, but actually
patiently waits for me to take this step so He *can* save me. He longs for
me to allow Him to do what only He can do—change my heart to
conform with the principles of happiness and eternal life. He cannot
force His will on me. He must wait for *my* decision. This surrender of my
will and life to Him must begin with surrendering my addiction. Taking
Step Three will not be accomplished instantly, but I have become
convinced I have no other option if I am to get well. I am finally willing
to begin this process and to **"give away all my sins" (Alma 22:18).**

THE WRESTLE I HAD TAKING THIS STEP

I am amazed at what a willful soul I can be. It's easy for me to believe I fought *hard* for my agency during the war in heaven, considering how stubbornly I have insisted on doing things *my* way since I've come to earth. And now, Step Three asks me to surrender this hard-won agency to the Lord? From another perspective, it's been quite a struggle to admit to myself that if I don't give my agency to the Lord, I'll be automatically giving it to Satan. I see the words of Step Three. I know I should surrender, but my stubborn will resists, just to prove I am in control of my own life. I've come to realize this obsession with control has been one of the roots of my addiction, one of the excuses I used to justify my acting out.

When I was a young father, for example, I was sure I would be able to raise wonderfully obedient children, despite the fact that I was secretly disobeying God. Never mind the mismanagement of my own agency—as a father I was supposed to manage theirs. Imagine my frustration when they became teenagers and developed opinions of their own! And my wife—how often I have decided she shouldn't feel the way she does! Then there's my boss at work. He always has an opinion about how I should perform my job, and it's not always the same as mine. And what about the weather, and the wars, and all the suffering that goes on in the world? Is it any wonder—in the face of all I had to worry about and stay busy trying to control—I didn't even notice when my own private, personal indulgences became an addiction that began controlling *me*.

In light of the mess the world was in, including especially the mess my own life had become, I was sorely tempted at times to wonder whether Heavenly Father's plan to allow us our own agency was such a good idea. But, then I was reminded that Satan is the one who seeks to take control of our souls and destroy the agency of man. The plan of the Father, in fact, the very path to Godhood, requires the correct use of agency, not the destruction of it. I began to realize that addiction was one of Satan's greatest tools against humanity, against *me*.

THE SUPREME PRINCIPLE OF AGENCY

Agency is such an important principle in the grand scheme of things that our Father in Heaven allows it to be the ultimate deciding factor in our lives. God respects our desires, our wills; that's why He doesn't step in and prevent us from making mistakes. How could we learn to properly use our agency if we never experienced the consequences of misusing it?

I think we sometimes underestimate the significance of the so-called "war in heaven." We think of it as a historical event. "That's when it was decided we would have agency here on the earth." In truth, Satan has never stopped trying to steal our agency from us, and so, in a sense, the war in heaven is still going on—the battleground has just moved to earth. At the same time, however, the Father and Jesus have never stopped respecting and honoring our agency. **"The agency of man" (Moses 4:3)** is an eternal principle that God continues to cherish and protect, placing it even above His own desires for us. Alma said:

> I ought not to harrow up in my desires, the firm decree of a just God, for I know that he granteth unto men according to *their* desire, whether it be unto death or unto life; yea, I know that he allotteth unto men, yea, decreeth unto them decrees which are unalterable, according to *their* wills, whether they be unto salvation or unto destruction. (Alma 29:4, emphasis added)

Notice that what is "allotted" or given to us is according to *our* will, not God's. In the Lord's Prayer, we pray, **"Thy will be done in earth as it is in heaven" (Matt. 6:10),** but the only way for that to happen is for *our* will to become one with *His* will, for He will respect what we choose. The Book of Mormon teaches this principle as the "doctrine of restitution":

> And it is requisite with the justice of God that men should be judged according to their works; and if their works were good in this life, and the desires of their hearts were good, that they should also, at the last day,

> be restored unto that which is good. And if their
> works are evil they shall be restored unto them for
> evil...The one raised to happiness according to his
> desires of happiness, or good according to his desires
> of good; and the other to evil according to his desires
> of evil; for as he has desired to do evil all the day long
> even so shall he have his reward of evil when the night
> cometh. (Alma 41:3–5)

There are really only two choices open to us. We can say unto God,
as the Savior did, "Thy will be done," or we can wait until our chances
for repentance are past and the Lord reluctantly says to us, "Very well
then, *thy* will be done. If you insist on having evil and what evil brings,
you may have it. The choice is entirely yours." Thus we will find that the
telestial kingdom is populated entirely by people who have chosen it.

I have always been impressed with the Lord's powerful counsel to us
in **Doctrine and Covenants 121.** He tells us in no uncertain terms that
we are to lead only with **"gentleness and meekness,"** and warns us that
power and influence cannot be maintained by the use of the priesthood
(or any other position of power, such as parenthood). I accepted that
principle of priesthood leadership in the home, and although I didn't
practice it perfectly in raising my children, I believed it and tried to
follow it. It was a great awakening for me, however, to realize that God
follows the same principles in His interactions with us. Because God
waits upon our will, He Himself follows the same standard to influence
others:

> Only by persuasion, by long-suffering, by gentleness
> and meekness, and by love unfeigned; By kindness,
> and pure knowledge, which shall greatly enlarge the
> soul without hypocrisy, and without guile. (D&C
> 121:41–42)

Therefore, the Lord continues to wait for us to decide to serve Him
with all our **"heart, might, mind and strength"** (D&C 4:2). And
perhaps the greatest thing we can do to help **"[His] kingdom come"**
(Matt 6:10) is to each bring our will into harmony with His perfect will.

Because the Lord leaves it all up to us, it is of utmost importance that we carefully examine our desires and motives. Our actions are one of the truest indicators of our desires, for our deeds spring from our desires. One of the hardest truths I have had to face is the fact that when I was acting out it was because that was what in my heart of hearts I truly wanted. I told myself that I wanted abstinence, but my actions proved otherwise. What I needed was not a transplant of willpower, but a "heart" transplant. I needed a new heart, new desires, new longings for God, instead of for the pleasure or comfort of pornography. The only person who could give me those desires, in place of the corrupt ones I had, was God. He has promised us:

> **Then will I sprinkle clean water upon you, and ye shall be clean: from all your filthiness, and from all your idols, will I cleanse you. A new heart also will I give you, and a new spirit will I put within you: and I will take away the stony heart out of your flesh, and I will give you an heart of flesh. And I will put my spirit within you, and cause you to walk in my statutes, and ye shall keep my judgments, and do them. (Ezekiel 36:25–27)**

ADDICTION—SATAN'S ENSLAVEMENT OF AGENCY

Addiction is "cunning, baffling and powerful," as AA puts it. That is as true of sexual addiction as of any other addiction. So much of my battle has had to do with my desires—wrestling with the fact that at times I really *want* to sin. It seems insane to look at the devastation that addiction brings into my life and then say that some of the time I don't *want* to give it up. It defies logic. It defies reason. That is what makes addiction so "cunning, baffling and powerful." The truth is, addiction subverts our will, our desires, and our very agency. My desire for righteousness dwindled as my desire for the "rush" I got from pornography increased. I saw myself becoming dependent on those feelings. It would be naive to pretend there was no "reward" in these behaviors. If I didn't get something from it, I wouldn't continue these behaviors, would I?

When I logically consider all that these behaviors have done to ruin my life, however, it clearly isn't worth it. But how do I hold on to that rational perspective when I am in the throes of a very enticing temptation?

I remember a General Authority telling of a visit he made to a man in the hospital who was dying of lung cancer caused by his years of addiction to smoking. Even though the man had no more access to cigarettes, his habit of reaching into his shirt pocket for them was so strong, he had worn a hole in his pajamas by repeatedly reaching for the cigarettes that weren't there. The General Authority then asked: "When this man passed into the spirit world soon after my visit, do you think he still wanted a cigarette? Of course he did! **'That same spirit which doth possess your bodies at the time that ye go out of this life...will have power to possess your body in that eternal world (Alma 34:34)'."**

Addiction to sensuality is no different. The addict continues to indulge, even though the enjoyment becomes less and less, while the craving becomes fiercer and fiercer. Soon the pain hugely outweighs the diminishing thrill. I can easily picture a person in spirit prison, wishing he could indulge in sexual behavior long after the chance to do so is gone. Even when the possibility of acting on his lust has disappeared, he would rather hold on to lust he can no longer satisfy than surrender it to the Lord and be set free. He is truly in prison.

As I struggled to take Step Three, I was amazed at the arguments Satan, the father of lies, used to keep me entrapped. For instance, I was tempted to see surrendering my will to God as just plain unnatural. I mean, isn't it a *natural* and desirable thing for children to grow up and become self-sufficient? After all, I worked hard to become an adult, independent from my parents. If I hadn't, I might still be living at home, using up their resources instead of earning my own way. Under the influence of this way of thinking, I was completely distracted from the testimony of the scriptures concerning the degree of dependence I needed to have *on the Lord*:

> **For the natural man is an enemy to God, and has been from the fall of Adam, and will be, forever and ever, unless he yields to the enticings of the Holy Spirit,**

> and putteth off the natural man and becometh a saint
> through the atonement of Christ the Lord, *and
> becometh as a child, submissive, meek, humble, patient,
> full of love, willing to submit to all things which the
> Lord seeth fit to inflict upon him, even as a child doth
> submit to his father.* (Mosiah 3:19, emphasis added)

Gradually, I began to realize Step Three was the step inviting me to finally heed these words from King Benjamin, to finally realize that, on an eternal scale, I am still a small child when compared to God. But still I resisted. I just could not find the *desire* to submit to Him in all things. It seemed all my desires were bound up in the shame and degradation of sexual addiction.

BECOMING MORE AWARE OF MY DESIRES

The human capacity for desire is perverted and corrupted by addiction. My addiction was no different. For many years I believed that the only way to overcome my addiction was to "stuff" my sinful desires as much as possible, to keep them contained or repressed. However, using this approach, I found myself virtually unable to resist a single urge to act out. Because I refused to *admit* my desires, to acknowledge the warning signs that were happening in my heart and mind, I was oblivious to my own danger. I was set up to act out without warning, and then found myself asking—after the act—"How did I get *here* again?"

Bill W., the founder of Alcoholics Anonymous, described this same experience in his battle with alcoholism. After a series of binges, he determined once and for all to quit drinking.

> Shortly afterward I came home drunk. There had been
> no fight. Where had been my high resolve? I simply
> didn't know. It hadn't even come to mind. Someone had
> pushed a drink my way, and I had taken it. Was I crazy?
> I began to wonder, for such an appalling lack of perspec-
> tive seemed near being just that.

Renewing my resolve, I tried again. Some time passed, and confidence began to be replaced by cocksureness. I could laugh at the gin mills. Now I had what it takes! One day I walked into a café to telephone. In no time I was beating on the bar asking myself how it happened. As the whisky rose to my head I told myself I would manage better next time, but I might as well get good and drunk then. And I did.

The remorse, horror and hopelessness of the next morning are unforgettable. The courage to do battle was not there. (*Alcoholics Anonymous*, Fourth Ed., 5–6)

Paradoxically, the recovery process has led me to the understanding that rather than deny my desires, I needed to pay *more* attention to them, including and most especially the sinful ones. Before I could start getting abstinent, I had to "step outside myself" enough to take a hard look at the desires I was harboring and the choices they were enticing me to make. Concerning the importance of our desires, Elder Neal A. Maxwell said:

Actually, everything depends—initially and finally—on our desires. These shape our thought patterns. Our desires thus precede our deeds and lie at the very cores of our souls, tilting us toward or away from God (see D&C 4:3)...

The end rule is "according to [our] desires...shall it be done unto [us]" (D&C 11:17), "for I, the Lord, will judge all men according to their works, according to the desire of their hearts" (D&C 137:9; see also Alma 41:5; D&C 6:20, 27). One's individual will thus remains uniquely his. God will not override it nor overwhelm it. Hence we'd better want the consequences of what we want! (*Ensign*, Nov. 1995, 23)

After a time of some bewilderment, I finally began to understand that if I was not willing to confront my desires, I would continue to be subject to their power to carry me away without my even considering the alternatives. It took a lot of prayer and surrender to the Lord before I could admit that at some level I *did* know what was happening, even though I desperately tried to pretend I didn't. As painful as it was, I had to admit to my Lord that I had wanted sin more than I had wanted Him. Then I had to petition Him to change my heart, to give me the desire for Him and His way of life. Only then could I start to change from the inside out. I had to stop and think about how fierce my craving for pornography had been at times, and realize that my desire for God had to be at least that desperate. I had to want God more than I wanted my addiction—but that desire was not something I could call up from inside me. The desire for righteousness was itself a gift from God.

LOOKING UNTO THE LORD IN EVERY THOUGHT

How, then, do we begin to turn back to the Lord and surrender our addiction to Him? We have talked about the importance of turning our desires over to Him. This begins with our very thoughts.

> If one "mind[s] the things of the flesh" (Rom. 8:5), he cannot "have the mind of Christ" (1 Cor. 2:16) because his thought patterns are "far from" Jesus, as are the desires or the "intents of his heart" (Mosiah 5:13). Ironically, if the Master is a stranger to us, then we will merely end up serving other masters. The sovereignty of these other masters is real, even if it sometimes is subtle...To the extent that we are not willing to be led by the Lord, we will be driven by our appetites, or we will be greatly preoccupied with the lesser things of the day...For many moderns, sad to say, the query "What think ye of Christ?" (Matt. 22:42) would be answered, "I really don't think of Him at all!" (Neal A. Maxwell, *Ensign*, Nov. 1995, 22–23)

Our thoughts and desires must be centered in Christ if we are to escape enslavement by our appetites. This doesn't mean we must first "have the mind of Christ" before we can give up "the things of the flesh," nor does it mean we must be clean before we can approach the Lord. The two processes happen simultaneously.

The Lord has told us that we are to first **"come unto Christ [as we are], and [then] be perfected in Him"** (Moroni 10:32). I have learned I can begin by doing things that bring Christ into my mind. I spend time every day in sincere, heartfelt prayer, and regularly ponder the scriptures. In addition, I must not only "think of Jesus" but also let Him become the center of my life, of my very thoughts, if I am to become free from the ravages of entrapment in sensuality. Even when I was still slipping back into acting out, I found that the more I turned to Christ, *even while I still felt I was a mess,* the more He blessed me and comforted me. Even so, I didn't automatically start turning to the Savior every time I was tempted. It took time to develop trust in Him, and time to develop the habit of relying on Him, but the more often I tried, the easier it became.

THE AMAZING POWER OF SURRENDERING TO CHRIST

A marvelously liberating principle fell into place when reading in the SA White Book. Instead of *automatically surrendering to temptation,* as I had done for years, I needed to *surrender the temptation to the Lord* and ask Him to take it away. Could it really be that simple? It seemed too easy, but I had already tried all the hard ways, and they didn't work. What could it hurt to give "surrendering" a try?

My attempts were rewarded, for I found, as Alma did, that I could cry out to Jesus for mercy **(Alma 36:18–19; 38:8).** Each time I found myself being tempted, I began to say: *"Lord, I am powerless over this temptation. I need you to take it from me. Please take it away and keep me safe from sin."* As I began asking the Lord to take each temptation away, I found to my great amazement and relief that "God could and would, if He were sought" (*Alcoholics Anonymous,* 60). What an amazing difference! Instead of automatically giving in each time the enticement to sin was thrown at me, I found I could surrender the temptation to the Lord and *not* give in. Frequently I have had to surrender a temptation several times until I succeeded in letting it go, but I have found that if I persist in giving each temptation to the Lord, over and over, for as long as it takes, I am delivered every time.

As I continued this practice, I began to have more and more success in allowing the Lord to take from me temptations I encountered in my daily activities—such as the temptation to rent a pornographic video or get on the Internet and surf for pornography. Then, since no new filth was coming into my brain, the adversary of my soul started calling to my mind images I had stored in my brain over the many years I indulged in this terrible addiction. After all, the mind retains everything we experience, and I had willingly put lots of garbage into my mind that could be called up at any time. In trying to deal with this new assault, I found I could apply the same principle of surrendering my *thoughts* to the Lord. After all, He said: **"Look unto me in every thought"** (D&C 6:36). I didn't really want to admit to the Lord what some of my thoughts were (as if He didn't know already!), but I was desperate, so I tried surrendering my memories, too. *"Dear Savior, I have put some awful images into my mind, and right now I am struggling with this one. Would you please take it out of my mind so I don't have to dwell on it?"* And He would! With rejoicing, I realized I had finally found a way the Lord and I together could win a victory over temptation. My surrender and the Lord's strength made it possible. As the apostle Paul stated:

> **There hath no temptation taken you but such as is common to man: but God is faithful, who will not suffer you to be tempted above that ye are able; but will with the temptation also make a way to escape, that ye may be able to bear it. (1 Corinthians 10:13)**

Again, the Lord is the One who makes the **"way to escape."** In fact, He *is* **"the Way."** As He said to his apostles anciently, **"I am the way, the truth, and the life: no man cometh unto the Father, but by me"** (John 14:6). And no man escapeth addiction but by Him, either. I could not do this on my own. But there was still another lesson I needed to learn from this scripture. The apostle Paul said the Lord would prepare a way to escape, **"that ye may be able to bear it."** Even with the Lord preparing a way for me, there was still something I had **"to bear."** I still had to exert whatever willpower or agency I possessed, but now it was suddenly possible. It seemed that either the intensity of the temptation was lowered, or something had been added to my previously inadequate ability to resist. Miraculously I saw myself begin to say "No" to the temptations. What a glorious feeling that brought! Gradually, I regained the hope that I was *not* condemned to repeat the sin over and over for the rest of my life. There *was* a way out.

I found it to be challenging to remember (and to *want*) to surrender to the Lord each time I was tempted to lust, but I also found that the Lord was willing to help me long before I could do it well. As I have struggled to surrender my will more completely to Him, the Lord has made it possible for me to give up the "right" to indulge in pornography, one step at a time. Each sacrifice of my will for His has been accepted and rewarded with an increase in "sobriety."

It is my testimony that as we offer the Lord whatever shred of agency we have left, He will take it and make it more. Perhaps we only have the courage or strength to cry for help, as Alma did, but we must do it. He will work with whatever we have, if we are willing to give it to Him. As Elder Neal A. Maxwell said:

> Only by aligning our wills with God's is full happiness to be found. Anything less results in a lesser portion (see Alma 12:10–11). The Lord will work with us even if, at first, we "can no more than desire" but are willing to "give place for a portion of [His] words" (Alma 32:27). A small foothold is all He needs! But we must desire and provide it. (*Ensign*, Nov. 1995, 23)

In Twelve Step circles, this is called "being willing to be willing." Maybe we don't have the willingness to give up the sin yet, but if we can summon the willingness to approach the Lord, and offer Him whatever willingness we have, He will help us. We can say: *"Dear Savior, I know I need to give this up, but I just don't want to. But if you will soften my heart and give me the willingness, I will do it."*

Alma's experience gave me a new understanding of the word "remission." I thought of a cancer, growing and spreading throughout the body, making it sicker and sicker, gradually robbing it of strength and vitality. Then help comes, perhaps in the form of medical treatment or maybe by divine intervention, and the cancer stops its advance, and even retreats. We say the cancer is "in remission." It no longer threatens. The potential for a recurrence may still be there, but for the present it is quiet. So it is with sin. Although we never lose the *possibility* of sin, through the Lord's mercy, we can experience a "remission" of our sins. They can become dormant, inactive, and no longer threatening.

MAKING THE DECISION TO SURRENDER OUR WILL

Step Three says, "Made a decision to turn our will and our lives over to the care of God." It's important to remember that this *is* a decision. It is a decision I have to make over and over again, because the opportunities to exercise my agency keep coming up over and over. And in that process, I am repeatedly tempted to follow my own will, to do what I want instead of what *God* wants. I have to admit I sometimes still want things that are not God's best choice for me. The decision to submit my will to His has to be continually re-made, many times each day, and each time it is a matter of choosing life, instead of death:

> **And now remember, remember, my brethren, that whosoever perisheth, perisheth unto himself; and whosoever doeth iniquity, doeth it unto himself; for behold, ye are free; ye are permitted to act for yourselves; for behold, God hath given unto you a knowledge and he hath made you free. He hath given unto you that ye might know good from evil, and he hath given unto you that ye might choose life or death; and ye can do good and be restored unto that which is good, or have that which is good restored unto you; or ye can do evil, and have that which is evil restored unto you. (Helaman 14:30–31)**

I can't overemphasize how important, how central, this decision is—to surrendering our will to the Lord. We think we make many sacrifices in our attempts to be obedient to the gospel. In truth there is only one sacrifice, although we make it over and over again. Quoting again from Elder Maxwell:

> In conclusion, the submission of one's will is really the only uniquely personal thing we have to place on God's altar. The many other things we "give," brothers and sisters, are actually the things He has already given or loaned to us. However, when you and I finally submit ourselves, by letting our individual wills be swallowed up in God's will, then we are really giving something to Him! It is the only possession which is truly ours to give! (Neal A. Maxwell, *Ensign*, Nov. 1995, 24)

It is an amazing principle that when we give up our agency to God, we receive greater power in return. It is one of those principles that sound so paradoxical, like **"the last shall be first, and the first last: for many be called, but few chosen" (Matthew 20:16),** and **"He that findeth his life shall lose it: and he that loseth his life for my sake shall find it" (Matthew 10:39).** Nevertheless, even if it sounds paradoxical, it is true. We have the Lord's word on it.

In each stage of my journey toward recovery, I have found there was something in front of me that, deep inside, I knew I needed to do, some step forward that the Lord, through His Spirit, was inviting me to take. Often I didn't have the courage or the willingness to do it, but I found that if I talked to Him and asked Him to soften my heart, before long I found the willingness to go ahead and take that next step. Before surrendering my heart to the Lord, it was as if the door was locked, bolted and barred. There was no way I could get through it. But when I called upon the Lord, offered Him my heart, and asked Him to change it, the door was suddenly open; I could see my way to walk through it. I suddenly felt, "I can do this or not. I have the power to choose." *I have learned that my recovery absolutely depends on my willingness to walk through the door when it opens.* Christ will open the door, but He will not push me through it; I have to walk through it myself. The Prophet Joseph Smith said: "I made this my rule: When the Lord commands, do it" (*History of the Church* 2:170). For me, that translates to, "When the Lord shows you a path and gives you the power to take it, do it."

MAKING THE MOST OF THIS CHAPTER

Please take time to answer the following questions in your recovery journal.

1. Write about any fears you have about surrendering your will to the Lord. What are the thoughts or feelings holding you back? What do you think your life would be like if you surrendered your complete will to Him?

2. Think of someone you feel has surrendered his life to God, such as one of the General Authorities, or perhaps a personal acquaintance. What is that person like? What is his/her personality? Has this "surrender" made him/her lifeless and robot-like, or does he/she strike you as real and vibrant?

3. In **Mosiah 15:7** we read about **"the will of the Son being swallowed up in the will of the Father."** Do you see Jesus as a person with no will of His own? How has surrendering His will to the will of His Father affected the Savior's life? How did it affect His ability to fulfill His earthly mission?

4. Write about the difference between surrendering your addiction to the Lord and surrendering your whole life to Him. What other areas of your life might need to be surrendered to the Lord? Are you able to see this surrender process as something you can undertake, one step at a time?

5. Write another letter to the Savior in your recovery journal. Express to Him your feelings about turning over your life and will to Him. Tell Him about any fears you have. Continue writing about how you feel after you have expressed these feelings. If you feel a response from Him, write that, too.

7 Step Three and a Half

Continuing in Surrender:
Living with Steps One, Two and Three

After attending recovery meetings and working through the Twelve Steps for a while, I was grateful to realize my addiction was beginning to lose its power over me. I had spent many years under the total control of this awful disease. Finally, when I admitted my need for the Savior in my life and started asking Him to take the temptations away, I began to find the ability to turn away and not act out each time I was tempted. It was as if the intensity of the temptation had been reduced. I was sure that from that point on, everything in my life was going to be better. I felt like a prisoner set free from a dark dungeon!

Then one evening, at a Heart t' Heart meeting, I listened as some-one described her current challenges. After several years of abstinence from her "primary addiction" (the problem that had first brought her to a Twelve Step program), she was feeling a need to give attention to another area of her life. "I have decided I need to work the Steps on this," she said. Her declaration hit me like a bucket of cold water! This was a completely new way of looking at recovery. I had pictured I would learn how to apply the Twelve Steps to my pornography addiction, and then, like graduating from a twelve-week course, I would be fixed. It might take a little longer than twelve weeks, but I hadn't imagined I would need to work through the Twelve Steps more than once—on this or any other problem. I still didn't realize that these principles described a *process*, a formula I would find helpful again and again. I thought a change as mighty as the one I was experiencing had to be permanent!

DISCOVERING THE MEANING OF *REMISSION*

After several days of being clean and feeling no inclination to act out, an almost overwhelming temptation hit me out of nowhere. I was stunned! I tried to push it away, but it kept returning, each time with more intensity than the last. I asked, "What do I do? I thought I was safe! I thought the problem had been taken away!" I was stunned that the Lord hadn't completely cured me of this addiction. After a period of reflection and prayer, it began to dawn on me that the Lord had something else in mind for me. As I mentioned in the last chapter, I began to realize that the word *remission* needed to be taken very literally. I needed to take another look at exactly what "remission" means.

Alma the younger related how he first *received* a remission of his sins by turning to the Savior:

> And never, until I did cry out unto the Lord Jesus Christ for mercy, did I receive a remission of my sins. But behold, I did cry unto him and I did find peace to my soul. (Alma 38:8)

This much I could relate to. I had turned to the Savior and surrendered my addiction and had even begun trying to give the rest of my life to Him. I had surrendered a number of temptations to Him, asking Him to deliver me from them—and He had. The challenging part was I seemed to have to renew this surrender—this turning my life over to God—on an ongoing basis!

Alma understood this process. Although he was blessed with a remission of his sins, he, too, had to *retain* that remission by continuing to be faithful in maintaining his relationship with the Lord. If he had not, he would have lost that remission, as suggested by his later question to some members of the Church.

> And now behold, I say unto you, my brethren, if ye have experienced a change of heart, and if ye have felt

to sing the song of redeeming love, I would ask, can ye feel so now? (Alma 5:26)

Suddenly I realized what Alma's question implied! A person could have a mighty change of heart and then lose it! This mighty change I was experiencing was merely a *reprieve*, not a *cure*! When I prayed for relief from one wave of temptation and received it, that did not mean I had prayed once and for all. The Lord's rescue of me from one tempta-tion was not a promise that I would never be tempted again. *Boy, what a letdown! That wasn't what I wanted!* I wanted to be free from the danger, the threat, the annoyance of continually being assailed by the adversary, by the enemy of my peace. I wanted a magic cloak that made me invisible to temptation and invulnerable to the darts of the adver-sary. No such luck. Apparently, it was possible for me to receive a remission of my sins, and then to become, as **"entangled again in the vanities of the world" (D&C 20:5)**

I found solid, practical advice and support in the SA White Book. In the following passage, I learned that the need for continued vigilance and dedication—in other words *surrender*—was actually typical of most people's recovery experience. I was relieved to know it wasn't just me who couldn't get it perfect the first time around. We all have to *practice* recovery.

> Sooner or later, the urge strikes again, sometimes out of nowhere, like a tidal wave crashing over us. Wham! Maybe it's the first time we feel rejected. Any of count-less triggers can do it; it really doesn't matter what they are. We all have them.
>
> *"It's too overpowering!...No one will know the difference."*
>
> *"A look never killed anyone..."*
>
> *"Everyone's doing it!"*
>
> *"I never thought I'd hear from him [or her] again. Now what do I do?"*

Often it begins in the privacy of our innermost thoughts, when we're alone, when we're living inside our head and the emotions we could never face overwhelm us. So what do we do? Naturally, we want to reach for the drug again; that's what we programmed ourselves to do. Instead, we surrender. Again. Just like the first time. And the cry for help goes up again: *I'm powerless; please help me!*

And we take the action of getting out of ourselves and making contact with another member. As soon as possible. The closer to the heat of the action the better. We use the phone. We make the call. Not because we want to, *because we don't want to.* We call because we know we have to. Our survival instinct comes to life. And we go to a meeting as soon as possible.

When we first come into the program, this cry for help is, in effect, a shotgun working of Steps One, Two, and Three. Surrender, of whatever sort. That's all it takes, and not one of us does it with all the right motives. When the craving hits again, we repeat this surrender at the very point of our terror, in the pit of our hell. For that's where the admission of powerlessness really works, when we're in the raw heat of temptation and craving. Again, it's the change of attitude that brings relief. Instead of, "I've got to have it or I'll die!" our attitude becomes, "I give up; I'm willing *not* to have it, even if I do die."

And we don't die! We get a reprieve. Again. For seconds, minutes, hours, perhaps even days and weeks. The tidal wave is spent. The craving passes. And we're okay. We are learning the truth of the program maxim, "One Day at a Time."

But there will be another wave behind it, and sooner or later we get hit again. This may knock us off balance.

> *"Why do I always feel recovered after each bout and then get caught off guard by the next wave?"*

Often, seeing we've stopped acting out our habit for a time, we feel we're free of it forever. This may just be the time it strikes again. So the realization slowly dawns that we may always be subject to temptation and powerless over lust. We come to see that it's all right to be tempted and feel absolutely powerless over it *as long as we can get the power to overcome.* The fear of our vulnerability gradually diminishes as we stay sober and work the Steps. We can look forward to the time when the obsession—not temptations—will be gone.

We begin to see that **there's no power over the craving in advance;** we have to work this *as it happens each time.* Therefore, each temptation, every time we want to give in to lust or any other negative emotion, is a gift toward recovery, healing, and freedom—another opportunity to change our attitude and find union with God. We didn't get here in a day; it took practice to burn the addictive process into our being. **It takes practice to make our true Connection.** (*Sexaholics Anonymous,* 67–69. Italics original; bold emphasis added)

In other words, *retaining* a remission of my addiction would happen in the same way *obtaining* it had happened—by humbly admitting my continuing need for a personal, daily relationship with my Savior. Like the manna the Lord sent the children of Israel, the sustaining power He sends to me that keeps me abstinent has to be replenished anew every day, too.

RETAINING A REMISSION BY CONTINUING TO SURRENDER

I can't overemphasize the importance of these principles learned from the experience of SA members. They helped me realize my need for *ongoing* humility and patience. Once I accepted that there was no quick cure for my addiction, these ideas helped me acknowledge my need for principles and tools I could use, day after day, one day at a time. Here are some of the statements from SA, translated into my own truth:

1. *"Often it begins in the privacy of our innermost thoughts, when we're alone, when we're living inside our head and the emotions we could never face overwhelm us."* Isolation is dangerous. It is both the result of our addiction and the means by which the addiction is perpetuated. As part of my own healing process, I must be willing to stay in touch with others who are practicing recovery.

2. *"And the cry for help goes up again: I'm powerless; please help me!"* The cry for help, the repeated surrender *must* become part of my daily experience, a way of life, a way of living clean. I cannot really enjoy the life God intended for me if I ignore or neglect my need to stay connected to Him.

3. *"And we take the action of getting out of ourselves and making contact with another member. As soon as possible. The closer to the heat of the action the better...And we go to a meeting as soon as possible."* Temptations and actions I have experienced in the past will continue to have a seducing influence over me as long as I remain ashamed and silent about them. In my isolation, the adversary can entice me to recall them to my mind over and over, each time tempting me anew. Telling another recovering person about my struggle has the miraculous effect of lessening the temptation's hold on my mind. The adversary revels in secrecy. Honesty neutralizes his power.

4. *"A shotgun working of Steps One, Two, and Three."* This phrase suggests a rapid, almost automatic reworking of these vital steps. "I can't. God can. I'll let Him." I have to be willing to take these steps again and again, as often as it takes. In doing so, I begin living the Savior's invitation to **"look unto me in every thought"** (D&C **6:36).**

5. *"We repeat this surrender at the very point of our terror, in the pit of our hell. For that's where the admission of powerlessness really works, when we're in the raw heat of temptation and craving."* I must remember that, *"there's no power over the craving in advance."* To change lifelong

patterns, I have to be willing to admit I am tempted *again,* face the temptation, and surrender it, rather than surrender *to* it. It has been said in great simplicity: "The only way to stop is to stop." In other words, while the Lord will lower the intensity of a temptation for me, He still requires me to exert whatever amount of courage and agency I can muster—no matter how small. I must remember that He said: **"My grace is sufficient for all men *that humble themselves before me"* (Ether 12:27, emphasis added).** Continuing surrender is an act of humility. It is an admission of my continuing need for Christ, acknowledgment of His power, and a petition for that amazing gift to be applied in my behalf (Steps One, Two and Three).

6. *"So the realization slowly dawns that we may always be subject to temptation and powerless over lust. We come to see that it's all right to be tempted and feel absolutely powerless over it as long as we can get the power to overcome."* For many years, I confused temptation with sin. In my perfectionism, I was disgusted and impatient with myself *just for being tempted*—acting as if temptation were the same as sin. I have since learned (and constantly try to remember) *it is not a sin to be tempted.* Temptation is a part of being mortal. Sin only comes in giving in to the temptation. Admitting powerlessness over lust does not mean I have to give in to it. Admitting powerlessness over lust means I must always remember that I will never outgrow my need for the Savior's grace (enabling power to *maintain* the good work of abstinence and recovery).

7. *"The fear of our vulnerability gradually diminishes as we stay sober and work the Steps. We can look forward to the time when the obsession—not temptations—will be gone."* There's a major difference between obsession and everyday exposure to temptation. I must remember that to deal with temptation does not mean I am obsessed, as I was before surrendering to Christ in recovery. When I was obsessed with sex, I couldn't stop thinking about it. As I have progressed in recovery, the obsession with sex and pornography has gradually been lifted, and the temptations I experience have diminished in intensity as well. I

can trust the Lord's wisdom in not removing them entirely, in order that I might learn from my weaknesses.

Coming to understand this process has helped me to appreciate and rejoice in the Apostle Paul's honest confession of his own ongoing struggle with a weakness of "the flesh":

> **And lest I should be exalted above measure through the abundance of the revelations, there was given to me a thorn in the flesh, the messenger of Satan to buffet me, lest I should be exalted above measure. For this thing I besought the Lord thrice, that it might depart from me. And he said unto me, My grace is sufficient for thee: for my strength is made perfect in weakness. Most gladly therefore will I rather glory in my infirmities, that the power of Christ may rest upon me. Therefore I take pleasure in infirmities, in reproaches, in necessities, in persecutions, in distresses for Christ's sake; for when I am weak [and give my weakness to Christ], then am I strong. (2 Corinthians 12:7–10)**

I have come to know for myself and not just from Paul's testimony that the Lord has a divine reason for giving me this need to stay in constant surrender to Him. I have lived the meaning of these words from the Book of Mormon:

> **And if men come unto me I will show unto them their weakness. I give unto men weakness that they may be humble; and my grace is sufficient for all men that humble themselves before me; for if they humble themselves before me, and have faith in me, then will I make weak things become strong unto them. (Ether 12:27)**

THE NEED FOR PATIENCE TO TRUST THE LORD'S PURPOSES

At first, it was really hard for me to adjust to this dawning realization that the Lord doesn't usually rush right in and make everything
perfect, even for those who genuinely seek His intervention. The experience of the elder Alma and his followers helped me begin to accept
this truth. Alma's people were in servitude to the Lamanites and had
prayed fervently for deliverance from their oppression. While the Lord
did not deliver them immediately, He made their situation bearable:

> And I will also ease the burdens which are put upon
> your shoulders, that even you cannot feel them upon
> your backs, even while you are in bondage; and this
> will I do that ye may stand as witnesses for me here-
> after, and that ye may know of a surety that I, the
> Lord God, do visit my people in their afflictions. And
> now it came to pass that the burdens which were laid
> upon Alma and his brethren were made light; yea, the
> Lord did strengthen them that they could bear up
> their burdens with ease, and they did submit cheer-
> fully and with patience to all the will of the Lord.
> (Mosiah 24:14–15).

Isn't this what we really need? Don't we just need enough help to get
through the challenges we are facing? That wasn't enough for me at
first, though. I wanted my problems to be wiped away completely, right
now. This "all or nothing" thinking—another expression of my perfectionism—was actually keeping me in my addiction. As life didn't unfold
the way I had insisted it should, I would numb my impatience through
the use of pornography and masturbation. Even in recovery, when I
finally found I could petition the Lord for relief from my addiction, I was
still impatient. I just wanted to ask once and be done with it. Obviously,
patience had never been one of my better qualities. Why then should it
seem strange to me that the same impatience I have had toward life
should also manifest itself in my recovery? I had to admit I had not
changed that much, not deep down inside. I was learning some
marvelous principles through the Twelve Steps, but so far the changes

had only reached the upper layers of my character. I still related totally to Colleen's confession of the same feelings during her own early recovery:

> That same defect [of character] that wanted *instant* relief from my pain—the defect that created my compulsive, addictive behavior—also wanted *instant* recovery. (Colleen C. Harrison, *Patterns of Light: Step 3*, 19)

Though I was just beginning the recovery process, I'm grateful to say I was awakening to the power of the scriptures to provide comfort and guidance. I found myself noticing how the prophets met afflictions and challenges with patience. The Prophet Joseph Smith provided me with a marvelous example, *if I would be humble enough to receive it.* As Joseph sat in Liberty Jail after months and years of watching the Saints go through unspeakable persecution, he longed for the Lord to show His hand in relieving their afflictions. In anguish, Joseph cried out:

> **O God, where art thou? And where is the pavilion that covereth thy hiding place? How long shall thy hand be stayed, and thine eye, yea thy pure eye, behold from the eternal heavens the wrongs of thy people and of thy servants, and thine ear be penetrated with their cries? Yea, O Lord, how long shall they suffer these wrongs and unlawful oppressions, before thine heart shall be softened toward them, and thy bowels be moved with compassion toward them? (D&C 121:1–3)**

The Lord had compassion toward Joseph, and comforted him with these words:

> **My son, peace be unto thy soul; thine adversity and thine afflictions shall be but a small moment; And then, if thou endure it well, God shall exalt thee on high; thou shalt triumph over all thy foes. (D&C 121:7–8)**

I always wanted God to be patient with my shortcomings, but gradually I realized that I also needed to have patience with Him and His timetable. I needed to be humble and meek and willing to be long-suffering, as He worked out His purposes in my life. This business of getting me through the lessons of this life really was a joint venture between God and me. I needed to trust that God knew best how to lead me through this recovery process—how much of my burden to lift and how soon.

In this spirit of trust and patience, I try now, when temptation returns, to surrender it to Him again, and then again, and still again, as many times as it takes. And with time and with patience, I find that I can be abstinent, one day at a time. I hadn't realized before how essential to recovery the virtue of patience was, but I find that it is indeed a central principle:

> **Let us lay aside every weight, and the sin which doth so easily beset us, and let us run *with patience* the race that is set before us, Looking unto Jesus the author and finisher of our faith. (Hebrews 12:1–2, emphasis added)**

One step at a time, I am learning to trust God with my life, and I am coming to know for myself the truth of the Lord's promise given through President Ezra Taft Benson:

> Men and women who turn their lives over to God will discover that He can make a lot more out of their lives than they can. He will deepen their joys, expand their vision, quicken their minds, strengthen their muscles, lift their spirits, multiply their blessings, increase their opportunities, comfort their souls, raise up friends, and pour out peace. Whoever will lose his life in the service of God will find eternal life (see Matt. 10:39). (*Teachings of Ezra Taft Benson* [1988], 361)

I know this truly is the Lord's promise, for I am seeing these blessings in my own life. The Lord has helped me through so many difficulties. Even if further trials and afflictions come, I know the Lord will be with me in those as well, and so I declare with Job, **"Though he slay me, yet will I trust in him"** (Job 13:15).

THE VERY PERSONAL NATURE OF JESUS' FEELINGS FOR US

As I continued to ponder the Lord's reasons for letting me struggle with addiction, an amazing truth began to dawn on me. I began to see that the Lord didn't just want a change in my *behavior*. He wanted *me*, and not just for now, but for always. One of the most powerful and most comforting witnesses I have received from the Lord in all this long, painful journey of recovery, is this: *He misses me.* Jesus is my older brother, who through eons of time has known and adored me. I trusted and adored Him. I sat at His knee in the eternal courts and learned from Him as one of my most influential teachers.

I sense that, with great interest, Christ has watched me grow through all the long ages of preparation for this life. He has also sorrow-fully watched me stumble and fall as I have gone through this mortal probation, and has ached with my pains and wept with my sorrows. And after all this, it is now time for me to come back to Him. He is calling me, inviting me. But He doesn't want to just give me some quick help, so that once healed I can run off to play and never think of Him again. His power is real in my life, each and every time I ask for it, but it is designed to be short-lived in order to encourage me to reach for Him daily, to stay near Him and continue to learn directly from Him. He wants me, my entire person, to come to Him so that *He* can make me a new person.

> Christ says, "Give me All. I don't want so much of your time and so much of your money and so much of your work: I want You. I have not come to torment your natural self, but to kill it. No half-measures are any good. I don't want to cut off a branch here and a branch there, I want to have the whole tree down...Hand over the whole natural self, all the desires which you think innocent as well as the ones you think wicked—the whole outfit. I will give you a new self instead. In fact, I

will give you Myself: my own will shall become yours."
(Elder Robert L. Backman, quoting C. S. Lewis, *Ensign*,
Nov. 1991, 10)

The Lord has so much more in mind for me than I first imagined!
And the surrender required is a much greater surrender than I first
anticipated. I was thinking much more along the lines of surrendering a
little bit here and a little bit there. The truth is, that kind of surrender
never freed me from addiction. Step Three says, "Made a decision to
turn our will and our lives over to the care of God as we understood
Him." The first thing I was willing to turn over to Him was my addiction, my temptations. But the Lord wanted more. He wanted me to turn
my whole will over to Him, and eventually my whole life, my whole self.
I have learned that the key to my ability to access the Lord's help is my
willingness to continually surrender my life to Him.

If I read the scriptures with open eyes, I see how the Lord, in His
incomparable love, constantly reaches out to help us:

> Come unto me, all ye that labour and are heavy laden,
> and I will give you rest. Take my yoke upon you, and
> learn of me; for I am meek and lowly in heart: and ye
> shall find rest unto your souls. For my yoke is easy,
> and my burden is light. (Matthew 11:28–30)

> Behold, doth he cry unto any, saying: Depart from
> me? Behold, I say unto you, Nay; but he saith: Come
> unto me all ye ends of the earth, buy milk and honey,
> without money and without price. (2 Nephi 26:25)

> Wo be unto the Gentiles, saith the Lord God of Hosts!
> For notwithstanding I shall lengthen out mine arm
> unto them from day to day, they will deny me; never-
> theless, I will be merciful unto them, saith the Lord
> God, if they will repent and come unto me; for mine
> arm is lengthened out all the day long, saith the Lord
> God of Hosts. (2 Nephi 28:32)

The Savior truly loves each and every one of us. It was this great love that enabled Him to carry out His marvelous Atonement for all mankind, and this love permeates and inspires His concern for us today. His love is everywhere in the scriptures. Pondering the word of the Lord in a spirit of love and trust will open an unfailing storehouse of help and support to each of us.

MAKING THE MOST OF THIS CHAPTER

Please take time to answer the following questions in your recovery journal.

1. Write about your willingness to practice patience as a tool of recovery. How are you blessed by being patient with the struggles addiction presents?

2. Write about the level of trust you have in the Lord's ability and willingness to meet your needs if you let Him direct your life. Do you believe you will be happier if you follow Him? How far do you need to come to believe the promises President Benson made to us as quoted on page 99 of this chapter?

3. When the Savior appeared to the Nephites after the destruction of their lands, He said: **"O all ye that are spared because ye were more righteous than they, will ye not now return unto me, and repent of your sins, and be converted, that I may heal you?"** (3 **Nephi 9:13).** Write about your willingness to be healed by the Savior. What do you need to do to contribute toward that healing?

4. The Savior told the Nephites: **"Yea, verily I say unto you, if ye will come unto me ye shall have eternal life. Behold, mine arm of mercy is extended towards you, and whosoever will come, him will I receive; and blessed are those who come unto me."** (3 **Nephi 9:14).** Picture yourself in the crowd that heard these words.

Where would you be standing in the crowd? Write about your feelings for the Savior. Would you approach Him? Why or why not? What would He say if He were talking just to you?

5. The apostle John wrote: **"Whosoever abideth in him sinneth not"** **(1 John 3:6).** Have you had the experience of finding that temptations were lowered when you were closer to the Lord? Write about this experience, or about some time you felt help in resisting temptation. What was the source of that help?

Chapter **8**

Step Four

Made a searching and fearless
moral inventory of ourselves.
(A.A. and Heart t' Heart traditional versions)

*Made a searching and fearless written inventory of
our past in order to thoroughly examine ourselves
as to our pride and other weaknesses with the
intent of recognizing our own carnal state and
our need for Christ's Atonement. (Alma 15:17;
Mosiah 4:2; Jacob 4:6–7; Ether 12:27)*
(Heart t' Heart scriptural version)

Do you have a "junk" drawer? Most people do. Some people even
have a "junk room" or two. Drawer or room, basement, garage, briefcase
or purse—we all have someplace where we've stuffed things and
forgotten them. At my house, my study is one of those places. I allow
half-finished projects to pile up along with unfiled papers, books, and
other "important" things. And since it looks more like a storeroom than
a study, I couldn't very well object when my daughter asked if she could
stash some stuff from the upstairs bedroom in my study when she moved
home for the summer.

Well, my daughter moved away again months and months ago, but
the displaced boxes and even more unfiled paperwork have remained
undisturbed in my study—until last night. Maybe it was because I've

been studying and praying about the Fourth Step process of inventorying that I finally felt willing to tackle the build-up. I'm not nearly finished clearing out my study yet, but you know what? Already, I feel fabulous. It looks like a whole new world in here. I can see the carpet along one whole end of the room, and I'm throwing away ten-year-old catalogs and Christmas cards! What a great principle the Fourth Step represents—a chance to reclaim our lives by sorting through our "stuff."

FACING THE TRUTH ABOUT
MY PAST BEHAVIORS AND ATTITUDES

I have sinned. And who hasn't? I admit it's much easier to talk about someone else's tragic choices than my own. Thinking about my own mistakes, my own *sins*, makes me pretty uncomfortable. Even so, I find it wonderfully encouraging to hear reassurances like Elder Boyd K. Packer's amazing apostolic promise:

> The gospel teaches us that relief from torment and guilt can be earned through repentance. Save for those few who defect to perdition after having known a fulness, *there is no habit, no addiction, no rebellion, no transgression, no offense exempted from the promise of complete forgiveness.* (*Ensign,* Nov. 1995, 19, emphasis added)

I was terrified to face Step Four. I'd messed up in a lot of ways for a lot of years. The things causing me the most pain had to do with sexual addiction, of course. First of all, there were all the times I had given in and indulged in viewing pornography and masturbating. And, even more numerous were the times I had indulged in lust, letting my mind wander into unacceptable and sinful paths. How could I face all that?

Still, I felt the witness of the truth to my heart and mind: In order to be cured of a disease, you must be willing to acknowledge that you have the disease, and then you must begin to pay strict attention to its symptoms. To become free from the behaviors of sexual addiction, I must first acknowledge I have engaged in them. I am only as sick as my secrets. My wounds must be opened to the air to be healed. It actually helped to review scriptures that testified that sooner or later, all men's secrets will be known:

> For there is nothing covered, that shall not be revealed; neither hid, that shall not be known. Therefore whatsoever ye have spoken in darkness shall be heard in the light; and that which ye have spoken in the ear in closets shall be proclaimed upon the housetops. (Luke 12:2–3)

> For verily the voice of the Lord is unto all men, and there is none to escape; and there is no eye that shall not see, neither ear that shall not hear, neither heart that shall not be penetrated. And the rebellious shall be pierced with much sorrow; for their iniquities shall be spoken upon the housetops, and their secret acts shall be revealed. (D&C 1:2–3)

Having come this far—having taken Steps One, Two, and Three—I was finally ready to get on with my Fourth Step inventory. I didn't want to wait for someone else to reveal my sins against my will. I wanted to get rid of my sins and secrets now and let the healing begin. I wasn't sure if I could do it thoroughly enough, but I became willing to make a first stab at it. I wanted to get out all the garbage and allow the Savior to save me from it. I didn't want to keep anything back.

LETTING GO OF EXCUSES—COMING OUT OF DENIAL

Still it was hard. I was so used to making excuses for myself. I was so bound up in the deceit of denial. I knew I would have to admit how deeply my life had become entrenched in the violation of the laws of chastity. As I began to face my past, I found trends and patterns in my *thoughts*, as well as the resulting deeds. For example, I noticed I repeatedly turned to pornography and/or masturbation for comfort or to escape from the emotional distress of a disagreement with my wife or a bad day at work. I found how quickly I used my circumstances to excuse or rationalize acting out.

Several years ago Elder Robert L. Simpson made some very insightful comments about excuses and rationalization:

> Satan is the master of deceit. He perverts man's God-given attributes from their noble and divine purpose onto a downward track. All seem to agree that one of man's most demanding and ever-present drives is centered in his desire for companionship and sexual fulfillment. To have this highly sensitive and divine human mechanism falsely aroused by unnatural processes creates a serious conflict in that vital control center, the mind. Rationalization quickly rallies to the side of the victim of off-color literature, because rationalization helps him to live with his conscience. He tells himself that his drives are God-given and, therefore, not that bad. He also tells himself, "Nearly everybody does it. I am not so different," and while he may not be so very different, he is just exactly 100 percent wrong in the eyes of God. (*Ensign*, Jan. 1973, 113)

One of the things I regained as I became more honest about my underlying thoughts and motives was ownership of my own actions. It is a lie to say, "She tempted me, and that's why I fell." I had to face the truth that the lying spirit I gave in to when I entertained such thoughts was the same spirit that convinced sexual perpetrators to blame their victims instead of themselves. I began to see the insane dishonesty of that kind of thinking. It irrationally cast *me* in the role of the victim. If I said to myself, "That girl made me lust after her by the way she dressed," I was making *her* responsible for what was, in truth, my own decision to lust. I was denying that I had my own agency and that I chose to look. Honestly examining my choices and becoming willing to own them has turned out to be one of the most liberating (saving) acts I have ever taken.

Do not endeavor to excuse yourself in the least point because of your sins, by denying the justice of God; but do let the justice of God, and his mercy, and his

long-suffering have full sway in your heart; and let it bring you down to the dust in humility. (Alma 42:30)

None but the truly penitent are saved. (Alma 42:24)

I have found it is just as Alma taught: when I allowed my guilt to bring me out of the darkness of denial and into the light of truth, I was troubled by them "no more."

I desire that ye should let these things trouble you no more, and only let your *sins* trouble you, with that trouble which shall bring you down unto repentance. (Alma 42:29, emphasis added)

PRIDE KEEPS US FROM GETTING HONEST

I have concluded that without pride there wouldn't be any addicts! Pride is perhaps the most subtle and yet pervasive of our faults. Pride is the addict's Achilles' heel. As we inventory our lives, we begin to see how pride has played a major role. President Benson gave a marvelous, landmark talk, entitled "Cleansing the Inner Vessel," on the things we need to eliminate from our lives, focusing especially on pride as the root of all other sins. I recommend that every reader find this talk and read it in its entirety. I will quote only a few passages here:

In the scriptures there is no such thing as righteous pride. It is always considered as a sin. We are not speaking of a wholesome view of self-worth, which is best established by a close relationship with God. But we are speaking of pride as the universal sin, as someone has described it...

Essentially, pride is a "my will" rather than "thy will" approach to life. The opposite of pride is humbleness, meekness, submissiveness (see Alma 13:28), or teachableness...

Pride does not look up to God and care about *what* is right. It looks sideways to man and argues *who* is right.

> Pride is manifest in the spirit of contention...Pride is characterized by "What do I want out of life?" rather than by "What would God have me do with my life?" It is *self-will* as opposed to *God's will*. It is the fear of man over the fear of God. (Ezra Taft Benson, *Ensign*, May 1986, 6–7, emphasis added)

I began to learn a great deal about myself when I was willing to finally face questions such as: "In what ways does pride govern my life? How have I put myself, my wishes, desires, and opinions first?" I had to admit I had been uncharitable and self-pampering (selfish) and that sexual addiction was one of the most devastating ways I had let that self-ishness run rampant. Though the Fourth Step would take some serious work, it was *essential* that I complete it if I wanted to let go of hypocrisy and find recovery.

WE MUST BE WILLING TO HUMBLE OURSELVES TO OBTAIN GRACE

Writing an inventory requires courage and honesty. I testify that the Lord will give each of us the necessary courage and power to take this step if we will turn to Him and ask Him to go through this process with us, thought for thought. In addition to courage and honesty, we also need a good deal of humility to make this inventory. I used to think humility was a very elusive and mysterious virtue. I remember people saying, "Humility is the hardest of all virtues to obtain, because as soon as you claim to have it, you have lost it." That called to my mind a picture of myself asking, "Am I humble yet?" And, of course, the answer was always "No," because if it was ever "Yes," then I had become proud and had to go back to the beginning and start over. There is something wrong with that picture. I don't think humility simply settles upon us like the dews from heaven, or is something you sneak up on, like a cat stalking a bird. Consider what the scriptures say about *"humbling ourselves."*

> **I would that ye should remember, and always retain in remembrance, the greatness of God, and your own**

> nothingness, and his goodness and long-suffering
> towards you, unworthy creatures, and humble your-
> selves even in the depths of humility, calling on the
> name of the Lord daily. (Mosiah 4:11)

In light of this gospel truth, I began to see the fallacy in asking, "Am I humble yet?" Rather, I should be continually asking, "Have I suffi-ciently humbled *myself?*" The difference in those two questions speaks volumes. Humility is not something that just happens to us, or a desti-nation at which we can arrive. *Humility is a choice.* It is not something we have, it is something we do. It is the decision we make to place ourselves under God and acknowledge our utter dependence upon Him.

If pride is a universal trait shared by all addicts, then humbling ourselves and letting go of our defensiveness is a key to placing ourselves in a position where the Lord can lift us out of our addiction:

> Submit yourselves therefore to God. Resist the devil,
> and he will flee from you. Draw nigh to God, and he
> will draw nigh to you...*Humble yourselves in the sight
> of the Lord, and he shall lift you up.* (James 4:7, 8, 10,
> emphasis added)

> Be clothed with humility: for God resisteth the proud,
> and giveth grace to the humble. *Humble yourselves
> therefore under the mighty hand of God, that he may
> exalt you in due time:* Casting all your care upon him;
> for he careth for you. (1 Peter 5:5–7, emphasis added)

> The people were checked as to the pride of their
> hearts, *and began to humble themselves before God,...*
> watching and praying continually, that they might be
> delivered from Satan, and from death, and from
> destruction. (Alma 15:17, emphasis added)

According to the Book of Mormon, then, being humble and **"watching and praying continually"** (staying in close, personal contact with God, all through the day, every day) are the keys to being **"deliv-**

ered from [the temptations of] Satan, and from [spiritual] death, and from destruction."

> And they had viewed themselves in their own carnal state, even less than the dust of the earth. And they all cried aloud with one voice, saying: O have mercy, and apply the atoning blood of Christ that we may receive forgiveness of our sins, and our hearts may be purified; for we believe in Jesus Christ, the Son of God, who created heaven and earth, and all things; who shall come down among the children of men. (Mosiah 4:2)

Like me, a lot of people initially back away from thinking of themselves as "less than the dust of the earth" or "nothing." Again, a humble, open-hearted, in-depth consideration of the scriptures brings one to understand that these phrases do *not* deny our infinite worth in the eyes of God. They simply describe the degree of humility we must exercise in order to recognize and admit that only by allowing His grace (power) to take over in our lives, can we overcome the world. Humility is essential to our eternal growth, because it helps us let go of defensiveness toward God and toward the truth about our past. Humility is essential to recovery because it connects us with the Savior's power of redemption.

THE FOURTH STEP IS ANOTHER STEP TOWARDS CHRIST

Taking Step Four brings us closer to Christ as we draw upon His role in our lives as **"the Spirit of Truth"** (John 14:16–17; D&C 93:8–11). Not only do we begin to understand general principles of truth, but even more important to our own salvation, we begin to experience *personal* insight and revelation. Truth attracts truth. Honesty attracts the Spirit of the Lord. Let's take a closer look at the principles of truth, insight, and honesty and at how they help us become closer to the Savior.

Truth. In looking at the character traits that contributed to my addiction, I had to admit I had become extremely adept at shading or completely avoiding the truth. Whether this was a contributing cause or a result of addiction, I'm not sure. I either minimized my behavior, claiming, "It wasn't *that* bad," or I blamed and shamed myself into the ground. Since Christ is the Spirit of Truth, connecting with Him helped me regain the ability to see the truth of my life more clearly—to see my actions as neither more nor less serious than they were.

Insight. Insight is understanding the truth as it applies to myself. Since I had gone to great lengths to hide the truth about my behaviors from my consciousness, I needed the Lord to help me see what I was doing and what I had done in the past. Recovery includes letting the Lord show us what we have previously hidden from ourselves:

> **Nevertheless, the Lord God *showeth us our weakness* that we may know that it is by his grace, and his great condescensions unto the children of men, that we have power to do these things. (Jacob 4:7, emphasis added)**

> **And if men come unto me I *will show unto them their weakness.* I give unto men weakness *that they may be humble;* and my grace is sufficient for all men *that humble themselves before me;* for if they humble themselves before me, and have faith in me, then will I make weak things become strong unto them. (Ether 12:27, emphasis added)**

In Step Two we talked about the need to trust the Savior, realizing He will only do that which will ultimately bring us peace and joy. Now, more than ever, we need to rely on that promise and let Him lead us through this inventory process.

Honesty. Closely related to insight is honesty about my addiction—particularly about my motives. Before I could see inside myself (insight) and examine not only my behaviors, but my skewed *reasons* and motives that supplied me with my excuses and rationalizations, I had to have the willingness to be honest. I have been much like Amulek, who said of his own past:

> **Nevertheless, I did harden my heart, for I was called many times and I would not hear; therefore I *knew***

> *concerning these things, yet I would not know;* therefore
> **I went on rebelling against God, in the wickedness of**
> **my heart. (Alma 10:6, emphasis added)**

For years, living with addiction felt like being trapped in a black hole. It *seemed* that I automatically gave in to temptation before I even knew what was happening. When I allowed the Lord to teach me more about addiction, I saw that before each episode of acting out, I made a number of choices that paved the way for the actual event. Perhaps I chose to feel sorry for myself, or to harbor a resentment, or to flirt with the "edges" of temptation—with things that weren't *that bad.* Each of those choices further clouded my thinking until acting out seemed inevitable. *When I got honest about my motives, I had to admit I only acted out when I wanted to, and whenever I was able to stay clean, it was because I wanted to be close to the Lord more than I wanted to sin.*

THE ACTUAL INVENTORY PROCESS

It was scary enough to start *thinking* about my past and remembering the things I had done, but when it came to actually committing my inventory to paper, I faced an even greater level of discomfort. Something about writing down these events symbolized a deeper commitment to recovery than before. More than once, like Lot's wife, I paused and looked longingly over my shoulder at the familiar haunts of my own personal "Sodom and Gomorrah." Did I really want to recover, to be free, to have my old ways and my old self changed forever? For a while it was definitely a wrestle before God.

Another fear slowing my recovery had to do with privacy. What if someone should find my inventory and read it? Some things I had not told a soul, except perhaps my bishop. How could I risk writing them down where someone could find them? A few suggestions helped me.

First, it helped to realize I was not making a permanent record, like a journal. I was just making notes to help me identify what I needed to haul out of my dark, musty "junk room." This inventory list was only for me. I could abbreviate, use code words or otherwise disguise what I was writing—whatever made me feel safe putting it down. I also chose to write my list on my computer and protect the file with a password. Some might want to keep their inventory in a different kind of safe place, perhaps under lock and key, until they are finished sharing it in Step Five. Once Step Five is done, many people burn their inventory in a symbolic gesture of leaving the past behind. Others keep it for a while to help them make their list of amends in Step Eight. Do what feels good to you. This is your program.

We also need protection from becoming overwhelmed in this process. Sometimes we are so burdened by the mistakes we have made that we lose the courage to go forward. Often, people agonize more over their Fourth Step than any other. Certainly the adversary would like us to get stuck here and sink back into shame and discouragement, where he can more easily influence us. It is my witness that the Lord stands ready to hold our hand as we go through this process. His mission is to help us repent, and He will help with each step, including this one.

I have included in Appendix B some suggestions on how to write an inventory, including a sample form. You can also find suggestions on making an inventory in a number of other books on working the Twelve Steps (see Appendix D).

WHAT DO I INCLUDE IN MY INVENTORY?

In talking about the different ways we sin, King Benjamin said:

> **And finally, I cannot tell you all the things whereby ye may commit sin; for there are divers ways and means, even so many that I cannot number them. (Mosiah 4:29)**

We are not trying to number them either, but rather to become honest, as King Benjamin said, about our **"thoughts, and [our] words, and [our] deeds..."** (Mosiah 4:30).

As you write your inventory, you may find things for which you haven't fully repented. Maybe there are things in your past that trouble your conscience, but you haven't yet confessed them to a bishop or stake president. If you are like me, there will probably be things for which you haven't yet made amends. Do not let any of these regrets or sorrows stop you from including them and completing your inventory up to the present. Later steps will help you with the job of confessing and making amends; for now you are just making a list.

Please remember the witness of those who have completed this process: this journey back into the past to clean out "old baggage" may feel painful at first, but it is the paradoxical means to an end that will be glorious. As AA puts it, we are "clearing away the wreckage of the past." If you feel the need, you can also make a separate list of your life's positive experiences in order to keep a more balanced perspective. However, we must not shy away from the fact that the healing in the Fourth Step comes primarily from facing the things we have done that have hurt others or ourselves. These may include:

1. Offenses toward God.

Here we list our "sins," things we have done that are clearly a violation of the commandments—things that have taken us away from God. This list will include ways we have violated the principle of chastity, but it should also include violations of the Word of Wisdom, the principle of tithing and other Church responsibilities. We can also include the neglect of our prayers, of the scriptures, and other ways we have lived **"without God in the world":**

> **Behold, I say unto you, wickedness never was happiness. And now, my son, all men that are in a state of nature, or I would say, in a carnal state, are in the gall of bitterness and in the bonds of iniquity; they are without God in the world, and they have gone contrary to the nature of God; therefore, they are in a state contrary to the nature of happiness. (Alma 41:10–11)**

2. Ways we have hurt others.

Many who have become trapped in sexual addiction, particularly addiction to pornography, have deluded themselves with the excuse: "I'm only hurting myself." What a lie! First of all, consider the damage pornography does to the people who pose for pictures. In how many ways are these people being exploited? I used to look at magazines in bookstores without buying them, and visit only "free" pornographic Internet sites, trying to numb my conscience with the rationalization that at least I wasn't putting any money into the industry—that way I wasn't guilty of supporting this vile business. (Eventually this barrier fell when I started renting pornographic videos.) But even when I wasn't giving money to the purveyors of this filth, wasn't I giving implied approval to the whole sordid business? Wasn't I voting on the side of the pornographers by viewing what they produced? Wasn't I giving assent to the exploitation and abuse of these women by viewing the products of that abuse? The apostle Paul stood by while Stephen was martyred, stoned to death. Was he free of guilt because he only held the coats of those throwing the stones and didn't throw any himself? I didn't actually click the shutter, but when I looked at the pictures and lusted, wasn't I giving my consent? Where were my desires? Which side was I on? These questions reveal much about what I had to inventory.

In the category of things I had done to others, I had to also include the effects of addiction on my family—how I had denied them the blessings of having a righteous priesthood leader in our home. I had avoided giving blessings to my family when I didn't feel worthy (which was much of the time). I had avoided teaching principles that had the potential to embarrass me if I ever got caught. As I participated in the actions of addiction, I also fulfilled a prophecy made by Elder Robert L. Simpson:

> Now a mind that has been deceived into receiving trashy input cannot but send false signals to the feet, the hands, and the tongue. Future decisions will all be colored by the impurity allowed to enter that control center of his entire being.

> As you invite unclean thoughts to become a part of your total being, be assured some of your faculties will become considerably sharpened. Your temper will be sharpened. Your tongue will be sharpened. Your desire for more trash will be sharpened. Your ability to shade the truth will be

sharpened. Yes, just about every negative part of your character will be enhanced.

There will also be a noticeable diminishing effect in your life. Your personality will be diminished. Your family relationships will be impaired. Your ability to pray will be lessened. Your spirit will be affected adversely, and your testimony of the truth will start to slip away, probably so gradually at first that you won't even realize it is happening until it is too late. (*Ensign*, Jan. 1973, 113)

Could I deny that my use of pornography had diminished me as a father and a husband? Wasn't I more impatient and less loving as a result of Satan's control over my mind? To deny this would be refusing to see the truth. Recovery asks us to accept the truth squarely and fearlessly. *We can't fix it until we face it.*

If we have involved others in our sexual transgressions, we will, of course, include that in our housecleaning. Admitting how much we have hurt others in our acting out may be the hardest part to face, but it must be included, above all.

3. Ways we have hurt ourselves.

While it is true that we have violated God's desires for us, and we have hurt others in the course of our addiction, very likely the person we have hurt most is our self. For years I rejected the dictionary definition of masturbation as "self-abuse." I thought it was a silly, old-fashioned phrase, but how accurate it really is! We don't realize how much we are hurting ourselves, especially when we are using addiction to numb our pain and avoid working through life's challenges.

In completing the inventory of how we have hurt ourselves by our addiction, some compassion is also called for. Like many others, I truly missed out on a lot of blessings in my life because of this addiction. For example, the blessing of feeling good about myself. The blessing of being able to hold my head up, to associate with others without feeling inferior, without having to hide who I really was. I couldn't even relax and participate in many innocent, enjoyable activities. I was sure I didn't deserve to. In addition, I missed out on many spiritual experiences because my unworthiness robbed me of the confidence to ask God to bless me with them. Even though I usually held a recommend, many times I stayed away from the temple because of my guilty feelings. When I avoided giving priesthood blessings to my family, I was deprived of the blessing as much as they were.

If we could truly see how many ways the adversary has diminished our lives through this abominable addiction, we would be amazed and greatly sobered. We all need to have that kind of awakening to convince us it's time to take our life back and receive the inheritance of love and joy the Father wants to give us.

4. Taking offense at others, life, and God.

Many people are seriously challenged by the circumstances of their lives. Some are born with a crippling deformity, with blindness, or some other physical or mental handicap. Others experience events that change the course of their lives. An accident cuts short a promising athletic career. A serious health condition limits another's options in life. Some are challenged by parents who abuse or neglect them. There are many ways life and the Lord allow challenges to come to us. Sometimes we respond to these challenges by indulging in negative thoughts such as self-pity or resentment. Such resentment may be directed toward individuals, life in general, or toward God. Our faith may be tried as we attempt to come to peace about our life. The "Serenity Prayer," often used in Twelve Step groups, has comforted many:

> God grant me the serenity to accept the things I cannot change, the courage to change the things I can, and the wisdom to know the difference.

Much of our sorrow and frustration comes from refusing to accept what we cannot change. Such things include realities of life, the choices of others, as well as everything that is in the past. As you look at your life, are there some facts that cause you distress but about which you can do nothing? Are there choices you made years ago that have taken you down a path you wish you hadn't followed? Have you suffered abuse at the hands of those who should have been your protectors? Has an important relationship in your life ended? Have you lost a loved one in death? Has a painful divorce shattered your hopes for happiness? We may try to cope with such situations by using our addictive behaviors. Inventorying these things can help us identify what we need to surrender to the Lord. As I invited Him to change my heart and replace sorrow and bitterness with a spirit of acceptance and trust, I could feel addiction's power weakening in my life.

What a marvelous reassurance to know that even sexual sin and addiction can yield to the repentance process! I want to add my testimony to that of Elder Packer, quoted earlier on page 105. *Any* addiction will yield to the power of the Savior's Atonement. I know this is true, for I have lived it. May I paraphrase the amazing testimony of the king of the Lamanites who was converted by the sons of Mosiah:

> **And I also thank my God, yea, my great God, that he hath granted unto [me] that [I] might repent of these things, and also that he hath forgiven [me] of [my] many sins…and taken the guilt away from [my heart], through the merits of his Son. (Alma 24:10)**

Because of this miracle in my life, today I can share my story with you without guilt, but instead with rejoicing, praying that it may encourage you to follow these same steps of repentance and mighty change, that you may also enjoy these same blessings.

MAKING THE MOST OF THIS CHAPTER

Please take time to answer the following questions in your recovery journal.

1. King David, who spent many years repenting of his sexual sins, wrote, **"Cast thy burden upon the Lord, and he shall sustain thee" (Psalm 55:22).** In what ways is writing an inventory of your

past casting your burden upon the Lord? Write about your willingness to let God take the burden of your past from you.

2. Write about humility as a tool of recovery. How is writing an inventory an act of surrendering pride?

3. Read the section "Making a Step Four Inventory" in Appendix B (277). Write about which of these approaches could work for you. What insight could this process give you into your own character?

4. If you are having a hard time writing your inventory, write about the blocks you are experiencing. Are you afraid to face your past? Are you more troubled by things you have done or by things others have done to you? Are you afraid to make a written record of your past for fear of someone reading it? Write about your willingness to surrender these fears to the Lord and let Him walk with you through this process.

5. If you haven't started writing down your inventory yet, start now. Use this moment as a springboard and begin today. Decide whether you are going to use a computer or write it on paper. Choose a specific time to write your inventory. Choose a place to write where you can be uninterrupted. Put aside all obstacles and simply start.

9

Step Five

Admitted to God, to ourselves, and to another
human being the exact nature of our wrongs.
(A.A. and Heart t' Heart traditional versions)

*Honestly shared this inventory with God and
with another person, thus demonstrating the
sincerity of our repentance, and our willingness
to give away all our sins that we might know Him.*
(Mosiah 26:29; Alma 22:18)
(Heart t' Heart scriptural version)

Addiction presents a serious challenge to our honesty. Addiction is always attended by secrecy and shame. When I was still in my addiction, I hid a lot of things. I not only hid what I did, I also hid what I thought of as my true self. I thought of myself only as a despicable sinner, a monstrous hypocrite, and a colossal weakling. I was sure if anyone knew the "real me," if anyone knew about my problem, they would despise me as much I despised myself. If my secret ever got out, I would be rejected, cast out and alone.

To protect myself from total abandonment, I kept this part of my life hidden from everyone. As my addiction grew and consumed me from the inside out, I had to repress more and more of my feelings. There was more and more to avoid being conscious of. As I drew further into myself, I became isolated emotionally. My mind and heart became prisons about which I couldn't let anyone else know. Thus, I *caused* the very abandonment I feared! Only it was *I* who was abandoning the rest of my life in order to be a slave to my addiction. What insanity! I truly became my own worst enemy.

If addiction is all about hiding and secrecy, Steps Four and Five are all about honesty and openness. In fact, the whole recovery process is a journey of becoming increasingly honest with ourselves and others. If we look back at the four steps we've already taken, we will see that every one of them has been an exercise in becoming humble and honest.

Step Five asks us to "admit...the exact nature of our wrongs." The word "admit" means "to allow entrance, to receive, to acknowledge, or to concede as true." Admitting the exact nature of my wrongs means accepting the truth of my wrongdoing and defects—letting the truth of my diseased thoughts and actions enter into my heart. Jesus said: **"Ye shall know the truth, and the truth shall make you free"** (John 8:32).

GETTING HONEST WITH GOD

The person we owe our *highest* degree of loyalty and obedience to is our Father in Heaven. It makes sense then, to start with Him. Take your list and sit down (or kneel) with Him in a private, one-on-one inter-view. Begin with a prayer. Let the Spirit guide you as you read through your Fourth Step list. Express to your Father in Heaven not only what you have done, but how you feel about it. Invite the Savior to be part of this conversation. He is the one who has paid the debt for your sins. He is the one who can lift your pain and sorrow, your guilt and shame. Christ is the source of all healing, including the healing we need from all our bad choices and the harm they have done. He understands what we are feeling:

> **Seeing then that we have a great high priest, that is passed into the heavens, Jesus the Son of God, let us hold fast our profession. For we have not an high priest which cannot be touched with the feeling of our infirmities; but was in all points tempted like as we are, yet without sin. Let us therefore come boldly unto**

the throne of grace, that we may obtain mercy, and
find grace to help in time of need. (Hebrews 4:14–16)

When we give our sins to the Lord, they are no longer ours. Jesus
bought them with His blood. We give up ownership of them, and
likewise, ownership of the guilt and shame they produced. Once we
have finished the repentance process by confessing to appropriate
persons and making restitution as best we can in Steps Eight and Nine,
these sins are no longer ours and need trouble us no more. As Paul said:

What? know ye not that your body is the temple of
the Holy Ghost which is in you, which ye have of
God, and ye are not your own? For ye are bought with
a price: therefore glorify God in your body, and in
your spirit, which are God's. (1 Corinthians 6:19–20)

Acknowledging our sins and asking the Lord's forgiveness is a
crucial part of repentance. In the words of King Benjamin:

Ye must repent of your sins and forsake them, and
humble yourselves before God; and ask in sincerity of
heart that he would forgive you. (Mosiah 4:10)

Nephi emphasized the need for total honesty before God:

Follow the Son, with full purpose of heart, acting no
hypocrisy and no deception before God, but with real
intent, repenting of your sins, witnessing unto the
Father that ye are willing to take upon you the name
of Christ. (2 Nephi 31:13)

For so many years, I pretended to be a disciple of Christ, but the
whole time I had been acting in **"hypocrisy"** and **"deception before
God."** Taking this part of the Fifth Step—coming 100% clean before
God—was one of the few things I had done "with full purpose of heart."
I began to realize that these steps were requiring me to *finally* become a
true disciple of my Lord. My full confession to the Father, required in
Step Five, was exactly what I needed in order to let Him know that, at
last, I wanted to take the name of Christ upon me worthily.

It was painful to think of reading my whole inventory—saying each one of those shameful words—to my Heavenly Father, but I knew, as with everything the Lord asked of me, this too was for *my* benefit. After all, admitting the nature of my sins before God is not informing *Him* of anything; He already knows all about me. Taking Step Five is another step in admitting to *myself* my need for God in all things.

GETTING HONEST WITH MYSELF

If it were easy to break free from pornography, it wouldn't be considered an addiction. During the early months and early steps, I experienced several "slips." Looking back, I realize that each of those slips, without exception, followed a slip in my willingness to be honest with myself. After a period of abstinence, I would be feeling good about myself, but then ever so gradually the most insane thinking would begin. A devious little thought would worm its way into my mind: "I've been 'good' for a couple of weeks now. Don't I deserve to let down a little? Don't I deserve a break from this constant striving? Don't I deserve to do something 'nice' for myself?" Imagine! Thinking that sinking back into the slavery of addiction is doing something "nice" for myself. And it all began with becoming dishonest with myself—again. There, in that thinking, was the "exact nature" of my "wrongs"! Like all addicts, I was a champion excuse maker. I once heard a man who had been trapped in addiction exclaim, "If I've had a good day, I think I deserve to celebrate by acting out. If I've had a bad day, I want to console myself by acting out. I never met an excuse I didn't like!"

We would do well to heed the counsel Alma gave to his son Corianton. Corianton fell victim to sexual temptation and did **"forsake the ministry, and did go over into the land of Siron...after the harlot Isabel"** (Alma 39:3). Alma counseled his wayward son, **"Do not endeavor to excuse yourself in the least point because of your sins"** (Alma 42:30). Like Corianton, I, too, had to let go of my excuses! All of them. Step Five was the step that took me out of lying to God *and to myself.*

LETTING GO OF "STINKIN' THINKIN'"

Since we are beings of truth and light (**D&C 93:29**), if we choose to participate in addictive behaviors we first have to deliberately deny the truth. Getting honest with ourselves and "admitting the exact nature of our wrongs" requires that we learn to recognize the "stinkin' thinkin'" that paves the way to acting out. Here are some of the "rational lies" we tell ourselves to excuse our acting out:

- I'm too tired. I can't keep up the effort of resisting any longer.

- I just feel like turning off my brain (conscience) and going with the flow.

- I've been working hard and I deserve a break.

- Just this once won't hurt.

- No one will know. I can keep it a secret.

- I can't take the pressure of the temptation any more. It's too hard.

- I'm not made of strong enough stuff. Maybe others can resist, but I can't.

- Everyone else does it (and seems to get away with it)!

- I can't get away from it—it's everywhere (*at least everywhere I have been looking*).

- I won't get really involved—I'll just take a quick peek.

- I'm just going to see if it's something I shouldn't be looking at.

- I want to see what's going on in the world. What is it that everyone else knows?

- This is that movie I heard about. It sure sounded exciting.

- Work didn't go well today and I need to let off some steam.

- I just argued with my wife. It's her fault I feel this way.

- My wife isn't available to me. She's cold and unfeeling. I need something for myself.

- I'm single and this is the only option I have.

- At least it's not adultery.

- I feel sad, lonely, tired, bored, hungry.

- My wife knows I have this problem, but she is patient with me—she will understand.

- I couldn't help myself. I wasn't even fully awake.

I hope the lie in each of these rationalizations is evident. Each one is a devious invitation to get back on the slippery slope and start sliding. There isn't any *safe* way to indulge. As President James E. Faust said in the Priesthood session of general conference, quoting President George Albert Smith:

> If you cross to the devil's side of the line one inch, you are in the tempter's power, and if he is successful, you will not be able to think or even reason properly, because you will have lost the spirit of the Lord. (*Ensign*, May 2003, 51)

I know the feeling of not being "able to think or even reason properly," as addiction carried me away. I listened to these lies from the adversary for years. Honesty demands I admit that when I listen to these rationalizations, I do so because I want to sin more than I want to obey God. Admitting that I am *choosing* my actions is the first step in moving on to a better place, a place where I want God more than anything else.

GETTING HONEST WITH OTHERS

When I read the Twelve Steps for the first time, the idea of sharing my inventory with someone else filled me with terror. I didn't want to tell anyone about the things I had done. As I said earlier, I was sure it would be the end of all earthly relationships; telling would make me a total outcast. Because of that fear, I put off doing Step Five far too long. In avoiding doing Step Four and then, later, in postponing Step Five, I used many of the same rationalizations that kept me in my addiction to begin with.

Notice how many of the justifications for acting out listed earlier also apply to the process of sharing your inventory with another person:

- I'm too tired right now. I'll do it later.

- I just feel like turning off my brain (conscience). I don't want to think about my past.

- I've been working hard and I deserve a break.

- It won't hurt to wait a little longer.

- No one knows about most of these things. Maybe I can still keep them secret.

- Everyone else doesn't have to go through this embarrassing confession.

And so on. But the truth is, when we finally get the courage to sit down and talk with someone face-to-face, soul-to-soul, and share our inventory with them, we discover an amazing thing. We don't die. Neither are we "cast off" or shut out. Instead, the person hearing our Fifth Step responds with compassion, and thus, lifts a huge load of fear from our hearts. Part of the reason for doing this step is to learn that we can be loved in spite of our sins. Many people, after giving their inventory away to another person, have felt an undeniable witness that surely, if another mortal can have such compassion, God can, too. If a finite mortal can feel patient and forgiving of us, then we are reassured because of the Father's love that He will also be patient with us. In giving our Fifth Step to another person, we are blessed to feel at least a portion of the Lord's willingness to not cast us off.

> And now, my beloved brethren, seeing that our merciful God has given us so great knowledge concerning these things, let us remember him, and lay aside our sins, and not hang down our heads, for we are not cast off. (2 Nephi 10:20)

WHY IS CONFESSION TO ANOTHER PERSON NECESSARY?

If you're like I was about taking Step Five, you're probably asking yourself, "Why? Why do I have to talk to anyone else about this problem?" Getting honest with others may present the greatest challenge we've faced so far in our recovery process. After all, we think, "God may be forgiving, but He's perfect. Others are not perfect. Will they be able to hear my truth without rejecting me?"

It took me awhile to believe this particular part of Step Five was also necessary—even essential—if I wanted to escape from the darkness of my addiction. It took some serious prayer before I could find the grace to humble myself *this* much. As I prayed about it, I began to see that admitting my sins only to God and myself was not the very *depths* of humility that the Lord required to open my prison doors and let me go free. I needed to do all I could do to humble myself; talking to another person, face-to-face and soul-to-soul, had to be part of it—even if it meant some humiliation for me. If I was to have a new heart and a new life, I had to get my pride and my ego out of the way entirely.

I could not keep my reality inside any longer and continue to get well. I had to start getting more honest than I had ever been, whatever the result. I came to believe what AA says: "We are only as sick as our secrets." I had to take the chance and start talking. To my utter amazement, when I finally bared my soul to another person in a Fifth Step inventory, keeping nothing back, nothing secret, something miraculous happened. I expected some negative reaction from the person I shared my inventory with—some drawing back in disgust, in judgment of me—but that never happened. Quite the opposite. And what a relief it was to finally have everything out there, "on the table."

WHEN SHOULD I DO MY FIFTH STEP?

It's probably a good idea to give your Fifth Step to someone as soon after finishing your Fourth Step as you can. This is not one of those experiences you should put off until you feel ready. I don't think anyone ever feels comfortable going into a Fifth Step, but it seems everyone feels better after doing it. It's sort of like jumping into a cold lake. You anticipate a tremendous shock diving in, but after you take the plunge, it's not as bad as you feared.

As I have said, most people postpone doing their Fifth Step because they worry how it will be received. However, there are others who, crazy as it may sound, are suddenly struck with a fit of perfectionism. They want to be sure to include everything the first time around, because they don't want to have to face doing this more than once. This sudden insistence on doing something perfectly may seem totally illogical, until you realize that most addicts are really frustrated "perfectionists." Ironically, their need to numb themselves with their addiction usually comes from being devastated and disgusted with their own imperfection. Don't let this trap stop you from getting on with your Fifth Step. As soon as you have a reasonably good list of your past behaviors, go ahead and share it with someone. You probably have the most important things written down. If other things come up later, you can deal with them then.

HANDLE THE FIFTH STEP WITH CONSIDERATION FOR OTHERS

Though it may sound contradictory at first, the other strongest guideline about doing the Fifth Step is to not become suddenly obsessed with unloading it all on a spouse or family member. The SA White Book has some good suggestions about making disclosures to loved ones:

> **A note of caution:** Here again we suggest that newcomers to Sexaholics Anonymous *not* reveal their sexual past to a spouse or family member who does not already know of it without careful consideration and a period of sexual sobriety...Of course, if there is any chance we have put others in danger, we take immediate steps to try to correct that.
>
> Few things can so damage the possibility of healing in the family as a *premature* confession to spouse or family where sacred bonds and trust have been violated. Unwittingly, such confessions can be attempts on our part to dump our guilt, get back into good graces, or

make just another show of willpower. (*Sexaholics Anonymous*, 127–128; emphasis original)

As suggested in the passage above, an examination of one's *motives* is essential. We may want to make confession to a spouse in order to unburden *ourselves*. We may be confessing to make *ourselves* feel better. We need to be sure that concern for our spouse and for our marriage, rather than guilt, shame, fear, or obsession with our own comfort, are prompting our confession. Above all else, we need to listen for and follow the guidance of the Holy Spirit in this most sensitive disclosure.

While some of us have to resist the urge to dump everything on our spouses, others of us wish we could totally skip telling them anything. It is my personal experience and my firm belief that the best path to take is somewhere in the middle. I believe eventually, our spouse will need to be included in *some portion* of our confession experience—possibly as part of the amends process addressed in Steps Eight and Nine. In both instances—with my first wife, Kathy, and then with Colleen after Kathy's passing—I was prompted, after much serious prayer, to share the truth of my weakness with each of them. I felt the Lord very plainly directing me and reassuring me that both women, with years of Twelve Step recovery themselves, would be able to deal with my disclosure.

When the time comes for you to talk to your spouse about your addiction, you must be sure to do it in a way that will be as considerate of her tender heart as possible. With this intent, it is not usually necessary to share any details with her. The details of your transgression need only be shared with your bishop. Instead of making up for the wrongs done to your spouse, a too detailed confession may only enlarge her wounds. The details may be impossible for your spouse to forget, even when the sin has been forgiven. She may demand to know the details, but remember that the "exact nature" of your wrongs to her has been in your infidelity and dishonesty. This is the basic truth she needs to know, in order to be assured that you are in the process of changing forever.

It will help if your spouse also has support as she works through her portion of this difficult time. The principles of the Twelve Steps are helpful to loved ones, as well as to the addict, and most Twelve Step organizations have meetings oriented toward helping the spouse with their issues, feelings, and concerns. Since it is common for the spouse of an addict to experience challenges related to codependency, these challenges are addressed in such groups. Some material on codependency is included in Appendix B (282).

Some people advise us not to ever let our spouses know about our mistakes. Personally, I believe that after violating my marriage covenant to my wife I owe her the truth as a sacrifice of my ego and a down payment on a future of genuine fidelity. I do not understand how we can be "of one heart and one mind" if we are not "as one" in knowledge and forgiveness of all of each other's weaknesses.

Sharing our past with a loved one carries some risk, but a foundation of honesty is absolutely essential to a healthy relationship. I know of several cases where the young man in question admitted his struggle with pornography to his fiancée. In most of these cases, the young woman has been willing to accept his humble admission and has chosen to remain in the relationship. In a few cases, the engagement was broken off. Either way, it is better that the truth be known than that the potential marriage partner should find out later and feel deceived. Support from a loved one through the recovery process can be a great help if both partners are honest with each other about challenges and feelings.

TO WHOM SHOULD I GIVE MY FIFTH STEP?

There are several appropriate people to whom you can give your Fifth Step inventory:

1. Your Bishop

Confession to the bishop is most definitely necessary to our repentance before the Lord. The bishop is a "common judge in Israel," meaning he has the responsibility to vouch for our worthiness before the Lord and the fellowship of the Church. The bishop issues temple recommends and callings based on our adherence to the standards of the gospel. He acts for the Church in matters of transgression against the laws of the Church. Therefore, any sin we have committed that may jeopardize our membership in the Church needs to be confessed to him. This especially includes sins of a sexual nature. Therefore, fornication (sex before marriage), adultery (sex outside of marriage), abortion, masturbation and even the viewing of pornography should all be confessed to the bishop as part of our repentance process. It is also beneficial to discuss with the bishop things some might consider trivial, such as lustful thoughts and sexual fantasizing. His calling is not simply to hear confessions and issue discipline, but also (and more importantly) to help us work through the repentance process. If a problem is ongoing, reporting periodically to the bishop can be an important act of accountability and an important motivation for abstinence.

Throughout the years that I struggled with sexual addiction, I counseled with several bishops and stake presidents. Each time I approached the task of disclosing my sins, I felt a knot in my stomach. I felt embarrassed and ashamed. But each time I confessed, I felt better afterwards. Even when we are still struggling with the actions of addiction, it helps to have someone share the burden with us. I have a testimony of the principle of confession as part of the Lord's plan for our healing.

If you made a rigorous and complete inventory of your life in Step Four, your list will include a number of transgressions that are not necessarily serious enough to require confession to a bishop. Whether you include these things in an interview with your bishop is a personal choice. It may depend on your relationship with him, and also on the amount of time he has available to spend with you. If you want to give him your whole inventory, let him know when you make the appointment that you need an extended period of time for the interview. Explain that you are trying to do a thorough job of repenting and would like to include some things other than what you are required to confess to him. If your bishop has experience with the Twelve Steps, he will understand the role of a Fifth Step inventory in your recovery program.

2. A Professional Counselor

If you have a trusting relationship with a professional counselor, you may want to ask him to listen to your inventory. You have probably already talked over some of your issues with him, so a complete inventory could be considered an extension of that effort. Professional counselors are trained to listen, which is the main requirement of someone who hears your Fifth Step. In general, working with a counselor can help you understand the dynamics of addiction and your particular pattern. Insight gained from listening to your inventory may also help your counselor work with you in subsequent visits. Since inventories usually take more time than is allotted in a standard appointment, you may need to schedule some extra time.

3. Your Twelve Step Sponsor

In traditional Twelve Step organizations, such as AA and SA, an inventory is often given to a "sponsor." If you choose to use a sponsor, it's best if they have worked through all twelve steps themselves. This is especially vital when dealing with giving a sexual inventory. They must be someone who is solidly grounded in the principles of recovery, and if at all possible, has at least a year of solid abstinence from any acting out. For anyone to be a "Fifth Step sponsor," they must have done their own Fourth and *Fifth* Step. Doing a Fifth Step with such a person can be very reassuring for two reasons:

First, they are someone who has been where you have been and where you are, and who has come back by the grace and mercy of God. Their testimony to you will be invaluable. President Harold B. Lee made the following statement that we can use in seeking someone to help us take this important step:

> You cannot lift another soul until you are standing on higher ground than he is. You must be sure, if you would rescue the man, that you yourself are setting the example of what you would have him be. You cannot light a fire in another soul unless it is burning in your own soul. (Harold B. Lee, *Ensign*, July 1973, 123)

Second, many who have participated in a Fifth Step experience with a well-grounded, experienced Twelve Step sponsor find it can have a special benefit, because unlike a bishop or professional counselor, your

sponsor has no official obligation to hear your inventory. It is very easy
to fall prey to the adversary's lie that your bishop's kindness or your
counselor's time is "just part of their job." This lie can find no root when
you give your inventory to someone who has no obligation to help you,
but who listens and accepts you anyway.

Just a couple more important guidelines about doing your Fifth Step
with a Twelve Step sponsor: Remember that what you are going to share
in your inventory is *not the details* of your actions, but rather an in-depth
discussion of your character defects—your false beliefs and erroneous
thinking that led up to your actions. Make certain that the person you
choose to share your complete inventory with is sympathetic and understanding. And finally: *It is very important when asking someone to help you
in this way, that you do not cross gender lines. A woman should only ask
another woman to be her sponsor, and a man should only ask another man.*

CONFESSION BRINGS PEACE

The spiritual reality is that recognizing our character
weaknesses and the unrighteous actions they have led us
to take, and acknowledging those things privately to
God, is not enough. Only when we are willing to bear
our witness to another person of the exact nature of our
need for Christ's atonement, are we ready to come to
peace with our past, to forgive it and let it be. Nothing
restores our mental and emotional well-being like the
feeling of innocence we gain when we have nothing left
to hide. (Colleen C. Harrison, *Patterns of Light: Steps
4&5*, 8)

Usually, people who have done their Fifth Step feel a great burden
has been lifted from them. We confess the things we have done and
then let them go. The Savior has told us that He would bear our
burdens, and He will. In many ways, we can also **"bear one another's
burdens, that they may be light"** (Mosiah 18:8).

Some have thought that if their sins had been forgiven, they would
not remember them. The Lord has told us, **"Behold, he who has**

repented of his sins, the same is forgiven, and I, the Lord, remember
them no more" (D&C 58:42). As far as I know, it doesn't say anywhere
in the scriptures that *we* won't remember our sins anymore, only that
the *Lord* won't remember them.

> But if the wicked will turn from all his sins that he
> hath committed, and keep all my statutes, and do that
> which is lawful and right, he shall surely live, he shall
> not die. All his transgressions that he hath
> committed, *they shall not be mentioned unto him:* in his
> righteousness that he hath done he shall live. (Ezekiel
> 18:21–22, emphasis added)

While we may remember our past sins after we have been forgiven
for them, those memories will no longer burden us with guilt. I am
willing to talk about my past with an openness and honesty that
surprises me. My feelings are so different now from the shame I used to
feel. The only reason I can talk and write openly about these things is
because the Lord has lifted the burden of shame and guilt from me. I no
longer feel unworthy of His love, but instead I rejoice with gratitude for
His tender mercy towards me. I rejoice in the opportunity to bear
witness of the miracle of repentance, forgiveness, and *rebirth*. After the
life of sin and indulgence I previously led, I have found a *new life*, a
glorious life filled with happiness and peace. A feeling of peace is a sign
the Lord provides us that our sins have been forgiven. Listen to the
experience of the people of King Benjamin:

> And they all cried aloud with one voice, saying: O
> have mercy, and apply the atoning blood of Christ that
> we may receive forgiveness of our sins, and our hearts
> may be purified; for we believe in Jesus Christ, the
> Son of God, who created heaven and earth, and all
> things; who shall come down among the children of
> men. And it came to pass that after they had spoken
> these words the Spirit of the Lord came upon them,
> and *they were filled with joy, having received a remis-*
> *sion of their sins, and having peace of conscience,*
> because of the exceeding faith which they had in Jesus

> **Christ who should come, according to the words**
> **which king Benjamin had spoken unto them. (Mosiah**
> **4:2–3, emphasis added)**

Many of the sins I included in my inventory are fading from my
memory. The ones I still remember do not trouble me. It's almost as if it
were someone else who did those things. But still, I think it is important
to remember enough about my mistakes to learn what I need to learn
from them. The statement that people who don't remember their
history are doomed to repeat it is true of individuals as well as nations.
If I stopped doing the things that have enabled the Lord to lift me out
of addiction, I could be right back where I was. I have no desire to go
there again, and so I sometimes remind myself what it was like and how
miserable I was. I need that sobering reflection from time to time.

Another reason we remember our mistakes is so others may benefit
from them. I think of Alma and how willing he was to share with his
sons (and with us) the mistakes he had made and the agonizing process
he went through in becoming humble enough to be cleansed by the
Lord **(Alma 36 and 38).** When moved upon by the Holy Ghost, we
may feel it appropriate to share our experiences with others. That is the
feeling that has motivated me to write this book.

May the Lord bless you in carrying out this difficult act of humility.
While it may be scary, it is well worth it. Humility only *looks* bitter. Once
swallowed, it is sweet indeed.

MAKING THE MOST OF THIS CHAPTER

Please take time to answer the following questions in your recovery
journal.

1. The Lord has promised us forgiveness if we repent: **"Come now,**
    and let us reason together, saith the Lord: though your sins be as
    scarlet, they shall be as white as snow; though they be red like
    crimson, they shall be as wool" (Isaiah 1:18). Write about how
    the words **"red like crimson"** make you feel, and then the words

"white as snow." Express in writing your desire to experience this amazing change from the one state of being to the other.

2. Think of someone who once offended or hurt you, but whom you have since completely forgiven. Do you still have bad feelings toward them? Write about the gift of forgiveness the Lord bestows upon us to help us forgive each other.

3. The Lord has told us how he regards the sins for which we have repented: **"Behold, he who has repented of his sins, the same is forgiven, and I, the Lord, remember them no more" (D&C 58:42).** Write about a mistake you have made in the past for which you feel you have been forgiven. Is there a peace that accompanies the memory of that act? Explain what you have learned as a result of your mistake.

4. In the very next verse in **D&C 58,** the Lord gives us this insight: **"By this ye may know if a man repenteth of his sins—behold, he will confess them and forsake them" (D&C 58:43).** In what way is confession a sign of forsaking our sins? Is it possible to confess our sins without truly intending to forsake them? As addicts, we often find that the "forsaking" part takes time to achieve. Write about your feelings about the Lord's patience with you in this process.

5. Have you ever gone through a difficult experience with someone and found that you were drawn closer to each other because of the experience? Sharing an inventory is often that kind of experience. Write about your willingness to **"bear...another's burdens, that they may be light" (Mosiah 18:8)** and to let another bear your burdens with you.

10 *Step Six*

Were entirely ready to have God
remove all these defects of character.
(A.A. and Heart t' Heart traditional versions)

*Became humble enough to yield our hearts and
our lives to Christ for His sanctification and purification,
relying wholly upon His merits, acknowledging even our
own best efforts as unprofitable. (Helaman 3:35;
2 Nephi 31:19; Mosiah 2:20–21)*
(Heart t' Heart scriptural version)

During the years I was caught in addiction, I wasn't ignoring the problem. As I have already related, I was actually repenting over and over, and unfortunately, relapsing over and over. Even after coming into the Twelve Step recovery program and sincerely slogging through the first five steps, I must admit, I was still having an occasional slip in my abstinence. By the time I got to Step Six, I realized I was going to have to dig deeper and change so much more than just my actions if I wanted to stay "clean and sober" permanently. Simply put, without a pure heart, my hands would not, *could* not, stay clean. I needed to have my thoughts and even my very desires changed, too. But how? How could I work such a miracle? I began to realize that, here again, as in Steps One and Two, I was facing something that only *God* could do. Did that mean I would have to surrender to Him again? Curiously, I found another layer of resistance—of pride—rising up in my character. Obviously, I needed another period of preparation; and conveniently enough, that's what Step Six is—a preparation step.

LEARNING THE VALUE OF PREPARATION

Having the humility to take the time to prepare for something has always been hard for me. I've always been impulsive, and as soon as I have the idea to do something, I've wanted to jump right in and do it. A perfect example of this happened when I was sixteen. Even at that young age, I was deeply moved by the beauty I saw in my surroundings—the majesty of the mountains, the beauty of the trees, the mysterious interplay of light and shadow in the clouds. All these things inspired me with awe and wonder. I longed to try to capture those feelings in a way I could share with others. I decided I wanted to learn oil painting. I bought some books and started reading them, and even took a correspondence class. Somehow, though, my budding career as an artist didn't go as smoothly as I expected. I was dismayed by the very first lesson. It began, "If you want to paint, *you must first learn to draw.*"

Learn to draw? But that wasn't what I was looking for! I didn't want to mess around with pencils and erasers and mere paper! I wanted to paint! I wanted to get into the messy, gooey oil paints and smush them around and make beautiful images on real canvas. After all, I had been "drawing" since I was old enough to hold a pencil. In comparison to the glamour of oil painting, drawing was boring. No color. No pizzazz. But still I was told: "Learn to draw." Why was that? As I later learned (the hard way), it was because drawing is an essential part of painting. Without good basic drawing skills, any effort to reproduce realistic landscapes would be sabotaged by poor composition, balance, perspective, and more. In a similar way, Step Six helped me prepare to surrender my character defects in Step Seven by asking that I humble myself and completely let go of any illusion that in some way I had the power to change my own nature.

The Book of Mormon tells how the poverty of the Zoramites humbled them and prepared them to hear the gospel. Alma recognized that they had been through this necessary preparation, and were finally ready to hear the truths he desired to share with them.

> **And he beheld with great joy...that their afflictions had truly humbled them, and that they were in a preparation to hear the word. (Alma 32:6)**

As you've worked through the steps to this point, you have also faced your own share of humbling experiences. Each step is based on our willingness to humble ourselves. Consider with me for a moment what this journey has taught us so far. What has facing our addiction in the first three steps taught us about humility, about powerlessness and our need for God? What has the inventory process taught us about our past behaviors, and about the character traits that have contributed to our addictive patterns? This process of being prepared by humility continues now in Step Six, as we come to grips with the weaknesses revealed in Steps Four and Five. We can't conquer them without the Lord, any more than we could conquer our addictive behaviors without Him.

FINALLY FACING LIFE WITHOUT OUR ADDICTION

I have heard many people in Twelve Step meetings express surprised discouragement. It seemed that just when they began to get abstinent from their addiction, everything else in their life started to go wrong. Suddenly, they were having more arguments with their wife, their children were acting up, work wasn't going well, and so on. "What's happening?" they cried. Like me, they thought that as soon as they tried to "straighten up and fly right," life would take off in a better direction.

A similar phenomenon was observed by the wives of the first alcoholics to get sober in AA: "He may not be drinking," they exclaimed, "but in every other way, he's as bad as he was when he *was* drinking!" This phenomenon has come to be called a "dry drunk." Sometimes the expression, "Can't get drunk, can't get sober" is used. The obvious acting out behavior has stopped, but the underlying causes of that behavior have not been addressed. This observation is almost universal throughout all kinds of addiction recovery. It makes sense when we remember and admit the reason we originally resorted to using our addiction was to numb ourselves to the stress of facing the challenging realities of our lives. When we stop using our "drug," we inevitably find that those challenges haven't gone away. We can't hide from them any more, and they now demand our attention. These challenges are actually symptoms of our underlying character weaknesses, just like our addiction was. Our problems with wife, children, job, etc., will not improve until we are ready to turn *all* our character flaws over to the Lord.

The truth is we can't overcome weaknesses, or even start surrendering them to the Lord, until we recognize that they exist *in* us and are not being imposed *on* us, or caused by some stimulus in our environment. I may think I am doing well, behaving kindly and patiently, and then some sudden provocation catches me off guard. Someone pulls in front of me in traffic, forcing me to immediately apply my brakes in order to avoid an accident, or my daughter needs to use my computer at the last minute to finish a homework assignment when I was planning on doing some important writing myself. When I catch myself reacting uncharitably in situations like these, my first impulse is to excuse myself because the event came on me so suddenly. I tell myself, if I had had more time to prepare, I could have acted more kindly. But on the other hand, isn't my first reaction—how I respond before I have time to think it over—a truer indication of what I really am, of how much of the natural man still exists in me?

I lived in the southern United States for several years, and while there I became acquainted with roaches. Since roaches live in out-of-the-way places and only come out at night, you can go for years without knowing you have them. When I would go into the kitchen at night and suddenly turn on the light, dozens of roaches would scatter for cover. The sudden turning on of the light didn't create the roaches, it merely caught them before they had a chance to hide. Similarly, when I am caught off guard by some upsetting circumstance, the circumstance doesn't make me impatient or unkind, it merely shows me how much impatience and unkindness still remain in my natural-man self. That self is a part of me that I don't seem to be able to change. It is a part of me that I must surrender to the Lord and ask Him to heal. That is the essence of Steps Six and Seven.

When I was still looking at pornography and masturbating, many "less serious" behaviors in my life went totally unnoticed. Compared to the struggle I was having with my addiction, these lesser faults just didn't seem worth worrying about. When I finally allowed the Lord to bless me with abstinence, I began to notice a lot of things that needed repentance. For example, I realized I needed to repent of being inconsiderate of others' time by being consistently late. I needed to repent of being impatient with my wife and children over what were actually trivial issues. I needed to stop trying to control everyone around me.

The major change in my perception of myself reminds me of an amusing, but at the same time, telling experience I had once in connection with a trip to the temple. Even if you haven't been through the temple yet, you probably know that everyone dresses in white clothing there. One morning, as I was getting ready to leave for the temple, I put on a white shirt that I could also wear during the temple services. Then I put on my Sunday suit and took the rest of my white temple clothes in a suitcase. In the dressing room at the temple, when I changed into my white pants, I was startled and disappointed to realize that my "white" shirt was not really white at all! It was actually a *pale yellow.* Hanging next to the darker clothes in my closet, it had only *appeared* white. When I put on pants at the temple that really *were* white, I could see my mistake. Fortunately I was able to rent a white shirt and participate in the session. Similarly, some of my "lesser sins" hadn't looked that bad when compared with my sexual acting out, but when I became abstinent, those other sins began to be apparent.

LEARNING WHAT REALLY NEEDS TO BE SURRENDERED

For years, I thought I knew what needed to be fixed in my life. I needed to stop looking at pornography! As I mentioned before, as far as I was aware, this addiction was my only real weakness. If I could just get this problem under control, I was sure I would be very nearly perfect! The Lord had something more in mind, however:

> And if men come unto me **I** *will show unto them their* **weakness. I give unto men weakness that they may be**

> humble; and my grace is sufficient for all men that
> humble themselves before me; for if they humble
> themselves before me, and have faith in me, then will
> I make weak things become strong unto them. (Ether
> 12:27, emphasis added)

I really used to wonder at that verse, thinking, "I don't need to go to the Lord and have Him show me my weakness! I *know* what my (one) weakness is—it's this darned addiction." What I didn't realize was that my constant obsession with my addiction—either doing it or resisting it—was helping me to ignore a lot of other problems in my life. It was kind of like having your house on fire. It doesn't leave you much time to worry about tidying up the living room.

One of the weaknesses the Lord showed me was how carnally minded I was. The obvious example was my addiction to sensuality, but being carnally minded also included my essential character flaw of relying on the "arm of flesh" in my life as a whole. The following verse was a real shock to me:

> For to be carnally minded is death; but to be spiritu-
> ally minded is life and peace. Because *the carnal mind
> is enmity against God:* for it is not subject to the law of
> God, neither indeed can be. (Romans 8:6–7, em-
> phasis added)

I could handle the accusation of having a carnal mind, but the phrase **"enmity against God"** hit me like a slap in the face! Enmity means "a state of ill-will, hostility or hatred." But I certainly didn't have any "ill-will" toward God! I loved God, or at least, I thought I did. I immediately rejected the suggestion that my bad choices grew out of hostility or hatred toward God—that language was simply too strong to describe *me.* But on the other hand, I couldn't deny how deep my rebellion against God had been. How many times had He prompted me through His Spirit to turn away from sin, and I had ignored Him? How many times had He invited me to turn to more enlightening, uplifting thoughts and actions? And how many times had I turned my back on those promptings and rejected His invitations? Too many to count.

Eventually I came to the point where something within me began to recoil from anything spiritual, even from the mention of the Savior's name! It got to where, whenever the Lord's Spirit would invite me to pray or read the scriptures or participate in some other faith-promoting activity, a dark spirit would whisper in my ear: *"Don't do that. If you do that, the Holy Ghost will start to work on you and then you won't feel like playing. It will ruin our fun."* Today, I look back with horror at how far I allowed the adversary's influence to penetrate my soul, and how slowly I began to turn away from it. Someone once said that when we first start to come back to God, we don't rush toward heaven as much as we back reluctantly away from hell. That was certainly true for me.

Thinking about how diligently I avoided the heart-deep changes Step Six and Seven require of us, I am reminded of an old-fashioned remedy for toothaches I learned from my parents. As a teenager, when I had a toothache, I would often put off going to the dentist; instead, I would use a drop of clove oil on the tooth to numb the pain for a while. Of course, it didn't do anything to stop the decay, but in my childishness, stopping the decay wasn't what mattered to me. Stopping the pain was all I cared about. My efforts at evading the dentist would continue until finally the pain became so intense the clove oil wouldn't mask it any longer. Sometimes the decay had gone so far that the tooth had to be pulled. A lot of the dental problems I deal with today are the consequence of my prior attempts to postpone genuine healing.

In the process of working Step Six, I began to realize I had been using my addiction like I once had used the clove oil, to hide from weaknesses in my character that were now coming to the surface. For example, I began to see that my impatience with others represented tremendous selfishness I would not see before. I also discovered a deep-rooted unwillingness to face the challenges and responsibilities of my life, wanting others to fix things for me. Gradually I realized these deeper faults were actually at the foundation of my addiction. I had to admit I had used pornography to avoid facing life and turning to the Lord for guidance and power. When at last I started to become abstinent, the inside-out work of Step Six could finally begin.

OUTSIDE–IN VS. INSIDE–OUT

From the beginnings of AA, Twelve Step groups have taught that the devastating condition we call addiction is primarily a spiritual disease, and that any lasting cure also has to be spiritual. The deeper we allow these healing spiritual principles to reach into our beings, the surer our freedom will be. The SA White Book puts it this way:

> We will use the word *spiritual* in referring to that aspect of ourselves underlying and determining all our attitudes, choices, thoughts, and behavior—the very core of personality, the very heart of the person. If we can see how the addictive process involves this most fundamental aspect of our being, we will be able to understand why recovery—whatever else we make it—must be a spiritual process. (*Sexaholics Anonymous*, 46; emphasis original)

I tried for years to conquer my addiction by using what *Alcoholics Anonymous* calls "half-measures" (p. 59). I attended innumerable self-improvement classes and workshops on motivation. Even after I started attending Twelve Step meetings, I was confused for awhile. I sincerely thought the program and all its tools or aids to recovery were the answer. So instead of attending classes on motivation, I attended Twelve Step meetings. Instead of self-help books, I read Twelve Step literature. But still the lasting peace I sought evaded me. During the preparation process of Step Six, I was brought down into the **"depths of humility"** **(2 Nephi 9:42)** to realize I was still resorting to "half-measures," using the tools as if they held the healing power that only one source can provide. Elder Richard G. Scott provided the answer to my confusion:

> No matter what the source of difficulty and no matter how you begin to obtain relief—through a qualified professional therapist, doctor, priesthood leader, friend, concerned parent, or loved one—no matter how you begin, those solutions will never provide a complete answer. The final healing comes through faith in Jesus Christ and His teachings, with a broken heart and a

contrite spirit and obedience to His commandments.
(*Ensign*, May 1994, 9)

We must be healed from the inside out. The change must happen in our hearts—a change that can only be brought about by the Master Healer. That is the testimony of President Ezra Taft Benson:

> The Lord works from the inside out. The world works
> from the outside in. The world would take people out of
> the slums. Christ takes the slums out of people. (*Ensign*,
> July, 1989, 4)

WHAT WE NEED, WE CAN'T DO FOR OURSELVES

I don't think anyone would argue that Alma the Younger and the sons of Mosiah were deep in the "slums" of worldly behavior and sinful choices. Yet, as Alma went through his three days of intense repentance, he cried out to the only One who could lift him out of those slums of unrighteous attitudes and behavior:

> **And it came to pass that I was three days and three
> nights in the most bitter pain and anguish of soul; and
> never, until I did cry out unto the Lord Jesus Christ
> for mercy, did I receive a remission of my sins. But
> behold, I did cry unto him and I did find peace to my
> soul. (Alma 38:8)**

For many years, I read this verse and interpreted Alma's words "and I did find peace to my soul" to mean he had finally repented for his sins and been forgiven. But in truth, much more than forgiveness took place in that moment when he cried out to the Savior for mercy. Christ didn't just forgive Alma. Christ did that thing for Alma that Alma couldn't do for himself. Christ gave Alma a complete *remission* of the effects of sin! In that moment, Alma's whole disposition or character was changed. Not only did he never return to the errors of his past, he devoted the rest of his life to repairing the damage he had done and to teaching others of Christ's redeeming love. Something was at work in Alma's heart and mind that was more than simply "being forgiven."

Looking back now, I realize how often my repentance was just a bandage to cover the deeply infected wound of addiction. I wanted to meet the requirements of talking with the bishop and doing what he asked, and then move on. Even though I told myself I was sincere in my intent to change, is it any wonder that in a short while I found myself back in the same situation, needing to confess again, and "be forgiven" still again? This kind of "serial repentance" is an indication of an attempt to change that has not yet connected with the Savior's power to redeem.

A story told by Elder Ronald E. Poelman illustrates the dilemma we will all have until we finish the preparation represented in Step Six:

> Recently I was in private conversation with one who, having committed a serious transgression, had also made intense effort to repent and receive forgiveness from those personally offended, from the Church, and from the Lord...
>
> He spoke of how he had forsaken his transgressive behavior of the past, confessed to proper priesthood authorities, and attempted to make restitution to those offended. He further described his efforts to live according to gospel principles and Church standards.
>
> *The Savior and his atoning sacrifice were not mentioned.* The underlying assumption seemed to be that divine forgiveness is obtained through those steps of repentance limited to changing one's behavior. Despite the brother's earnest efforts to repent, he appeared to be burdened still by remorse and regret and to feel that he must continue to pay for his sins...
>
> One who assumes that he can or must pay the price for his sins and thereby *earn* divine forgiveness will not feel free to continue progress toward realizing his divine potential, that is, eternal life.
>
> The fact is *we cannot save ourselves.* (*Ensign,* Nov. 1993, 84, emphasis added)

Until we forsake our self-centered approach to repentance and surrender our need *totally* to the Savior, we remain in danger of slipping into addiction again. Elder Dallin H. Oaks talks about how deep the change needs to go if we are to have a real remission of our sins:

> We tend to think of the results of repentance as simply cleansing us from sin. But that is an incomplete view of the matter. A person who sins is like a tree that bends easily in the wind. On a windy and rainy day, the tree bends so deeply against the ground that the leaves become soiled with mud, like sin. If we focus only on cleaning the leaves, the weakness in the tree that allowed it to bend and soil its leaves may remain. Similarly, a person who is merely sorry to be soiled by sin will sin again in the next high wind. The susceptibility to repetition continues until the tree has been strengthened.
>
> When a person has gone through the process that results in what the scriptures call a broken heart and a contrite spirit, the Savior does more than cleanse that person from sin. He also gives him or her new strength...We must, as the scripture says, "[become] a saint through the atonement of Christ the Lord." (Mosiah 3:19.) This is what the scripture means in its explanation that a person who has repented of his sins will "forsake them." (D&C 58:43.) Forsaking sins is more than resolving not to repeat them. Forsaking involves a fundamental change in the individual. (*Ensign*, July 1992, 72–73)

HIS YOKE IS EASY

Maybe changing our character wasn't what we were looking for when we started into this recovery process, but in time we learn that the Lord has much more in mind for us than just freeing us from our addiction. In His goodness, He wants to take us all the way to perfection and complete happiness. Elder James E. Talmage taught:

We believe that our spirits are the offspring of Deity, and we hold that when Christ said to His apostles, "Be ye therefore perfect, even as your Father which is in heaven is perfect," He was not talking of a merely idealistic yet impossible achievement; but that on the contrary He meant that it was possible for men to advance until they shall become like unto the Gods in their powers and in their attainments, through righteousness. (*Conference Report*, April 1915, 123)

While the journey may be long, and in places very difficult, even painful, we are destined for eventual greatness. The Lord intends to make us over in His glorious image:

And we know that all things work together for good to them that love God, to them who are the called according to his purpose. For whom he did foreknow, he also did predestinate [foreordain] to be conformed to the image of his Son, that he might be the firstborn among many brethren. Moreover whom he did predestinate [foreordain], them he also called: and whom he called, them he also justified: and whom he justified, them he also glorified. (Romans 8:28–30)

Of course, in this remaking process, many things will have to be left behind. In truth, I thought the prospect of giving up not only my addiction, but actual portions of my character or heart, sounded dauntingly painful! After all, being your typical mortal, I don't like pain. Obviously. My addiction was proof of how far and how long I could run from the discomforts of everyday life. But finally I had to accept the fact that if I wanted to be delivered from my addictions, I would have to allow all these painful changes in my innermost self. I had to face the fact that my surrender had to be to the very depths of my heart. As I humbled myself and started to listen to the Spirit guide me into recovery, I was relieved to find that the Lord didn't ask me to change all at once, but instead was gentle and patient, showing me the next thing I could let go of, and then the next after that. Step by step, He led me out of the quagmire my life had become.

For example, when I first became abstinent, I knew I needed to get rid of any materials that were triggering me. I owned some movies that were definitely in this category, and one by one, the Lord gave me the willingness to let go of them. Finally, I was left with just a few, some that I really wrestled with the Lord about. "Come on," I reasoned. "Artistically, these are really top-notch movies. What if I just keep them and edit them?" Now, you have to understand that I had no experience at editing videos or access to the necessary equipment. It wasn't until months later, as I went through the process of Step Six, that I was able to honestly admit my deeper intentions—that some part of me wanted to keep those movies around *just in case.* Only when my heart was pure in this matter, could my "hands" become truly clean. Finally, even those movies went in the trash—where they belonged. Step by step, the Lord led me to where I needed to be, and He was with me every step of the way, patiently making my reformation possible.

When we are facing such *mighty* change head-on, the truth we often haven't recognized is that the Lord can bring to pass that which would be impossible for us to do on our own. Bit by bit, as we turn our hearts over to Christ, our desires begin to change and we begin to loosen our grasp on the false supports we have used. In time we find many changes have happened without our even being aware of them. He never asks more of us than we can do in *His* strength, but patiently prepares us to receive that strength.

President Benson taught that when we put God first in our lives, other things take care of themselves:

> We must put God in the forefront of everything else in our lives. He must come first, just as He declares in the first of His Ten Commandments: "Thou shalt have no other gods before me. (Exodus 20:3)

> When we put God first, all other things fall into their proper place or drop out of our lives. Our love of the Lord will govern the claims for our affection, the demands on our time, the interests we pursue, and the order of our priorities.

We should put God ahead of *everyone else* in our lives.
(*Ensign*, May 1988, 4. Italics original.)

Thus, we find we don't have to spend a tremendous effort on each one of our character defects individually—we only have to let God be in charge of our lives, and the transformation will follow:

> **But if ye will turn to the Lord with full purpose of heart, and put your trust in him, and serve him with all diligence of mind, if ye do this, he will, according to his own will and pleasure, deliver you out of bondage. (Mosiah 7:33)**

What a marvelous promise! What glory to be free of the bondage, not only of addiction, but of so many faults that have plagued my life. But this promise is conditional: it is based on my willingness to put my trust in the Lord. The Lord can make marvelous changes in our lives for us when we finally ask Him, or more accurately, when we finally give Him permission, but He won't violate our agency by doing it without our involvement. As we read in *Sexaholics Anonymous* (p. 96):

> *Without God, I can't.*
> *Without me, God won't.*

ONE FINAL FEAR—WILL MY NEEDS BE MET?

As I contemplated making a more complete surrender to the Lord than I had ever made before, one final fear still haunted me: What will happen to me if I let go of everything I have used to prop myself up? Will the Lord really take care of me as He has promised? I wasn't too sure. I wasn't sure that following Him would bring me the happiness I sought. What about the pain in my life? I only knew one way to deal with it, and that was to submerge myself in my addiction. Even if that didn't work for long, it was very effective in distracting me in the short run. Could the Lord do as much for me as I pretended I could do for myself? If I had only known how good the Lord really is, and how willing to take my burdens from me, I would never have fallen into the addictive patterns I did—seeking happiness and relief where there is truly only pain. President Benson's reassuring promise bears repeating:

Men and women who turn their lives over to God will discover that He can make a lot more out of their lives than they can. He will deepen their joys, expand their vision, quicken their minds, strengthen their muscles, lift their spirits, multiply their blessings, increase their opportunities, comfort their souls, raise up friends, and pour out peace. Whoever will lose his life in the service of God will find eternal life (see Matt. 10:39). (*Teachings of Ezra Taft Benson*, 361–71)

I praise my Savior that at some point I finally became willing to test His promises. What relief and joy I found! When I finally made the decision to let the Lord direct my life, I found things went so much more easily and joyfully than I had ever dreamed they could. I have truly come to know for myself the truth of the Lord's promise:

> **Come unto me, all ye that labour and are heavy laden, and I will give you rest. Take my yoke upon you, and learn of me; for I am meek and lowly in heart: and ye shall find rest unto your souls. For my yoke is easy, and my burden is light. (Matthew 11:28–30)**

With such goodness awaiting me, why did I delay so long? The Lord's way is much better than mine! Indeed, we can trust Him with our lives.

MAKING THE MOST OF THIS CHAPTER

Please take time to answer the following questions in your recovery journal.

1. Step Six is a preparation step. Alma's records, **"The Lord did pour out his Spirit on all the face of the land *to prepare the minds* of the children of men, or *to prepare their hearts* to receive the word which should be taught among them at the time of his coming"** (**Alma 16:16, emphasis added**). Write about the difference between having your mind prepared and having your heart

prepared. Write about the state of preparation you feel you are at in these two areas.

2. Review your response to Question 1 in Chapter Four (p. 57) and the list you made about the efforts you have made up until now to repent of your addiction and underlying character flaws. How do the results of these efforts compare with the promise of "remission"? Can you identify any problems from your past that you feel are now in remission, that do not trouble you like they used to?

3. King Benjamin admonishes us to watch ourselves in the areas of **"your thoughts, and your words, and your deeds" (Mosiah 4:30).** Write about the character traits your thoughts, your words and your deeds reveal. Do they tend to be overly aggressive ones—anger, control, etc.—or overly passive ones—fear, placing others' opinions above God's, etc.?

4. Nephi said, **"I know in whom I have trusted" (2 Nephi 4:19),** referring, of course, to the Lord. Write about your willingness to **"offer your whole souls as an offering unto Him" (Omni 1:26).** How much trust do you have in the Lord to manage your life and bring you happiness? How can you increase your faith in the Lord? Write about how Alma's sermon on faith **(Alma 32)** applies here.

5. Read "Step Six Inventory of Character Defects" in Appendix B (281). Write about each character trait you identify with, how your life would be better if that particular character flaw were removed from you. Write about your willingness to surrender each character defect to the Savior.

Chapter **11** *Step Seven*

Humbly asked Him to remove our shortcomings.
(A.A. and Heart t' Heart traditional versions)

*Humbly cried unto the Lord Jesus Christ in our
hearts for a remission of sins that through His
mercy and His grace we might experience a
mighty change of heart, lose all disposition to do
evil, and thus be encircled about in the arms of
safety because of His great and last sacrifice.*
(Alma 36:18; Alma 38:8; Moroni 10:32;
Mosiah 5:2; Alma 34:15–16)
(Heart t' Heart scriptural version)

If I am going to have a pure heart as well as clean hands, I must
petition the Lord to create such a heart in me. He is the only one who
has the power to make such a dramatic change in my disposition or
nature. Only He can replace my selfishness with generosity, my doubt
with faith, my stubbornness with willingness. Nevertheless, He waits for
me to become convinced of my need for Him and for me to ask Him to
change my heart. He will begin to work this miracle in my life just as
soon as I am ready and willing to exercise faith in Him and invite Him
to do so.

SANCTIFICATION—THE GOAL OF RECOVERY

In order to fully comprehend the blessing Step Seven can be to us, we need to review the wording of the scriptural version of Step Six. It reads, "Became humble enough to yield our hearts and our lives to Christ for His sanctification and purification..." In other words, what we became *willing* to do in Step Six—yield our hearts and lives to the Lord in order for Him to sanctify and purify us—we will actually carry out in taking Step Seven.

A scriptural example of yielding one's heart to the Lord is found in Helaman's day, when many of the Nephites were beginning yet another descent into pride and wickedness. Still, those who remained faithful received a most amazing spiritual blessing:

> **Nevertheless they did fast and pray oft, and did wax stronger and stronger in their humility, and firmer and firmer in the faith of Christ, unto the filling their souls with joy and consolation, yea, *even to the purifying and the sanctification of their hearts*, which sanctification cometh because of their yielding their hearts unto God. (Helaman 3:35, emphasis added)**

If you are like me, you have probably wondered, "Just what *is* sanctification?" The Latin root of sanctification is *sanctus*, which means "holy." Sanctification, then, is "the process of being made holy." Elder Bruce R. McConkie adds further light to that definition:

> To be *sanctified* is to become clean, pure, and spotless; to be free from the blood and sins of the world; to become a new creature of the Holy Ghost, one whose body has been renewed by the rebirth of the Spirit. (*Mormon Doctrine*, 675; Italics original)

Sanctification always sounded wonderful to me, but so far from my grasp! How I longed to be free of the filth I had invited into my mind and allowed to pollute my eternal spirit. I truly wanted to be pure, spotless, and holy, but hell only mocked my righteous desires. Satan had me captive and wasn't about to let me go. He knew full well that my willpower alone would never be enough, that only the Savior's power could free me. I am humbled to realize how much I was like the children of Israel, lost in the wilderness:

> He sent fiery flying serpents among them; and after they were bitten he prepared a way that they might be healed; and the labor which they had to perform was to look; and because of the simpleness of the way, or the easiness of it, there were many who perished. (1 Nephi 17:41)

As I look back on the years I spent in voluntary slavery, I am amazed that I missed understanding how easy the cure was, and puzzled at how many years I spent **"perishing."** **"The labor [I] had to perform was to look"**—to look to the Savior. I suppose I thought by going to church and fulfilling my church assignments, I *was* looking to the Savior. In reality, though, my personal attention to Him hadn't amounted to more than an occasional, almost casual glance. More recently I have learned that to "look" to Him means to do so with an eye *single to His glory*—in other words, to stand amazed, adoring, worshiping Him, recognizing Him as one with the Father in *everything*.

As mentioned earlier, Helaman's people experienced true sanctification, **"because of their yielding their hearts unto God"** (Helaman **3:35).** "Yielding" is such a perfect word for how we must respond to the Lord. The Lord never forces us. He only *entices* or *invites* us through the "still" and "small" promptings of the Holy Ghost. We, in turn, *choose* to either *resist* those promptings, or *yield* to them. The outcome from hour to hour, and day to day, depends entirely on our choice. So many times over the years the Lord invited me, offering the very help I needed, but I resisted His help and His love.

> For the natural man is an enemy to God, and has been from the fall of Adam, and will be, forever and ever, *unless he yields to the enticings of the Holy Spirit,* and putteth off the natural man and becometh a saint through the atonement of Christ the Lord, and becometh as a child, submissive, meek, humble,

> **patient, full of love, willing to submit to all things which the Lord seeth fit to inflict upon him, even as a child doth submit to his father. (Mosiah 3:19, emphasis added)**

During all those years of addiction, I was anything but submissive, meek, or humble. Nor was I willing to submit to **"all things which the Lord [saw] fit to inflict upon [me]"**—at least, not without comforting myself by using my addiction. While I made an outward pretense of obeying, I kept my heart **"far from [Him]" (2 Nephi 27:25)**. It took wading through the process of Step Six to help me realize I was still holding on to my willful, stubborn attitudes.

Eventually, I began to realize that if I was ever going to triumph over my character defects, I had to surrender them at a much deeper level than I ever had before. That realization led me to Step Seven. I was so tired of the negative attitudes and tendencies that continually kept me from any lasting peace with God and with myself. I was moved to cry, "Lord, I don't want any more of these characteristics *and I don't want my stubborn, self-sufficient pride either!!* Please take *all* of me—just as I am—and make me over in Thine image!"

Even at this point, the adversary was waiting to tempt me with another lie. "You're just falling into the trap of perfectionism, praying to become like Christ. Who do you think you are, anyway?" As I prayed to the Father, seeking the counsel of the Lord, I was blessed to see that Step Seven is the furthest thing from perfectionism. He showed me that perfectionism is an obsession with being perfect *right now* and by one's own achievement. To take Step Seven, on the other hand, is to turn the process of perfecting myself over to the Lord and to exercise faith *in Him* and in His timing.

SURRENDERING VS. ASKING FOR HELP

Surrendering my heart to the Lord in Step Six required even more humility of me than did surrendering my addiction in Step Three. I felt a great deal of resistance to an act of such total surrender. It seemed like "chickening out," or abdicating my responsibility to do what I should do on my own. Looking back now, I see that this was pride in its most pious and subtle form.

Eventually, I realized taking Step Seven meant I had to surrender everything to Jesus Christ, even ownership of my victory over self. There is a big difference in asking, "Lord, please give me the strength to..." and saying "Lord, I don't have the strength. Will you please..." If I only ask for His help, I am holding on to some of the credit if I succeed. On the other hand, when I surrender the problem to His might, I also give up all glory for the victory, and this was the depth of humility I desperately needed. This was the **"nothingness"** King Benjamin declared we must embrace **(Mosiah 4: 5–7)**. I was finally required to admit my total nothingness, or powerlessness without God. In other words, my efforts to overcome my weaknesses are nothing compared to the Lord's part in my salvation. The ultimate fulfillment of the command to **"work out [my] own salvation" (Mormon 9:27)** meant I must surrender all my weaknesses—my whole soul—unto Him. I do that by asking Him to "relieve me of the bondage of self" or, in other words, to take my character weaknesses away, according to His will and timing.

One brother, in discussing his efforts to obtain this heart-deep character change, wrote:

> I think God has given us the right—as His begotten sons and daughters—to ask Him to work upon us and upon our hearts to perform that "mighty change" so needed for our salvation. I have worked on changing my heart but was not successful until I asked God to do it for me. I had to be willing to accept His hand in my life. I could not even do 1% of what I needed—I was completely at His mercy. All I was capable of was a weak plea for Him to work miracles within me.

TRUE CONVERSION

Sometimes we use words rather casually, not thinking of their true meanings. The word "conversion" or "convert," in connection with joining the Church, is one of those instances, I'm afraid. It is our common habit to speak of a person becoming converted to the Church when they have simply become *convinced* it is true. We forget that to convert something actually means to change it from one state or condition to another. Quoting President Marion G. Romney, Elder Richard G. Scott explained:

> Sometimes the word *converted* is used to describe when a sincere individual decides to be baptized. However, when properly used, *conversion* means far more than that, for the new convert as well as the long-term member. With characteristic doctrinal clarity and precision, President Marion G. Romney explained conversion:
>
> "Converted means to turn from one belief or course of action to another. Conversion is a spiritual and moral change. *Converted* implies not merely mental acceptance of Jesus and his teachings but also a motivating faith in him and his gospel. A faith which works a transformation, an actual change in one's understanding of life's meaning and in his allegiance to God in interest, in thought, and in conduct. In one who is really wholly converted, desire for things contrary to the gospel of Jesus Christ has actually died. And substituted therefore is a love of God, with a fixed and controlling determination to keep his commandments...
>
> "Membership in the Church and conversion are not necessarily synonymous. Being converted and having a testimony are not necessarily the same thing either. A testimony comes when the Holy Ghost gives the earnest seeker a witness of the truth. A moving testimony vitalizes faith. That is, it induces repentance and obedience to the commandments. Conversion is the fruit or the reward for repentance and obedience." (*Conference Report*, Guatemala Area Conference, 1977, 8–9)
>
> Stated simply, true conversion is the fruit of *faith, repentance,* and *consistent obedience.* Faith comes by hearing the

word of God [see Romans 10:17] and responding to it. You will receive from the Holy Ghost a confirming witness of things you accept on *faith* by willingly doing them [see Ether 12:6]. You will be led to *repent* of errors resulting from wrong things done or right things not done. As a consequence, your capacity to *consistently obey* will be strengthened. This cycle of *faith, repentance,* and *consistent obedience* will lead you to greater conversion with its attendant blessings. True conversion will strengthen your capacity to do what you know you should do, when you should do it, regardless of the circumstances. (*Ensign,* May 2002, 24–25; italics original)

Isn't that what we are looking for in recovery, to have our "capacity to consistently obey strengthened?" That is the kind of change true recovery or true conversion signifies. We find that when our hearts have been consecrated to the Lord, good works automatically follow. These important changes are not something we can do of ourselves, however. The change is a miracle we allow God to work in us, according to His mercy and grace. This is the "mighty" change. We must never forget that it is granted and maintained from day to day, only by our surrendering our lives to Him. As B. H. Roberts so masterfully taught:

Through water baptism is obtained a remission of past sins; but even after the sins of the past are forgiven, the one so pardoned will doubtless feel the force of sinful habits bearing heavily upon him. He who has been guilty of habitual untruthfulness, will at times find himself inclined, perhaps, to yield to that habit. He who has stolen may be sorely tempted, when opportunity arises, to steal again. While he who has indulged in licentious practices may again find himself disposed to give way to the seductive influence of the siren. So with drunkenness, malice, envy, covetousness, hatred, anger, and in short all the evil dispositions that flesh is heir to. *There is an absolute necessity for some additional sanctifying grace that will strengthen poor human nature, not only to enable it*

*to resist temptation, but also to root out from the heart concu-
piscence—the blind tendency or inclination to evil.* The
heart must be purified, every passion, every prosperity
made submissive to the will, and the will of man brought
into subjection to the will of God. Man's natural powers
are unequal to this task; so, I believe, all will testify who
have made the experiment. *Mankind stand in some need
of a strength superior to any they possess of themselves, to
accomplish this work of rendering pure our fallen nature.* (B.
H. Roberts, *The Gospel and Man's Relationship to Deity,*
179, emphasis added.)

BEING REBORN

As I searched for further understanding of this concept of being
completely changed in our nature and reborn as a child of Christ
(Mosiah 5:7), I found the following statement that so beautifully
describes the miracle of taking Step Seven:

Sometimes we tend to focus so much upon the fact that
Jesus Christ died for us that we do not attend to an
equally important facet of his redemptive enterprise—
the fact that he also came to live in us. It is marvelous
beyond the power of expression to contemplate that the
Savior can and does forgive our sins. There is no way in
our present state to comprehend how and in what
manner this miracle of miracles was and is brought to
pass. It simply happens. And thanks be to God that it
does happen. *But we cannot enjoy the full and complete
powers of the atonement of Christ until our redemption from
sin entails the re-creation of a nature which is foreign to sin.*
That is to say, Jesus came to cleanse us from guilt and the
taints of transgression; he also came to renovate our
nature and empower our souls that we are delivered, in
process of time, from the effects and pull of those transgressions. We are not in the ultimate sense, therefore,

redeemed from our sins, to use Amulek's and Helaman's words, until those sins have no more power over us. *The additional wonder and beauty of the Atonement is that we are not expected to resist sin by will power and personal resolve alone, though such things are essential; rather, as we come to gain that life which is in Christ—a life which comes as we seek for and cultivate the Spirit of the Lord—we receive that enabling power which extends to us the strength to forsake and overcome, a power which we could not have generated on our own.* (Monte S. Nyman and Charles D. Tate, Jr., eds., *Helaman through 3 Nephi 8: According to Thy Word* [Provo: BYU Religious Studies Center, 1992], 22, emphasis added)

That enabling power which gives us strength to resist temptation and thus releases us from our slavery to addiction is the same power that changes our hearts and gives us a new life in Christ. This is the power that changes the basic character faults that have led us into addiction in the first place. This is the power to find help for the central cause of our problem, of which addiction to certain behaviors is merely a symptom. President Benson spoke of this vital change, echoing the words of President McKay and President Kimball:

When you choose to follow Christ, you choose to be changed. "No man," said President David O. McKay, "can sincerely resolve to apply to his daily life the teachings of Jesus of Nazareth without sensing a change in his own nature. The phrase 'born again' has a deeper significance than many people attach to it. This *changed feeling* may be indescribable, *but it is real.*" (*Conference Report,* Apr. 1962, p. 7; italics original)

Can human hearts be changed? Why, of course! It happens every day in the great missionary work of the Church. It is one of the most widespread of Christ's modern miracles. If it hasn't happened to you—it should.

Our Lord told Nicodemus that "except a man be born
again, he cannot see the kingdom of God." (John 3:3.)
Of these words President Spencer W. Kimball said, "This
is the simple total answer to the weightiest of all questions....To gain eternal life there must be a rebirth, a
transformation." (*Conference Report*, Apr. 1958, p. 14.)

President McKay said that Christ called for "an entire
revolution" of Nicodemus's "inner man." "His manner of
thinking, feeling, and acting with reference to spiritual
things would have to undergo a fundamental and permanent change." (*Conference Report*, Apr. 1960, p. 26.)

In addition to the physical ordinance of baptism and the
laying on of hands, one must be spiritually born again to
gain exaltation and eternal life.

Alma states: "And the Lord said unto me: Marvel not
that all mankind, yea, men and women, all nations,
kindreds, tongues and people, must be born again; yea,
born of God, changed from their carnal and fallen state,
to a state of righteousness, being redeemed of God,
becoming his sons and daughters;

And thus they become new creatures; and unless they do
this, they can in nowise inherit the kingdom of God."
(Mosiah 27:25–26) (Ezra Taft Benson, *Ensign*, July 1989,
2)

This idea of having such a significant change in my nature was
almost beyond my ability to believe when I first read about it in *He Did
Deliver Me from Bondage*. I struggled for so many years with aborted
attempts to change that I had begun to think change was impossible.
What I was not considering was the infinite power the Savior has to
change us from the inside out, once we give Him our permission.
Continuing the quote from President Benson:

The world would mold men by changing their environment. Christ changes men, who then change their

environment. The world would shape human behavior, but Christ can change human nature.

"Human nature can be changed, here and now," said President McKay, and then he quoted the following:

"You can change human nature. No man who has felt in him the Spirit of Christ even for half a minute can deny this truth...."

You do change human nature, your own human nature, if you surrender it to Christ. Human nature has been changed in the past. Human nature must be changed on an enormous scale in the future, unless the world is to be drowned in its own blood. And only Christ can change it. (Beverly Nichols, in David O. McKay, *Stepping Stones to an Abundant Life*, Salt Lake City: Deseret Book Co., 1971, p. 23.) (Ezra Taft Benson, *Ensign*, July 1989, 4)

I bear my solemn testimony to you that this comprehensive change in our very nature can include our attitude toward sex, even though it has been an area of life that has been filled with turmoil, temptation and maladjustment. This rebirth experience can include having **"weak things become strong" (Ether 12:27)** in our lives! The ability to feel a powerful degree of sexual desire is not an evil thing, in and of itself. It is a God-given and godly attribute to feel sexual attraction and physical passion. Only when this trait has been enslaved and perverted by Satan's lies does it become lust. Our ability to feel intense desire is only evil when it is misused and misapplied. This and all other attributes must be cleansed and purified by the influence of the Holy Ghost on our hearts. Elder Parley P. Pratt declared:

The gift of the Holy Ghost...increases, enlarges, expands, and purifies all the natural passions and affections, and adapts them by the gift of wisdom to their lawful use. (*Key to Theology*, 101–2)

THE MIGHTY CHANGE

There are many names in the scriptures for the kind of change we are seeking in Step Seven. It may be referred to as being **"born again"** (John 3:3–8; Mosiah 27:25), undergoing **"a mighty change"** (Mosiah 5:2; Alma 5:11–14), or coming **"unto Christ"** (Omni 1:26; Moroni 10:30–33). I keep coming back to the story of Alma the Younger because he is such a great example to me of someone who came to this mighty change "later" in life, after a period of turning away from the righteous teachings of his upbringing. We can be sure Alma was taught well by his prophet-father, and still he strayed. While my own father was not a prophet, I was definitely taught from the time I was small what I should and should not do. I cannot claim that any of my mistakes were born of ignorance of the commandments, but I made them nonetheless. And, like Alma, I came to a place where I was **"racked with eternal torment,…harrowed up to the greatest degree,…tormented with the pains of hell"** (Alma 36:12–13). As I learned to apply Step Seven, I once again felt that intense desire for change. However, this time it was not about my "sins" only, but about all the character traits that continued to keep me from being like my Savior. Again, I found myself turning to Him for the power to change:

> **Now, as my mind caught hold upon this thought, I cried within my heart: O Jesus, thou Son of God, have mercy on me. (Alma 36:17–19)**

And the Lord has indeed had mercy on me. As I have attempted the degree of surrender represented in taking Step Seven, I have watched my heart soften and my inspiration brighten. Although I am far from perfect, today I often see myself responding to life in ways that humble me—with faith, hope, peace, and charity far greater than my own. I know the Lord has accepted me and forgiven me, not only of my grosser sins, but is strengthening me **"in the inner man"** as well (Ephesians 3:16). He is doing for me, once again, what I could not do for myself. His act of Atonement for me was not an event that merely took place 2,000 years ago, but is an ongoing relationship He is pleased to have with me every day of my life. It is as if His continued walk with me is like a treasure box that is constantly replenished. Of course, the treasure

I receive from Him is far greater than any earthly possession, and this miracle has engendered a feeling of deepest gratitude in my heart. What the Lord did for the people who were taught by Alma the Elder at the waters of Mormon has now happened to me.

> Behold, he changed [my heart]; yea, he awakened [me] out of a deep sleep, and [I] awoke unto God. Behold, [I was] in the midst of darkness; nevertheless, [my soul was] illuminated by the light of the everlasting word; yea, [I was] encircled about by the bands of death, and the chains of hell, and an everlasting destruction did await [me]. And now I ask of you, my brethren, [was I] destroyed? Behold, I say unto you, Nay, [I was] not. And again I ask, were the bands of death broken, and the chains of hell which encircled [me] about, were they loosed? I say unto you, Yea, they were loosed, and [my soul] did expand, and [I] did sing redeeming love. (Alma 5:7–9)

I feel such joy and happiness and love and gratitude; "singing redeeming love" is a perfect description of my feelings. I don't know how to even begin to pay the Lord back for this marvelous gift. All I know is that I must bear witness of the good He has done in my life—in other words, share the message of redemption with those who are still suffering as I suffered. This is my message—to share the love God has shared with me, and to tell all who will hear that this amazing gift can be theirs as well.

I pray we may each surrender our weaknesses to the Lord and do what is in our power to prepare the way for this rebirth experience, this mighty change, that thereby we may all come unto Christ.

MAKING THE MOST OF THIS CHAPTER

Please take time to answer the following questions in your recovery journal.

1. Write about your *readiness* to ask the Lord to change your *character*. Copy **1 Nephi 3:7** into your journal and capture from it. In what ways has the Lord prepared a way for you to take this step? What obstacles do you need to ask Him to remove so that you may surrender to Him?

2. In Hebrews we read, **"For this is the covenant that I will make with the house of Israel after those days, saith the Lord; I will put my laws into their mind, and write them in their hearts: and I will be to them a God, and they shall be to me a people"** **(Hebrews 8:10).** Write about your feelings about letting God write His law in your mind and heart. What hesitancy do you still feel about having the Lord be "a God" to you, and you being part of His "people?"

3. The Lord said through Ezekiel, **"A new heart also will I give you, and a new spirit will I put within you: and I will take away the stony heart out of your flesh, and I will give you an heart of flesh. And I will put my spirit within you, and cause you to walk in my statutes, and ye shall keep my judgments, and do them"** **(Ezekiel 36:26–27).** Write about your willingness to have the Lord give you a totally new heart, disposition, attitude and personality. Copy this verse into your journal and capture from it.

4. After Alma the Younger was struck dumb by the angel of the Lord, he endured three days of **"repenting nigh unto death."** When he was restored to speech, he bore his testimony in these words, **"Nevertheless, after wading through much tribulation, repenting nigh unto death, the Lord in mercy hath seen fit to snatch me out of an everlasting burning, and I am born of God. My soul hath been redeemed from the gall of bitterness and bonds of iniquity. I was in the darkest abyss; but now I behold the marvelous light of God. My soul was racked with eternal torment; but I am snatched, and my soul is pained no more"** **(Mosiah 27:28–29).** Write about your feelings about being

"snatched" from eternal torment through the process of rebirth. If you have not yet had this experience, write about your hopes and desires for it. If you have experienced this marvelous change, write your testimony, as Alma did.

5. Look up the entire talk by President Ezra Taft Benson, "Born of God," (*Ensign*, Nov. 1985, 5 or July 1989, 2) and read it, capturing from any passages that impress you. Identify passages that relate to Step Seven and write about their significance in your life. (Articles published in Church magazines, including talks given in General Conference, can be accessed through this Church website: http://library.lds.org).

Chapter **12** *Step Eight*

Made a list of all persons we had harmed and
became willing to make amends to them all.
(A.A. and Heart t' Heart traditional versions)

Made a list of all persons we had harmed and
became willing to make restitution to all of them
(even those we had harmed in what we might
have considered righteous anger), desiring instead
to be peacemakers and to do all that we could to
come unto God by being first reconciled to others.
(3 Nephi 12:9; 3 Nephi 12:24; 3 Nephi 12:44–45)
(Heart t' Heart scriptural version)

No matter how we get into addiction, the result is always a deep preoccupation with self. I was no different. My addiction demanded more and more of my time, my attention, my resources, my *self*. In blind selfishness, I neglected and hurt others. Unfortunately, while I lived in "blissful" denial, my character defects weren't hidden—especially from those who lived with me and needed me the most. The rigorous honesty required for genuine recovery, though, has demanded that I look squarely at the harm I've done others. Some, I hurt directly through the practice of my addiction. Others, I hurt by the wholesale refusal to recognize and forsake the defects in my character. If I am to fully repent,

I need to be willing to recognize all the people I may have hurt and be prepared to make appropriate amends to all of them.

ANOTHER PREPARATION STEP

I guess when the Twelve Steps were originally formulated, it was decided that some of the steps were too challenging to tackle "head on," that people needed an intermediate step on which to pause and gather their resources. For example, in Step Four we only *wrote* our inventory; we didn't share it with anyone else until Step Five. In Step Six we *became ready* to surrender our character defects. We didn't actually surrender them until Step Seven. Once again in Step Eight, we are simply going to *identify* the people to whom we owe amends. As we make our list in this step, we don't need to worry about actually interacting with anyone. We don't have to be stalled out by the thought, "I could never go to this person and admit, face-to-face, what I did to them." Step Eight isn't asking us to face anyone. We don't have to decide what we will do about making amends—that is a separate process, reserved for Step Nine.

You may remember that in Step Five, we discussed the inappropriateness of making confessions primarily for the purpose of unburdening our guilty conscience—by dumping our Fourth Step inventory on people who would be hurt by it. That same warning is true for Step Eight. It seems that while some of us back away from making an amends list, others of us don't want to "waste" time making a list at all. Instead, we want to just leap-frog right into Step Nine. However, like our confession in Step Five, our amends-making must not be done to salve our own conscience. There may be people who would be harmed, not helped, if we rushed back into their lives and dredged up our past indiscretions. Thus, we need to take time to prayerfully prepare. We need to take Step Eight.

I have heard it said that if we want to be completely thorough in taking Step Eight, we actually need to make *three* lists of harms done, not just one. I found this approach worked for me. Let's take a look at each of these lists.

LIST ONE: THOSE I HAVE HARMED

On the first list, write down everyone you have harmed. If you have kept the inventory you wrote in Step Four, you can refer to it in making this list. Even if you destroyed your written inventory as a symbol of letting go of your past in Step Five, the things you wrote down then will help you remember the people who need to go on your amends list.

As with the inventory, you may want to consider your life in increments such as "during grade school," "during junior high," or from ages ten to twenty, twenty to thirty, and so on. Be sure to include not only people you have harmed as a direct result of your addiction, but also people you have harmed through the various character defects you have discovered in working Steps Four and Six. Since it is absolutely true that we hurt most those who are closest to us, we can be sure our spouse, children, and perhaps other family members, will have a prominent place on this list.

As I began my amends list, my heart ached because I immediately thought of my dear wife, Kathy. We were married for almost 29 years before she died from heart disease. She lived with me through most of my years of addiction, and even though I hid it from her much of the time, I can't deny that it hurt her and diminished our relationship. I sincerely tried to love her, and I think she was genuinely happy most of the time, but I had to admit I could have been a far better husband to her if I had not been enslaved to lust. How many times was I not there for her emotionally, physically, spiritually, and even sexually because I was focused on my addiction? How many hours did I steal from her to feed my habit? How many lies did I tell her in order to hide my actions? There are so many things for which I want to ask her forgiveness. Furthermore, in addition to the actions that hurt her as a direct result of my addiction, I have to acknowledge she was hurt by my other faults as well.

I always thought of myself as a good husband, but now I know I could have been more unselfish and more thoughtful. I could have made life better for my wife than I did. I don't say this to needlessly dump guilt on myself, but rather to honestly inventory my relationships and see where repair was needed. Kathy and I started attending Heart t' Heart Twelve Step meetings together only five months before she died. I am immensely grateful she was here to at least see me begin my recovery. I often wish she had been able to stay until I got to Steps Eight and Nine, so I could have made amends to her, face to face. At times I have thought, "What can I do *now* to make amends to Kathy—she's dead!" But in the quieter moments, I know her death does not stop her from knowing my heart. She may be on the other side, but some very personal and sacred experiences have taught me that communication across the veil is possible. I know Kathy still lives, and we can still feel each other's heart. I know she is aware of my willingness to make amends to her.

The next people on my amends list were my children. I had to face the hard questions concerning them: How *have* I harmed my children? Was I ever too severe in physically punishing them? How many times was I unavailable to them? How many opportunities to be with and enjoy them did I miss? And what about the missed teaching opportunities? How many times did I not bear my testimony to them, because I didn't feel the Spirit in my own life at the moment? How many principles did I not teach them because doing so made me feel like a hypocrite? And how many times did I blame them or put them on the defensive to hide my own sins? The Lord has told us:

> **The powers of heaven...may be conferred upon us, it is true; but when we undertake *to cover our sins,* or to gratify our pride, our vain ambition, or to exercise control or dominion or compulsion upon the souls of the children of men, in any degree of unrighteousness, behold, the heavens withdraw themselves; the Spirit of the Lord is grieved; and when it is withdrawn, Amen to the priesthood or the authority of that man. (D&C 121:36–37, emphasis added)**

I still wonder how much my failings have contributed to problems my children have had or will yet have in their lives. They are grown now. I can't go back and raise them all over again, but putting them on my amends list is the first step I can take in behaving differently toward them in the future.

Next we might include on our amends list people we have interacted with in the different activities in our lives, such as work, recreation, and church. Think about your financial dealings—is there anyone you owe money to or have dealt with dishonestly? Ask yourself, "Is there anyone I would be embarrassed or feel awkward about meeting today?" If there is, put them on the list, identifying why you might feel uncomfortable around them.

As I prayerfully searched my heart to answer the question, "Whom would I be embarrassed to meet today?" I found the Lord prompting me to consider two groups of people I would have never thought to include. First, I had to admit that I had actually contributed—albeit in an indirect way—to the harm done to the women who posed for the pornographic pictures I had looked at. While I didn't personally operate the camera, and even though these women have no idea who I am, I still hurt them nonetheless. I participated as a consumer in the pornography industry, and thus I helped create the demand for more pornography. Even if my contribution was infinitesimal in comparison with the billions of dollars spent on pornography each year, I did contribute. Not only did I contribute financially, but perhaps more importantly, I contributed morally. When I agreed to look at pornography, I was giving my consent that such materials be produced and that the abuse these women had already suffered, continue. I definitely must put these ill-treated women on my list.

Second, I was led to think of those who traffic in such filth, the pornographers themselves. How had I done *them* any wrong? The answer pierced my self-righteous heart and humbled me. I saw, in my mind's eye, that there would be no livelihood for people like them, if it were not for people like me. And if there had been no market for their filth, might they have sought honorable employment instead of producing pornography? I don't know—that is their "inventory," their choice to make. But I knew I owed even them—my worst enemies— amends for my half of the dishonorable exchange I participated in. As hard as it may be to accept, I know the Lord loves them too and desires for them to come unto Him and repent. Even *they* are not beyond the Atonement. The Lord has commanded me to forgive my enemies:

> **Ye have heard that it hath been said, Thou shalt love thy neighbour, and hate thine enemy. But I say unto you, *Love your enemies,* bless them that curse you, do good to them that hate you, *and pray for them which despitefully use you,* and persecute you; That ye may be the children of your Father which is in heaven: for he maketh his sun to rise on the evil and on the good, and sendeth rain on the just and on the unjust. (Matthew 5:43–45, emphasis added)**

I know that no one has more "despitefully used" me than those people who have produced the pornography that entrapped me, yet the Lord requires me to pray even for them. It is out of obedience to this commandment of the Lord to pray for our enemies that we come to make our second list.

LIST TWO: THOSE WHO HAVE HURT US

Thus, because the Lord requires me to pray for those who have despitefully used or otherwise hurt me, I needed to make a second list— one that would include all those I felt had harmed me throughout my lifetime. Whether I owed them an apology or not is a separate question, but I definitely needed to at least let go of any bitterness I felt toward them.

Now, if you are like me, you won't have any trouble thinking of people to put on this list. Most addicts are champions at holding on to resentments and using those feelings as an excuse to act out. Making this list can represent finally letting go of resentments we have carried far too long. And just as we hurt most those who are closest to us, we are also hurt most by them.

Let's start at the beginning. What resentments do you have towards your parents? Did they discipline or shame or ridicule you in ways that still hurt? Did you need more love and gentleness than they were able to give you? Were you provided with the necessities of life, or did you have to go without sufficient housing, clothes, medical care or even food? Even if you have excused your parents with the very likely observation that they did the best they could, are you still hurting over what they could not give you? What about brothers or sisters? What injuries from the past involve them? Put all these hurts on your list—they need to be acknowledged and dealt with. If you have married, are you carrying around pain that you attribute to your spouse? Chances are, neither of you came from a perfect home, and chances are, neither of you has been a perfect marriage partner. Marriage provides plenty of opportunities for hurt feelings. Do you have some unresolved issues from your marriage (or from dating, if you are single) that need to be inventoried?

Now think of people outside your family circle. How many of us remember painful episodes from our childhood and adolescence—being shunned or otherwise hurt by our peers. Consider employers, friends, church leaders, anyone else who has wounded you. Put down anyone you would feel uncomfortable meeting today. If either you or the other person has hard or strained feelings, then something is not resolved. It doesn't matter whether the other person meant to hurt you or not, if it still hurts, put it down. Remember, we are not making this list to drudge up old resentments, but to inventory them and surrender them to the Savior.

The Lord has defined the standard for forgiveness:

> **Wherefore, I say unto you, that ye ought to forgive one another; for he that forgiveth not his brother his trespasses standeth condemned before the Lord; for there remaineth in him the greater sin. I, the Lord, will forgive whom I will forgive, but of you it is required to forgive all men. And ye ought to say in your hearts—let God judge between me and thee, and reward thee according to thy deeds. (D&C 64:9–11)**

We are clearly commanded to forgive all men (and women). This is not the same as saying that what they have done is good or correct or right. Their actions may have been very wrong, but that is not for us to judge. The Lord will take care of that. Our job is to forgive.

Colleen wrote a beautiful parable of forgiveness that she included in *He Did Deliver Me from Bondage* (pp. 111–114). It is a truly powerful story and with her permission I want to share it with you.

A PARABLE

One day I dreamed a dream and saw myself in a scene that was almost like something out of *Gone with the Wind*. I was walking up a long, tree-lined lane, and though I was ragged and wounded and still using a crutch to steady myself, I was full of excitement. I had just entered into the last stretch in what had been a long and perilous journey home. Just over the next rise was "the green, green grass of home" and my family waiting to greet me. Even there along the lane, every tree was filled with yellow ribbons. And when the breeze carried just right, and I had my good ear turned, I could hear the music and smell the feast at the great party they were having.

Suddenly I noticed that another figure was hobbling along just ahead of me. Whoever this poor soul was, I could tell that he was in at least as bad a shape as I was. But even with all his wounds, he had made it this far too. My heart went out to him in fellowship, and quickening my pace, I hurried to overtake him, calling out to him, "Brother, wait! Wait for me!"

He stopped and turned. My heart went chill as all feelings drained from it. I recognized his face. He had been my enemy, the very one who had inflicted the deepest wounds—wounds that had made my journey so slow and painful—wounds that I still bore, unhealed. Not him! How could he be here too?

I halted my steps, unable to approach him any further, unwilling to say anything. As he called out, "Who's there? I can't see you," I realized that he was blind. Rather than answer his plaintive cry, I held my breath. Soon he turned, dejected, and shuffled on his way.

I didn't have far to follow him, for just ahead of us was a shining, glorious gate. The boundary that it marked was as definite as if it were guarding night from day. Even though the beauty of the country through which the lane passed was exquisite, what lay beyond the gate was beyond description, but not recognition. It was Home. Upon seeing it, childhood memories seemed to flood my mind. Every path and byway was familiar to me. The longing to be there once more became an overwhelming ache within me. It caused me to totally forget my reluctance to approach my enemy, who was even now standing at the gatehouse, speaking to the gatekeeper.

The gatekeeper had his back to me. Still I recognized Him immediately as my Lord and Good Shepherd, He who had carried me throughout much of my journey, ministering to my stubborn wounds. Just as He had promised, He employed no servant here. Still I could see only my enemy's face. There was light shining either from it or on it. I could not tell which. Suddenly I realized his eyes were bright and clear, focused upon the face of the Gatekeeper. I realized he was not blind anymore! Then I noted how straight he stood. Eagerly I threw down my crutch and rushed forward. Maybe I, too, could be made whole!

Before I could take more than a step or two, I was suddenly aware of the Gatekeeper's words to my lifelong enemy. "There is only one last thing before you are ready to enter in, one last question I must ask."

My enemy! This person who had been responsible for my deepest wounds? He was about to enter in?

The Gatekeeper continued, breaking through my shock, "Are you a friend to every man?"

Taking his gaze from the Gatekeeper's face, the man looked steadily into my eyes, and I knew he was seeing me, *really* seeing me, for the first time. Somewhere inside I trembled. I had known all along that I would have to face the Lord to enter in, but my enemy?

His words pierced my soul. "I am willing to be," he said quietly. Healed and no longer blind, he loved me. Could I, still maimed and crippled as I was, say the same? Could I answer this one last question with an honest yes?

The Gatekeeper seemed to disappear from between us, though I knew He was near. Nothing stood between my enemy and me. He waited for my response with longing meekness in his eyes, unable to enter in without my approbation. And just as surely, I knew I could not enter in without him. My long-harbored resentment and bitterness, or all that lay beyond this last barrier—which would it be? Which would I choose? Why had I waited so long? How had I thought I could avoid this moment?

My first step toward him was still halting, as if crippled, but with each step my strength grew greater and greater. I could feel my wounds healing as I reached for his hands and then his embrace.

And as the dream ended, I saw us wrapped in more than each other's acceptance and forgiveness. The Gatekeeper and still another figure stood with us. With shining countenance the Gatekeeper turned to the other, and speaking my name in unison with that of my former adversary, He said, "Father, these are my friends." As I awoke from the dream, the last impression I had was hearing the voice of the Father, so long awaited, *"Well done. You may all enter in."*

We cannot tell who will repent and who will not. We have not been given the privilege of judging others and saying who will be recipients of the grace of the Lord's Atonement and who will not. For myself, I am grateful not to have the burden of making those decisions.

LIST THREE: MAKING AMENDS TO OURSELVES

The last list is a short one, with only one name on it. Your own. Take the time to consider how many ways you have caused yourself pain.

Write down all the things you have denied yourself because of your addiction. What blessings could have come into your life if you had not been caught up in these foolish behaviors? What opportunities have passed you by? How unkind have you been to yourself? What names have you called yourself, names that you would never call any other child of God? How have you torn yourself down and denied your God-given worth and potential?

Next, write down all the positive, worthwhile things you have wanted to do in your life but, for one reason or another, didn't. Are there opportunities you let pass by? Are there talents you haven't allowed yourself to develop? Perhaps some of these things you gave up in a spirit of honest and willing sacrifice, and I'm sure the Lord has blessed you for that. But maybe it still hurts—maybe there is still an empty place in your soul. It might be helpful to list these things, count them, weigh them, and then give them to the Lord. On the other hand, what things have you passed up because you didn't feel you deserved to enjoy them? What blessings have you denied yourself, that you could have had, if only you had felt better about yourself? All of these are amends you can make to yourself, so put them on the list.

When I inventory the wrongs I have done to myself, I am deeply moved, often to tears. At first they were tears of bitterness, guilt, and shame, but with the passing years they have turned to tears of compassion for the person I was then. I think about how I accepted the adversary's lies that I was worthless and deserved to be despised. I remember how I listened to the names Satan put into my head, and how I readily started calling myself terrible things, unkind and untrue things. I even believed the adversary's ultimate lie: That all these negative feelings about me were coming from my Father in Heaven! What a tragedy! What an injustice against God *and* myself!

The wrongs I committed against myself were more than just the direct consequences of addiction. In my shame, I often shortchanged myself and denied myself a lot of good things I might have enjoyed. I denied myself friendships because I felt no one would want to be my friend or because I imagined everyone else was better than me. I stayed away from church softball games because I wasn't very good and I was sure no one would want me on the team. As a result, I denied myself the chance to develop those skills and I remained a mediocre player. And the list goes on.

I passed up opportunities because I didn't feel I deserved them. There have been times I said "no" to some pleasurable activity, because I felt I had to keep working, that I hadn't earned a break yet. As I think back, I recognize this pattern from my childhood. I was always a "slow-poke" and took forever to do my chores, because I was continually finding ways to play instead of work. Thus, I never felt the satisfaction of completing a job and enjoying the fun afterwards. That tendency is still with me today. I still have a hard time finishing anything. (In fact, if you're reading this book, I can promise you it is because God intervened and made it possible. Believe me, in my own strength I could never have accomplished it.)

As you make your own amends list, please remember to be thoroughly honest, but also equally diligent in your mercy and long-suffering towards yourself. The power of taking Step Eight lies in calling on the Savior's counsel and comfort—recognizing continually that His Atonement is equal to all the mistakes and sins ever done in this world—*including yours!*

MAKING THE MOST OF THIS CHAPTER

Please take time to answer the following questions in your recovery journal. Remember, you are keeping this journal just for you, not for anyone else. Writing honestly and plainly will move your recovery forward.

1. If you have not made the three lists suggested in the chapter, do so now. Those lists are:

    a. People I have harmed throughout my lifetime, whether I have contact with them or not, whether they are living or dead.

    b. People who have hurt me in significant ways; anyone about whom I feel, or have felt, resentful.

    c. Ways in which I have harmed or neglected myself. Things I would like to have accomplished, but have not because of shame or guilt.

2. Write about the fears you have of approaching people to whom you owe amends. What do you picture will happen if you go to them with an apology? How realistic do you think your fears are?

3. Imagine that someone came to you to apologize for some past wrong done against you. Write the story of this imaginary encounter. Compare your response with how you pictured someone responding to you in the last question.

4. The Savior said to His Nephite disciples, **"Yea, blessed are they who shall believe in your words, and come down into the depths of humility and be baptized, for they shall be visited with fire and with the Holy Ghost, and shall receive a remission of their sins"** (**3 Nephi 12:2**). Write about how the willingness to make the lists suggested in this chapter requires you to reach a deeper level of humility than you have experienced before.

5. Robert Frost wrote: "Forgive, O Lord, my little jokes on Thee, and I'll forgive Thy great big one on me" (*The Poetry of Robert Frost*, 428). In all seriousness, write about your willingness to forgive God for things He's allowed to happen in your life. How do you think He would react if you told Him you thought *He* had wronged *you*?

13 *Step Nine*

Made direct amends to such people wherever possible
except when to do so would injure them or others.
(A.A. and Heart t' Heart traditional versions)

*Made restitution directly to those we had harmed,
confessing our own wrongdoing in each instance except
when to do so would further injure them or others.
(Mosiah 27:35; 3 Nephi 12:25; Mosiah 26:30)*
(Heart t' Heart scriptural version)

The scriptures demonstrate that when we repent and turn our lives
over to the care of God, He will inevitably lead us by the promptings of
the Holy Ghost to try to make restitution or amends for our past
misdeeds. Consider the example of certain Nephites who had fallen
away, but were re-converted by the preaching of Nephi and Lehi, the
sons of Helaman:

> **They came forth and did confess their sins and were
> baptized unto repentance, and immediately returned
> to the Nephites to endeavor to repair unto them the
> wrongs which they had done. (Helaman 5:17)**

As I faced taking Step Nine, I felt tempted to turn and run. How
could I possibly make amends to others for the kind of wrongs I had
done? What could I say or do? What would *they* say or do if I

approached them? I knew that in most cases, an apology was all I could offer. Gradually, I began to realize, however, that a *sincere* apology was far from being inadequate, because it would mark the beginning of a whole new attitude in my life. In surrendering my life to the Lord, I needed to approach Step Nine with a genuine willingness to make restitution for the wrongs I had committed. Humbly, I asked Him for the courage to admit my mistakes and for the ability to listen patiently to the feelings of those I had hurt. More than just an apology, even more than a promise, taking Step Nine sets yet another pillar of truth in place in our ongoing journey to complete the *mighty* change. It is another step in turning our lives over to the Lord so He can make something better of them than we ever did.

Even when we have decided to make the amends, and have put the results in the Lord's hands, it is only natural to feel uncertain about how our amends will be received. After all, the people we have hurt are human too and capable of holding resentment—just as we have done ourselves. I was afraid the loved ones I had harmed would still be angry or hurt over my actions. I cringed, fearing their reaction. Would they reject me? Would they use my confession of acting out as an excuse to act out themselves?

ALMA'S RESTITUTION

When I consider how terrifying taking Step Nine can feel, I cannot help but think of Alma the Younger yet again. I know I have referred to his story frequently in these pages. I make no apology for that. I believe his experiences are in the Book of Mormon specifically for the sake of those of us who have walked the path of addiction. Who knows but that part of his wild behavior might have been a result of such bondage in his own life. I am thrilled and amazed at how closely his story parallels the Twelve Step process (which is simply the process of repentance), even including this step of making amends. Listen to the course he and the sons of Mosiah took as part of their repentance:

> **And now it came to pass that Alma began from this time forward to teach the people, and those who were**

> with Alma at the time the angel appeared unto
> them...And they traveled throughout all the land of
> Zarahemla, and among all the people...*zealously
> striving to repair all the injuries which they had done* to
> the church, confessing all their sins, and publishing
> all the things which they had seen, and explaining the
> prophecies and the scriptures to all who desired to
> hear them. (Mosiah 27:32,35, emphasis added)

Alma's story is even instructive for those who are afraid others will
react negatively to our public disclosure of previous wrongdoing and our
efforts to be different. He and his friends encountered just such opposition and hardship as they went about trying to **"repair all the injuries
which they had done."** The record shows that they were **"greatly
persecuted by those who were unbelievers, being smitten by many of
them" (v. 32).** Still they did not shrink from this stage of their repentance process. The record continues:

> They did impart much consolation to the church...
> And thus they were instruments in the hands of God
> in bringing many to the knowledge of the truth, yea,
> to the knowledge of their Redeemer. And how blessed
> are they! For they did publish peace; they did publish
> good tidings of good; and they did declare unto the
> people that the Lord reigneth. (Mosiah 27:33, 36–37)

Many of us might be sorely tempted to skip Step Nine if we thought
we were going to receive such violent responses from others, as Alma
and his brethren did. Nevertheless, if we persist in our course, even in
the face of opposition, we will find that the Lord will bless us as He did
these men. Like them, we can also publish peace and declare that we,
too, have come to know that the Lord lives, because He has given us
power to change our lives!

SOME CONSIDERATIONS ABOUT MAKING AMENDS

A closer look at the wording of Step Nine gives us some important
guidelines in working this step. Let's take several important phrases, one

at a time, borrowing from both versions of Step Nine, and explore their application:

1. *"Made restitution directly to those we had harmed..."* Amends should be made directly to the person involved. It is not an amends to your wife to tell your sponsor or your bishop that you are sorry you betrayed or otherwise mistreated her. You have to tell your wife, and the more directly, the better. For example, sitting down together in a face-to-face conversation—though requiring the highest degree of valor on your part—is, for that very reason, much better than writing a letter. Wanting to take the "easier, softer way" may still tempt us, as it did in all the years of our acting out, but it is not part of our new life. We must consider the needs of the person to whom we are making amends above our own comfort. Simply put, healing their heart is more important than saving our face. In a face-to-face conversation, they can see our face and feel our sincerity. Much is communicated by a touch of the hand. In this most tender and delicate of situations, the final answer is to let the Spirit guide you.

2. *"wherever possible..."* In some cases it may not be possible to contact someone to whom you owe amends. Maybe they have moved away or died. A contentious divorce may make contact inadvisable. In these cases the only way to express your desire to make amends may be through a letter, whether it can ever be mailed or not. Again, let the Spirit guide you in this. Using the tool of writing in this way serves a powerful purpose in helping us lay down our burden of guilt and sorrow. Later in this chapter I have included an example of a letter I wrote.

3. *"confessing our own wrongdoing in each instance..."* This is an important caution. As we have noted before and need to continually remind ourselves, as addicts, we have developed to the level of a fine art the practice of shading the truth and shifting responsibility. We have become so expert at this kind of denial that we may not even be aware of it. For example, it is a great temptation to include with our amends some justification as to why we weren't *really* responsible for our misdeed. We might make an apology, but slyly sneak in some blame of the person to whom we are apologizing. For

example, instead of saying, "I was wrong to yell at you the other day," we say, "I'm sorry I yelled at you when you were so inconsiderate to me the other day." The point of our amends is to confess *our own* wrongdoing, despite any supposed wrongdoing of the person to whom we are apologizing. Without this humility, the potential benefit of making the amends is spoiled. It takes courage and honesty to mind our *own* business—to "sweep *our* side of the street" (*Alcoholics Anonymous*, 77).

4. **"except when to do so would further injure them or others."** While it is uncomfortable to go to someone and admit our wrongs against them, we probably have the expectation that doing so will make us feel better in the end, and it usually will. But as we noted in Step Eight, we need to also consider whether our sudden reappearance in someone's life will be good for them. For example, an old girlfriend may have moved on with her life, gotten married and had children. Would a reminder of some situation from the past be a blessing in her life or would it be an unwelcome intrusion? This is a very delicate situation, and it needs great humility and openness to the Spirit to be sure that in making the amends, we consider the interests of the person we have offended, and are not just an attempt to unburden ourselves. These are things we need to let the Lord tell us, and act only with the confirmation of His Spirit.

AMENDS OWED TO YOUR SPOUSE

Probably, of all the amends we owe to others, the most important (and scariest) is to our eternal companion. I recognize that some of you may have already lost your marriage because of your addiction. Others of you are reading these things because you are desperate to keep your marriage together. Some of you may be engaged, but not yet married. Others have not yet met that special someone. In every case, however, we must realize that part of our amends will include being honest with our sweetheart—sooner or later—about this most difficult challenge in our own lives. If you are not currently involved in a committed relationship, this section is still of great importance, and the counsel will apply to you—you can be sure—now or at some future time. Remember though, that each of you will need to prayerfully adapt these suggestions to your own situation. To simplify the following section, I have addressed it to a man concerning his wife. If you are a woman and need to make amends to your husband, please reverse the genders.

Here are some things you can do to make amends to your spouse:

1. *Get honest.* It may be one of the hardest things you have ever done to tell your sweetheart about your transgressions. You may be in mortal fear for your future relationship, sure that if you tell her about your actions, she will leave you. At this point, you must ask yourself some pretty tough questions. Even if your marriage may be seriously threatened by your confession and attempt at amends, what is the alternative? How celestial can a marriage ever become if it is based on lies and deception? Over the years, as I have been involved in recovery work, I have seen many cases—the vast majority, in fact—where the wife, though deeply hurt, has been willing to remain with her now humble and honest partner. For many of us, our sweetheart becomes our greatest ally in facing these truths in our lives. While she cannot save us—something only the Savior can accomplish—she can be our most beloved friend and supporter in our recovery efforts. We must be willing to give her the chance to make that choice for herself. As I have mentioned before, this honesty requires revealing "the *nature* of our wrongs"—our character weaknesses, mistaken thoughts, feelings, and beliefs (see Chapter 9, Step Five)—not the details of our actions.

2. *Admit your own responsibility for what you have done.* This point cannot be made strongly enough, so if it sounds repetitive, bear with me: One of the most hurtful things you can do is blame your wife for *your* acting out. Likewise, blaming parents, employers, anyone or anything else besides yourself is denying your own agency and "playing the victim." Taking responsibility for your own choices is essential to recovery.

3. *Get into a recovery program.* Whatever you do to contribute to your own recovery can actually be seen as a part of the amends owed to

those you have hurt. Meeting regularly with your priesthood leaders, being diligent in daily personal prayer and scripture study, regularly attending Church and Twelve Step meetings, and studying recovery materials, if done with a sincere desire to get well, will all contribute toward recovery and give hope to your sweetheart.

4. *Participate willingly in family activities, both spiritual and recreational.* Addiction has probably pulled you away from your family and robbed them of your time, attention, and spiritual leadership. Even if you don't do it perfectly, you can humbly try to fill the assignment the Lord has given you to teach and to guide your families, paying particular attention to the principles taught in **D&C 121** about leading with patience, gentleness and meekness.

5. *Reestablish a spirit of courtship with your spouse.* Here is another tough question you must face. While you've been obsessed with your own secret sins, how have you treated her? How have you been selfish, both in practicing your addictive behaviors and in other ways? In most cases, the addict needs to start over again in his marriage, begin courting his wife anew and rebuild the relationship from the ground up.

6. *Listen to your wife's side of the story without justifying or blaming.* Be teachable. Your wife knows your weaknesses better than anyone else. You can learn much if you will humbly listen without reacting defensively to what she has to say.

7. *Reexamine your marital intimacy.* It is important to inventory the different ways sexual addiction has affected physical intimacy with your spouse. Sexual experiences with your wife need to grow out of a mutually respectful relationship. Some couples find that including prayer before sharing themselves with each other sexually helps restore the experience to the sanctity the Lord intends it to have.

8. *Include your wife in your recovery efforts.* Some men go through an initial confession of the problem, but don't continue to include their wife as time goes by. They just say "Everything's fine," when she asks how they're doing. This is most often a reassurance that doesn't reassure. Your wife needs to be in on the daily progress of your

recovery. It's all right to say, "I had a struggle today over _____ ." Whether you did well with the struggle or not, reporting to your wife is a commitment to continuing effort, assuming she is willing to hear these reports. If that degree of involvement in the day-to-day progress of your recovery is too difficult for her to hear, you might give those reports to a sponsor. But no matter how you do it, it is important for you to be honest with your wife at all times about how you are doing.

There will certainly be other things that will occur to you (or to your wife) as you prayerfully consider this together. Rebuilding a marriage that has been damaged by addiction is a team effort. If the two of you have not been a team before, now is the time to start.

AMENDS TO OTHERS BESIDES YOUR WIFE

There will be many others in your life besides your wife to whom you owe amends. It's impossible to have the kind of character defects that allow one to become addicted to sex and to not have hurt others. Now would be the time to refer to the list you made in Step Eight. Sort the names into three categories: 1) those you still have contact with, 2) those you could probably get in touch with if you tried, and 3) those you can't reach, either because they've passed away, you've lost all knowledge of their whereabouts, or because contact would harm them.

As we face making contact with those we have hurt, our shame and embarrassment can feel overwhelming. Contrary to the usual expectations, however, these experiences can be profoundly healing. I can assure you, it is possible to meet these people again in the spirit of Step Nine and have it turn out to be a positive experience. Often, you will find they have already forgiven you. For example, my wife and I recently encountered someone I had not seen for many years. I had put her on my amends list because I had been inappropriately intimate with her in my youth. Imagine my surprise when we accidentally met that day and were able to genuinely smile and greet one another amiably. I have never felt it was necessary or advisable to intrude into her present life by bringing up the past, but the experience of seeing her in a safe situation, after I had gained some recovery, was a healing experience. Some might define this "chance" meeting as a coincidence, but I prefer to believe, as others have said, that "coincidences are just God wanting to remain anonymous." Taking Step Nine has filled me with a powerful testimony that, as Colleen suggested through her parable, someday we will all be together again, able to look one another in the face without shame or regret, and rejoice in the miracle of our redemption through the Savior's Atonement.

A LETTER OF AMENDS

Earlier in this chapter, I mentioned the power of writing letters to those we have harmed, whether we actually send them or not. I used that technique to offer a very unique kind of amends to some people I felt I had seriously wronged, even though we had never met. In Step Eight, I listed among the people to whom I owed amends the women who posed for the pornographic pictures I had viewed. In the letter below, I have addressed one of these women as a representative of them all, although they are in truth, all individuals with individual lives.

Dear Sister,

You don't know me, and I don't know you either, but I feel I have hurt you and want to do something to make amends. I have been one of the men who has used you as an object of lust, caring nothing for the real person behind the images I saw of you. I recognize now that the whole experience was part of a lie that intimacy could be found in that way.

I try to think about your real life. I wonder about your parents, your family. I don't know whether they have been everything to you that you needed, but I suspect there have been serious deficiencies, even abuse, which put you on the path that led finally to your posing for pornographic pictures and movies. I wonder if you have ever been married. I wonder if you have been coerced into this tawdry business by drug addiction or financial problems. I can't imagine that being a porn star is what you always dreamed of becoming when you were a little girl.

I also wonder how you must feel about yourself. My involvement in illicit sexual behavior has brought me nothing but sorrow and shame. I imagine you know something of those feelings, too. Maybe because of experiences in your young life, you have been taught the lie that sex equals love. I wish I could convey to you how sorry I am for playing a role in your debasement and abuse. I know it was wrong. I pray that both you and God will forgive me, and that He will bless you and help you out of the world of shame and pain you must be in. Maybe, by now, He already has. Perhaps one day, on the other side of the veil, we will meet, and I will have a chance to tell you in person how sorry I am, and hopefully see that we both have healed. I know our Beloved Savior has the power to heal you, even from this. I pray you will let Him, for my sake as well as for yours.

Your brother, Phil

WHEN AMENDS WON'T MAKE IT BETTER

Sometimes, as much as we want to repair the damage we have done, it just isn't possible. We may have hurt someone in a way that will take years to heal. We may have destroyed trust that is not easily rebuilt. These are some of the greatest burdens connected with our sins. In times like these, we are forcefully confronted with our own powerlessness. At the same time, it is a great comfort to know the goodness of our Redeemer, and that He can repair things we cannot. Elder Boyd K. Packer wrote:

> To earn forgiveness, one must make restitution. That means you give back what you have taken or ease the pain of those you have injured.
>
> But sometimes you *cannot* give back what you have taken because you don't have it to give. If you have caused others to suffer unbearably—defiled someone's virtue, for example—it is not within your power to give it back.

There are times you cannot mend that which you have broken. Perhaps the offense was long ago, or the injured refused your penance. Perhaps the damage was so severe that you cannot fix it no matter how desperately you want to.

Your repentance cannot be accepted unless there is a restitution. If you cannot undo what you have done, you are trapped. It is easy to understand how helpless and hopeless you then feel and why you might want to give up, just as Alma did.

The thought that rescued Alma, when he acted upon it, is this: Restoring what you cannot restore, healing the wound you cannot heal, fixing that which you broke and you cannot fix is the very purpose of the atonement of Christ.

When your desire is firm and you are willing to pay the "uttermost farthing," [see Matthew 5:25–26] the law of restitution is suspended. Your obligation is transferred to the Lord. He will settle your accounts.

I repeat, save for the exception of the very few who defect to perdition, there is no habit, no addiction, no rebellion, no transgression, no apostasy, no crime exempted from the promise of complete forgiveness. That is the promise of the atonement of Christ. (*Ensign*, Nov. 1995, 19–20)

Some of the hardest things I have faced are things I have done that I can't undo. It comforts me to know that *all* these situations can and will be helped, as soon as the people involved bring their hurts to the Lord. This is another way in which I have been humbled—to realize that in some cases, all I can do is pray for those I have harmed and trust that the Lord will heal them as soon as they seek Him. What a great comfort it is to know there is Someone whose power to fix things is greater than my power to mess up. What I can and must do, however, is take this burden gratefully and deliberately to the Lord and lay it at His feet.

AMENDS TO MYSELF

The first thing I did to make amends to myself was to stop using my addiction. However, coming to know the Lord and His patient love for me was closely intertwined with that process. As I have communed with Him in my personal recovery journal, I have felt and recorded expressions of His love for me, which have been exactly the opposite of the nagging, self-blaming diatribe that used to run incessantly through my brain. Trying to follow His example of mercy, I have begun to let up on myself. The fruit of true repentance is a sense of peace, a sense of being forgiven. Elder Neal A. Maxwell wrote:

> The infinite Atonement is so vast and universal, but finally, it is so very personal! Mercifully, through the Atonement we can be forgiven and, very importantly, we can know that we have been forgiven—that final, joyous emancipation from error. (*Ensign*, May 2001, 61)

I don't think there is a better way to make amends to ourselves than to allow the Savior's healing influence into our hearts. Allowing the Savior into my life has given me a healing that astounds me. This healing has expanded to all areas of my life, giving me joy in many opportunities that I had previously denied myself. One of these joys has been writing this book, and sharing with you the miracle I have experienced. Thank you for sharing my joy!

MAKING THE MOST OF THIS CHAPTER

Please take time to answer the following questions in your recovery journal.

1. In Chapter 9, Step Five, I asked you to write about this verse: **"By this ye may know if a man repenteth of his sins—behold, he will confess them and forsake them" (D&C 58:43).** Now consider this verse in the context of Step Nine. Write about the importance of going to the person we have wronged, if there is any way to do it

appropriately. Why is it not enough just to stop doing what is wrong? Write about a situation in your life to which this principle applies.

2. The Savior taught these words to the Nephites: **"Therefore, if ye shall come unto me, or shall desire to come unto me, and rememberest that thy brother hath aught against thee—Go thy way unto thy brother, and first be reconciled to thy brother, and then come unto me with full purpose of heart, and I will receive you"** (3 Nephi 12:23–24). Apparently the Lord felt that unresolved conflicts in our relationships with others block us from coming close to Him. Write about someone you know who may have hard feelings toward you, whether you feel they are justified or not. Does the Spirit prompt you to seek a reconciliation with this person? Have you included this person in your prayers, even if their present attitude won't let you approach them?

3. When Joseph Smith went to Carthage, Illinois, to surrender himself to the authorities on trumped-up charges, he declared, **"I am going like a lamb to the slaughter; but I am calm as a summer's morning; I have a conscience void of offense towards God, and towards all men"** (D&C 135:4). Yet in Carthage a mob of men waited who hated Joseph enough to murder him. These men were certainly "offended" by Joseph, yet *Joseph's* conscience was clear. How is it possible to find peace when others do not act peacefully toward you? Write about someone in your life who harbors ill will toward you. Can your conscience be free, even if they don't forgive you?

4. In the Lord's Prayer, the Savior taught us to pray, **"And forgive us our debts, as we forgive our debtors"** (Matthew 6:12). He then followed up the prayer immediately by saying: **"For if ye forgive men their trespasses, your heavenly Father will also forgive you: But if ye forgive not men their trespasses, neither will your Father forgive your trespasses"** (Matthew 6:14–15). In working Step Nine, we are trying to set things right with others and are

inevitably hoping for forgiveness. Write about the importance of forgiving others as we, ourselves, seek to be forgiven. List someone you still need to forgive for their offense(s) against you. If you feel you can honestly do so at this time, ask the Lord to soften your heart toward this person, so His Spirit may have fuller influence in your life.

5. Write about repentance as a form of amends to yourself. When the Savior said, **"I, the Lord, will forgive whom I will forgive, but of you it is required to forgive all men" (D&C 64:10),** do you think He included forgiving ourselves? In *He Did Deliver Me from Bondage,* Colleen said in essence, that he that refuses to forgive others denies the Atonement of Christ in their behalf, and he that refuses to forgive himself denies the Atonement in his own behalf (66, A–11). Write about forgiving yourself. Why is continuing to hold a judgment against anyone, including ourselves, usurping the Savior's role as Judge of all?

14 *Step Ten*

Continued to take personal inventory and
when we were wrong promptly admitted it.
(A.A. and Heart t' Heart traditional versions)

*Realizing that the weakness to be tempted and to sin
is a part of the mortal experience, we continued to
take personal inventory and when we were wrong
promptly admitted it, being willing to repent as often as
needed. (2 Nephi 4:18; 2 Nephi 10:20; Mosiah 26:30)*
(Heart t' Heart scriptural version)

I'm embarrassed to admit that Step Ten was yet another hurdle for me. I had sincerely hoped that once I had gone through the "fearless and thorough" process of a Fourth Step, the rigorous honesty of a Fifth Step, the complete surrender of the Sixth and Seventh Steps, and the risk of humiliation involved in doing the Eighth and Ninth Steps, I could finally relax. Looking at myself and my past so closely had often been exquisitely painful, and I was sure I'd be eligible to be translated by the time I completed the repentance and transformation required by those steps. I thought I would have arrived at a place so spiritually advanced that I'd never make another mistake. I'd never have to offer another apology to another person. How successful do you think that was?... Right!

I was dismayed to find that, though I was abstinent from my addiction, I was still able to goof up in a lot of other ways and still needed to repent. What a let-down to realize this business of humbling myself was going to be a life-long challenge! I still make mistakes and I still have a lot of growing to do. I have learned that *recovery is not an event—it is a process*. I find I need to continually re-live the principles in all of the steps and re-learn the lessons in each one at a deeper level. It is the only way I can keep my "natural man" tendencies in remission. As Colleen has written about Step Ten:

YOU MEAN IT'S NOT OVER?!

You mean we could come to a place of mighty change and still have to deal with imperfection, even in ourselves?! Oh, how we are challenged and repelled by that realization.

Yes, people can come to a place of mighty change, in fact even a sealing up by the Holy Spirit of Promise to a sure place with Him in Eternity, and still be vulnerable, even able to sin (think, speak, or act in a way that separates themselves from God).

Speaking of those who have come to a place of knowing they are sealed up by the Holy Spirit of Promise, Elder Bruce R. McConkie wrote:

> The prophets and apostles from Adam and Enoch down, and all men, whether cleansed and sanctified from sin or not, are yet subject to and do in fact commit sin. This is the case even after men have seen the visions of eternity and been sealed by the Holy Spirit of Promise...

> Obviously the laws of repentance still apply, and the more enlightened a person is, the more he seeks the gift of repentance, and the harder he strives to free himself from sin as often as he falls short of the divine will...It follows that the sins of the godfearing and the righteous are continually remitted because they repent and seek the Lord anew every day *and every hour*. (Bruce R.

McConkie, *Doctrinal New Testament Commentary, Vol. III*, pp. 342–343; emphasis added)

(Colleen C. Harrison, *He Did Deliver Me from Bondage*, 131)

If you're reading straight through this book and haven't yet given the steps a chance to work in your life, you may be asking, "So, Phil, what was the benefit of going through all the honesty and contrition represented in the first nine steps?" I would have to answer with rejoicing, "*The benefit? Only one of the most amazing benefits that I, as a sex addict, could ever report: The things I have to inventory each day are no longer of such magnitude that they threaten my standing in the Church or the respect and trust of my loved ones.* It is actually a joy to do the Tenth Step, because—thanks to the grace of the Lord and my faith in Him demonstrated in living these principles daily—I find my mistakes are much less serious and a lot further apart than they used to be. Also, I can tell I have grown *stronger* in my humility as promised in **Helaman 3:35**."

Why? Because, today, I can face my need to repent daily without being tempted to shame myself or blame others.

In other words, I am different—much different—right down to my personality or **"disposition,"** as the Book of Mormon promises **(Mosiah 5:2)**. Through these principles or steps, I have surrendered my life into the hands of the Master Healer—Christ, Himself. It is actually my greatest joy, now, to remain in a state of repentance, or in other words in a state of continual acknowledgment of my need for Him—His Spirit, His word, and His power to keep me abstinent. Immediately repenting of each of the smaller offenses of which I am guilty keeps me connected to my Lord, and saves me from the bigger mistakes that would inevitably follow if I were without His constant forgiveness and support.

EVEN PROPHETS NEED REPENTANCE

Taking Step Ten is admitting that repentance and humility are not occasional Band-Aid® events in my life, but actually a new way of life based on rejoicing and remaining in the grace of Christ. Reading the words of the prophets has helped me to accept this fact. Nephi, for instance, has set the example by admitting his continuing struggle with sin and temptation—even into the mature years of his life.

> **Nevertheless, notwithstanding the great goodness of the Lord, in showing me his great and marvelous works, my heart exclaimeth: O wretched man that I am! Yea, my heart sorroweth because of my flesh; my soul grieveth because of mine iniquities. I am encompassed about, because of the temptations and the sins which do so easily beset me. And when I desire to rejoice, my heart groaneth because of my sins; nevertheless, I know in whom I have trusted. (2 Nephi 4:17–19)**

I know I've said it before, but I don't think I can say it enough: *I love the prophets of the Book of Mormon!* Each of them, without exception, model the manner of life that comes from being one with the Lord Jesus Christ. Who could imagine a life more filled with revelation and dedication to the Lord than Nephi's? From his boyhood until the day of his death, Nephi loved the Lord and sought and received revelations from Him, yet remained so amazingly humble. His honest disclosure that he was tempted and even sinned at times, has helped me gain a very valuable perspective: even though repentance brings improvement in my life, complete perfection is still a long way off, and that's okay. Even Nephi acknowledged his need to continue improving. As the prophet Joseph said concerning perfection:

> *When you climb up a ladder, you must begin at the bottom, and ascend step by step, until you arrive at the top; and so it is with the principles of the gospel—you must begin with the first, and go on until you learn all the principles of exaltation. But it will be a great while after you have passed through the veil before you will have learned them. It is not all to be comprehended in this world; it will be a great work to learn our salvation and exaltation even beyond the grave.* (Teachings of the Prophet Joseph Smith, 348; italics original)

OUR NEED TO BE "CONSTANT" CHRISTIANS

Taking Step Ten is admitting you will have to continue to invest in your newly obtained spiritual and physical "sobriety" for the rest of your life, even though the goal of perfection remains beyond your reach during mortality. Referring to our need to retain perfection as our ideal, even though we will not be able to obtain it while in this life, Elder Neal A. Maxwell said:

> The first thing to be said of this feeling of inadequacy is that it is normal. There is no way the Church can honestly describe where we must yet go and what we must yet do without creating a sense of immense distance. Following celestial road signs while in telestial traffic jams is not easy,...thus the feelings of inadequacy are common. So are the feelings of fatigue; hence, the needed warning about our becoming weary of well-doing. (See D&C 64:33.)...True, there are no *instant* Christians, but there are *constant* Christians! (*Ensign*, Nov. 1976, 12–14; italics original)

As long as we are in this life, we will be faced with temptation and have to continue to surrender it to the Savior. Pride will be constantly trying to wear down our humility. It is so important to remember that in each small moment of renewed commitment to our abstinence, the foundation of a "great work"—a lifetime of moral purity—is being laid:

> **Wherefore, be not weary in well-doing, for ye are laying the foundation of a great work. And out of small things proceedeth that which is great. Behold, the Lord requireth the heart and a willing mind; and the willing and obedient shall eat the good of the land of Zion in these last days. (D&C 64:33–34)**

These beautiful words remind me that though it may seem only a small thing, each and every time I resist a temptation by turning to the Savior and calling on His power, great results accumulate. The amazing thing about the perpetual attitude of repentance and reliance on the Lord represented in Step Ten is that it is exactly the *opposite* of the constant acts of "serial repentance" that filled my old life. Today, by the grace of Christ, I am able to turn to Him and find power to move away from temptation *before* I slide into its clutches. Temptations still assail me, but it is as if His presence weakens them and gives me a chance to escape. I think this is what the Apostle James meant when he spoke of "enduring" temptation.

> **Blessed is the man that endureth temptation: for when he is tried, he shall receive the crown of life, which the Lord hath promised to them that love him. (James 1:12)**

I can promise you that each time you choose to turn to the Lord *before* you actually sin, while you are still only at the temptation stage, you will be **"laying the foundation of a great work."** Those moments of endured temptation will eventually add up to days, weeks, months, and finally years of abstinence. We must always remember that "the heart and a willing mind" (D&C 64:34) constitute not an *event*, but instead represent a continual re-commitment to Him.

WHY THE LORD REMOVES US FROM SIN, BUT NOT FROM TEMPTATION

I don't know how you're feeling about Step Ten, but as I said, I faced it with a fair amount of disappointment. I so desperately wanted to be free from any possibility of sin! Why hadn't the Lord granted me absolute immunity from temptation? I wrestled with this perplexity for some time, until the day came when Paul's words rang in answer through my heart:

> **There was given to me a thorn in the flesh, the messenger of Satan to buffet me, lest I should be exalted above measure. For this thing I besought the Lord thrice, that it might depart from me. And he said unto me, My grace is sufficient for thee: for my strength is made perfect in weakness. (2 Corinthians 12:7–9)**

Like previous steps, Step Ten asked me to surrender my life to the Lord! Here again, I was required to wait upon Him and return continually to Him in order to receive *His* grace (power to maintain a good work). The Lord told Paul his "thorn in the flesh" would remain to remind him that only the Lord's grace was sufficient to save him. Paul received the Lord's strength, because he remained continually aware of his own weakness. Taking Step Ten is the equivalent of admitting the exact same thing about my own life. I began to see my moments of temptation, and their intensity, as warning signals. Like the lights on my car's dashboard, moments of temptations warn me I'm running low on something—humility and the willingness to **"always remember"** the Lord, **"that [I] may always have his Spirit to be with [me]" (Moroni 4:3)**. Today's moments of temptation, though much fainter, fewer, and further apart, keep me in remembrance of my early days in recovery when I had to call on the Lord a multitude of times every day—sometimes every hour—to keep from being swept away by Satan's lies.

I testify to you that learning to live in a state of constant repentance, of continual awareness of our need for the Savior, is not an act of weakness, but actually the retention of His strength. Today, it is second nature to "converse" with Him and "counsel" with Him in my mind, and not just when I'm facing temptation. He has become my best friend, my counselor, my salvation! As you continue to absorb and live by the true principles embodied in these steps, I hope you will rejoice with me in the realization that the words "I Need Thee Every Hour" (*Hymns*, no. 98) must remain the constant song of our souls.

As I continue to live in and practice this new way of life, I feel a growing conviction, not born of overconfidence or bravado, but of the quiet reassurance of the Spirit, that I will never again turn my back on the Lord. Still, I am willing to remember the history of the Nephites. The Book of Mormon, generally, is a sobering reminder of man's ability to backslide and turn away from amazing blessings. Perhaps if the Lord lifted this affliction from me, I might become neglectful of my relationship with Him and slide back into sin. If my addiction serves to remind me on a daily basis of my need for the Lord, I am blessed by it. I am infinitely grateful to have Him in my life, and if something as unsavory as sexual addiction was the vehicle that brought me to Christ to begin to be perfected *in Him* **(Moroni 10:32),** so be it. How could being conscious of Him and His love and power—day by day and hour by hour—be regarded as anything but a blessing?!

> **Most gladly therefore will I rather glory in my infirmities, that the power of Christ may rest upon me. Therefore I take pleasure in infirmities, in reproaches, in necessities, in persecutions, in distresses for Christ's sake: for when I am weak [and give my weakness to Christ], then am I strong. (2 Corinthians 12:9–10)**

Has my weakness been turned into a blessing and my sorrow into praise? Amazingly, they have! I would never encourage anyone to go out and sin as a path to discovering God, but looking at my life as a whole, I can only say I have been incredibly blessed, and I am at peace with how my life has unfolded.

FURTHER EXAMINATION AND FINER REPENTANCE

As I look for a metaphor to represent the power in living Step Ten, I am reminded again of my life-long interest in oil painting. When I was in college, I took an oil painting class from an artist whose work I had long admired. As we students wrestled with the process of creating our own pictures, someone asked the teacher, "How do you know when you're finished with a painting?" He smiled and replied that every so often, as he worked on a piece at home, he would take it off his easel and set it on the mantle above the fireplace in his living room. Then he would sit down on the couch and look at it long and hard. (He said his wife could never understand why he couldn't push a vacuum cleaner around while he was studying the painting!) But as he studied it, some part of the painting would stand out because it "didn't look quite right." Then he would take the painting back to his studio and work on the part that bothered him the most. He said he would usually repeat this process several times—each time fixing smaller and smaller problems. When he got to the point where nothing about the painting bothered him, he decided it was finished. Like this accomplished artist, I, too, in the spirit of Step Ten, must be willing to see my life as "a work in progress." As long as I am mortal, I will need to look for areas to improve at a deeper and finer level of repentance. Living Step Ten results in our being enabled to recognize and attend to smaller sins, as the bigger ones are put behind us.

LETTING GO OF LUST

Lust is a habit, a frame of mind. It says, "I want something that doesn't belong to me." The Savior warned about lust when he said:

Whosoever looketh on a woman to lust after her hath committed adultery with her already in his heart. (Matthew 5:28)

In typical fashion, the adversary convinced me to apply this scripture to myself in the most negative way possible. Under the influence of his lying spirit, I believed that even though I had never committed adultery, by looking upon women and lusting after them I was just as far gone as if I *had* committed adultery. In hindsight, I can see that this train of thought was an enticement to lead me on into a degree of sin I had not yet committed. If you have also felt this way, I plead with you to recognize Satan's attempt to lead you carefully down to hell **(2 Nephi 28:21).** As I have prayed and pondered about the Savior's statement, I have come to believe that what He was really saying to us is that our actions always begin with our thoughts and desires. If we don't want to end up at the end of the road, we'd better not even start on it. I found this was a true principle, even when applied to acting out with pornography instead of another living person. In other words, if I wanted to avoid being lured into viewing pornography, I had better pay attention to every lustful thought as soon as it appeared and surrender it to the Lord.

The fact that lust is usually the last stronghold of sexual addiction to be conquered as we recover, is illustrated by SA's statement that "True sobriety includes progressive victory over lust." (*Sexaholics Anonymous,* 4). As my acting out with pornography lessened and eventually stopped, I was still plagued with the persistent habit of lust.

Lustful thought patterns had become like deep ruts in a dirt road. The wheels of my mind seemed to automatically slide into them, even when I tried to stay on the "straight and narrow." In the refining process required in Step Ten, I had to eventually recognize that I could not allow even one lustful thought to cross my mind without immediately taking it to the Lord. If we are to truly become clean, we must eliminate this habit, too.

We need to also be careful that we do not interpret the word "progressive" in SA's statement as an excuse to allow our recovery to be so "gradual" we never get there. Another trap we need to avoid is the excuse of thinking, "Since God has given me this weakness, He can hardly blame me for having it." As the apostle James wrote:

> **Let no man say when he is tempted, I am tempted of God: for God cannot be tempted with evil, neither tempteth he any man: But every man is tempted, when he is drawn away of his own lust, and enticed. Then when lust hath conceived, it bringeth forth sin: and sin, when it is finished, bringeth forth death. (James 1:13–15)**

While it is true that God does not tempt us, it is equally true that He allows Lucifer, our common enemy, to tempt and try us. Even so, though Satan may whisper lying thoughts into our minds such as, "Just once more won't hurt," or "No one will ever know," he has no power to force us to obey his enticements. As James puts it, **"[we are] drawn away of [our] own lust."** James' statement is echoed in the words of the Prophet Joseph Smith: "The devil has no power over us only as we permit him" (*Teachings of the Prophet Joseph Smith*, 181).

In other words, we must face the truth that if we act on Satan's temptations, if we succumb to his attacks on our weaknesses, we are actually exercising our own self-will. And this is not only true of sexual desires. "Lust" is an appropriate word to describe that nervous feeling of longing every addict of any kind feels when he is "hungering" to act out in his addiction. This giving in to one's own desire—one's own lusts—is at the core of all addiction, even from the beginning stages.

One of the things I've come to recognize in taking a daily Tenth Step is how many other forms of lust I deal with that have nothing to do with sex! Today I realize I am practicing lust any time I want something—no matter what that "something" is—that God has not allotted to me in righteousness. For instance, when I long for and consume more food than I need and feel jittery or even surly if I can't have it—I am practicing lust. When I keep thinking of more and more things to buy, just for the thrill of buying or owning them—I am practicing lust. And in every case, succumbing to lust in any area breaks down my defenses against sexual lust. Thus, in taking Step Ten, I must counsel with the Lord in **"all [my] doings"**—in all areas of my life—so that He can direct me **"for good" (Alma 37:37),** or in other words, so that I will be able to conduct myself without lust. I must continue daily to surrender my desires to the Lord. Only then, can I become free from the many forms lust can take.

The glorious part of all of this is that Jesus is more powerful than Satan and my lust combined. When I take my lustful feelings to Him, and humbly and honestly admit they are plaguing and tempting me yet again, I find He responds to my plea and takes away my desire for sin and I become like the people of King Benjamin **(Mosiah 5:2).** I have a miraculously and mysteriously changed heart and no more desire for the sin that only minutes before was about to pull me over the edge of sanity. May I say it one more time, in plain testimony to all who have ears to hear: *I am not abstinent today because I have a wonderful amount of willpower. I am abstinent because Jesus has taken away my desire for sin.* It is my testimony that all who will surrender their lives to the Lord can have this same blessing. It is my testimony that there is nothing else in all this world that can, or will, complete us and make us whole except "conscious contact" with the Lord and His love for each of us, individually. Listen to the invitation of the Lord through His prophet:

> **Come, my brethren, every one that thirsteth, come ye to the waters; and he that hath no money, come buy and eat; yea, come buy wine and milk without money and without price. Wherefore, do not spend money for that which is of no worth, nor your labor for that**

which cannot satisfy. Hearken diligently unto me, and remember the words which I have spoken; and come unto the Holy One of Israel, and feast upon that which perisheth not, neither can be corrupted. (2 Nephi 9:50–51)

What then is lust? Couldn't we say that it is looking for God in all the wrong places, or looking in all the wrong places for what *only* God can give us? Looking for happiness or satisfaction in sex, overspending, overeating, excessive recreation or any other behavior that temporarily distracts us from the quest to place God and Christ first in our lives is practicing lust. Seen this way, we come to realize that lust is really just another name for idolatry.

ARE SENSUAL DREAMS EVIDENCE OF LUST?

One phenomenon that often plagues those who have indulged in sexual addiction is that of having sensual or erotic dreams, even after they have dedicated themselves to a life of abstinence. I have also had this experience, and have been distressed by it. How could I consider myself free of lust, if it kept resurfacing in my dreams? At first I wondered, "Are these dreams my fault? How can I possibly be responsible for something that happens in my sleep?" And what does a person do to get such a dream out of his mind? I found that the same process I had learned in surrendering my temptations and thoughts to the Lord, in the very moment of having them, also worked for dealing with my dreams. I could ask the Lord to take the memory of the dream from my mind, and He would. In some cases, when a dream continued to bother me, I found it helpful to talk to someone about it. Here again is an example of how important it is to bring temptations out in the open and not keep them secret. The truth remains that anything negative that we keep secret gains power over us. When I admit to someone else that I've had a disturbing dream—to my sponsor or to a counselor or to my spouse (if she has learned to practice the principles of recovery herself)—the dream loses its power to bother me. Here again, I've found it's best not to go into explicit details. Details are not necessary to receive the healing effect of the disclosure, and furthermore, it's not wise to burden anyone else with troubling details.

Becoming honest about such dreams after they happened required a lot of humility. Still, I wanted to do all I could to decrease and hopefully eliminate such dreams in the future. Once again, the literature of SA offered a suggestion I have found extremely helpful. Considering that our dreams are often the result of feelings or thoughts we have ignored or suppressed in our waking hours, a thorough Tenth Step before bedtime is imperative. Each evening, during my prayers before I go to sleep, I have learned to review the day's thoughts and feelings very carefully. If I find there was some temptation I failed to fully surrender to the Lord during the day, I give it to Him in my evening prayer, and ask Him to keep me safe from lust during my sleeping hours. Making this Tenth Step effort each night has virtually eliminated such dreams from my subconscious. I have found that the Lord can reign even in my subconscious if I will let Him.

Taking Step Ten has the power to help us *keep* the cleanliness and peace that are the fruits of earlier steps. This continual review of our lives is a marvelous gift, a means to continually *retain* a remission of our sins. What a blessing!

MAKING THE MOST OF THIS CHAPTER

Please take time to answer the following questions in your recovery journal.

1. Consider once more King Benjamin's counsel in **Mosiah 4:30** to **"watch yourselves, and your thoughts, and your words, and your deeds."** Imagine applying that kind of thorough humility on a daily basis. Think about your progress so far. Make a list of those thoughts and feelings—or even actual behaviors—that require you to do a Tenth Step every evening. Invite the Lord to show you any hidden motives you might have for hanging on to the things on your list.

Listen honestly and with an open mind, and then record His counsel to you.

2. The Lord counsels us in **D&C 101:38** that **"in patience"** we may **"possess"** our souls. Write about how Step Ten involves yet another call to patience with ourselves, and the fact that growth happens gradually over a season. What things do you find in yourself that still require patience in your recovery, even at the level of Step Ten? Write about the importance of balance, being neither too critical nor too lenient in assessing your progress.

3. Joseph Smith counsels us, **"Therefore, dearly beloved brethren, let us cheerfully do all things that lie in our power; and then may we stand still, with the utmost assurance, to see the salvation of God, and for his arm to be revealed"** (D&C 123:17). Write about how doing a daily Tenth Step to catch ourselves in our weaknesses manifests our willingness to do all that lies in our power. How does Step Ten also remind us to **"stand still"** and allow the Lord's **"arm to be revealed?"** What does it mean to be **"still?"**

4. Read "Sex, Love and Lust in Marriage" in Appendix B (286). If you are married, do you identify areas in your intimate relations where lust might be present? Write about any changes you feel you should make in your marriage to eliminate lust. If you are single, write about how you can avoid lust in your present dating relationships, as well as in a future marriage.

5. Write about the role humility and repentance play in a healthy marriage. If you are married, discuss Step Ten with your spouse and express your desire to live each day in a state of continuing repentance. Write about your thoughts and her response. If you are single, discuss this topic with a trusted friend. Make a record of your conversation in your personal journal.

Chapter 15 *Step Eleven*

Sought through prayer and meditation to improve
our conscious contact with God as we understood
Him, praying only for knowledge of His will for
us and the power to carry that out.
(A.A. and Heart t' Heart traditional versions)

*Sought through prayer and meditation to improve
our conscious contact with God, seeking the words
of Christ through the power of the Holy Ghost that
they might tell us all things that we should do,
praying only for a knowledge of His will for us
and the power to carry that out. (2 Nephi 32:3;
Alma 37:37; Helaman 10:4)*
(Heart t' Heart scriptural version)

Step Eleven is about improving and deepening my sense of "At-one-ment" with my Savior, with my Jesus. This step marks the most glorious reward of living the gospel principles represented in the Twelve Steps. Practicing the "conscious contact" with God that is the focus of Step Eleven feels as if I've obtained a bit of heaven while still on earth. By opening my heart and mind to the Holy Ghost, I receive the First Comforter, who, in turn, prepares the way for the Second Comforter, even Jesus Christ. Thus, I am simultaneously inviting the Savior and my Heavenly Father to abide with me.

OUR GREATEST NEED, THE ONE NO ADDICTION CAN FILL

If anyone had suggested to me a few years ago that my sexual addiction had anything to do with my unfulfilled need for God, I would have laughed. As I've said, I was sure I didn't need God as much as I needed more willpower. Studying and living the true principles represented in the Twelve Steps' spiritual approach to addiction recovery has helped me see past my addiction to the great emptiness I was trying to fill by acting out. Today I see my past sins, and those of others, in the same light President Kimball described the Savior seeing sin:

> Jesus saw sin as wrong but also was able to see sin as springing from deep and unmet needs on the part of the sinner. This permitted him to condemn the sin without condemning the individual. (Spencer W. Kimball, *Ensign*, August 1979, 5)

Through coming to the oneness of mind with the Lord, or establishing the "conscious contact" encouraged in Step Eleven, I now know that Jesus does not condemn me and never has. I know, because I have felt for myself His great compassion for me. I understand through the Spirit that He recognizes the unmet needs I have suffered. In fact, He has revealed those hidden needs to me with undeniable authority. Through my counsel with Him, He has shown me how my earliest experiments with delving into the world of pornography were simply a mistaken attempt to pacify my adolescent insecurity about being acceptable to girls. He showed me how the adversary's influence twisted my mind and led me on. Using the pseudo-intimacy of pornography, I was quickly deceived into imagining I was somehow acceptable to the women in the photographs. Today, restored to sanity by the counsel of the Lord, I recognize the foolishness of this lie which I wanted so desperately to believe. Of course, Satan was more than willing to use any natural drive, curiosity or need in my immature soul to entice me. And, like the following passage from the SA White Book explains, I let these things take the place of the one connection that would have *genuinely* assured me I was okay—a connection with God.

It seems that with all our human drives—hunger, thirst, sex, power, and the like—the most basic is what we might call the Person-drive, the drive to have union with another. This drive *must* have its Connection. Without this essential core of our being plugged in somewhere, life is unbearable. We can't just leave the plug of our soul dangling. We can't survive alone, cut off, disconnected. But most of us confused the personal with the sexual, as though only the sexual aspect of this union would satisfy what essentially is a spiritual drive. So, we used sex or lust or relationships to satisfy this drive, letting them take the place of God *as the source of our lives*. Idolatry. (*Sexaholics Anonymous*, 55; emphasis original)

DESTROYING THE IDOLS IN MY LIFE

This interpretation of my addiction as "idolatry" is not an idle comment, nor is it off the mark. In active addiction, I put these inappropriately intimate images of women in the place of God; I relied on them to comfort me, energize me, to make me feel reassured and whole. And because pornography has such a powerful effect, detaching from that pattern did not come easily or overnight. Even after I started my earliest recovery efforts and began to accumulate some abstinence from pornography, I found myself relying on my wife to keep me abstinent, either by meeting my sexual needs or by being an instrument of correction if I slipped. I still had not turned to God. Instead, I made legal, marital sex and my wife, herself, my god. I was much more concerned about what my wife thought of me than what God thought of me. If that isn't idolatry, I don't know what is.

I think I can honestly say that by the time I reached Step Eleven, I was finally ready to "fire" all my old "gods" and make the Eternal God (as He is referred to on the title page of the Book of Mormon) my *one, true God*. He has become "the source of my life," as SA puts it. That says it all. He is the only source that can truly meet all my needs and, even more, He is willing and eager to meet them—even the ones I mistakenly tried to fill with pornography. He cares about my longing for the approval of others, for the reassurance that I am "okay," and about my need to not be alone. When I came to Him and began to let Him take care of my needs, I felt reassured in the knowledge of His love for me. Consequently, I have learned my deepest needs were ones that not even my loving and tender wife could fill. They could only be met by my Lord and Savior, and He was only waiting for me to come to Him so He could take care of me.

This greatest of all relationships, this means of having all our needs and concerns taken care of by coming into conscious contact with God, is the ultimate purpose of the Twelve Step program. In the LDS version of recovery, all of the steps and all of the principles have but one purpose: to bring us to Christ, where we will find all we need. One of my favorite hymns says it so beautifully:

> The Lord my pasture will prepare,
> And feed me with a shepherd's care.
> His presence will my wants supply,
> And guard me with a watchful eye.
> My noonday walks he will attend,
> And all my silent midnight hours defend.
> (*Hymns*, no. 109)

SEEKING THE LORD

Down through the ages, the prophets have pled with us to **"seek this Jesus" (Ether 12:41).** There is a good reason why Jesus is mentioned specifically. While we do indeed owe our highest allegiance to the Father, Jesus is the One the Father has commissioned to be our Savior. As King Benjamin taught:

> **And moreover, I say unto you, that there shall be no other name given nor any other way nor means whereby salvation can come unto the children of men, only in and through the name of Christ, the Lord Omnipotent. (Mosiah 3:17)**

I believe the Savior has ascended to this unique position because He is the One who suffered for our sins and therefore has all power to judge given to Him by the Father **(John 5:22).** Jesus is our advocate with the Father **(D&C 45:3–5)** and no one comes to the Father but through Christ **(John 14:6).** If we continue faithful, one day the Savior will introduce us to the Father; but in the meantime, when we pray to the Father, as we are commanded, He directs us to the Son, saying, **"This is My Beloved Son. Hear Him!"** (Joseph Smith–History 1:17). That is why I emphasize the importance of developing our relationship with the Savior, Jesus Christ. My own recovery has progressed in exact proportion to how much I have been willing to embrace the following counsel of Brigham Young:

> The greatest and most important of all requirements of our Father in Heaven and of his Son Jesus Christ....is to believe in Jesus Christ, confess him, seek him, cling to him, make friends with him. Take a course to open a communication with your Elder Brother or file-leader— our Savior. (*Journal of Discourses*, vol. 8, 339)

The Lord does not hide from us, but, in our fallen and sinful state, it is sometimes hard for us to find Him. At one time or another, like Job, we have all cried, **"Oh that I knew where I might find him! that I might come even to his seat!"** (Job 23:3). Most often our inability to find Him is a result of our own reluctance to approach Him. We long for Him, but we are afraid to seek Him. And after years spent seeking comfort in addiction instead of in the Lord, we are numb with shame. Coming out of this shame takes a great deal of willingness and persistent desire. Someone once wrote to me, asking how one comes to know the Savior after so many years of avoiding Him:

> *I have a question for you. My biggest obstacle in all of this is that everyone is telling me I need to rely on the Savior. The problem I am having is I have no relationship with Him and when I pray, I feel nothing. I don't know if you felt like this when you first started trying to overcome this obstacle. I feel that forming this relationship with God is a starting point, but I can't do that if I don't feel anything for Him. I think my*

*feelings are mostly intellectual and not spiritual. How can I
get started?*

This struggling brother's questions represent the challenge all
addicts—and particularly sex addicts—have in coming out of the anes-
thesia created by years of addiction. We can be sure the adversary will
do all he can to convince us that attempting such a personal relationship with the Savior is useless, that we are the one soul who is beyond
the Lord's ability or inclination to love or reach. This is a lie. Opening
a communication with Jesus Christ is the single most important connection we will ever make in all of our mortal journey. I don't think there is
a subject of greater importance, and while much more could be written,
I hope the ideas presented here will at least be a beginning.

NOT A NEW RELATIONSHIP

The first thing we need to know is that we already have a relationship with Jesus. We all do. We knew Jesus long before any of us came
into mortality. And though we have forgotten our past with Him since
coming to earth, He has not forgotten us. This isn't a process of getting
to know someone we have never met. Because He was the Firstborn in
the Spirit, He is the Elder Brother of us all. He was there when we were
born as spirit children. Inspired by His own witness to my heart and
mind, I am able to picture Him lovingly watching us grow and develop
over eons of time as the earth was being prepared for us. I also imagine
Him as one of our most significant teachers during those formative
years. So what we are undertaking is not a process of "getting to know
the Lord," but of *recovering* the relationship we already have with Him.

In my experience, the process of renewing our relationship with
Jesus is not any different than developing any other friendship we might
have. If it surprises you to think of this relationship as a friendship,
please recall what He told His apostles anciently:

> **Greater love hath no man than this, that a man lay
> down his life for his friends. Ye are my friends, if ye do
> whatsoever I command you. Henceforth I call you not
> servants; for the servant knoweth not what his lord**

> doeth: but I have called you friends; for all things that
> I have heard of my Father I have made known unto
> you. (John 15:13–15)

How do you become friends with someone? You spend time together. You do things together. You talk to each other and share your deepest feelings. The process of becoming the Savior's friend is no different. How do we spend time with Jesus? One way that works powerfully for me is "on the page," as I read what others have written and as I record my own thoughts about Him, to Him, *and from Him*. That means, of course, reading the scriptures, especially the parts where His own words are recorded and being willing to "liken them to myself." (This process is covered in depth in Appendix A.) The four Gospels, the part of Third Nephi in the Book of Mormon that talks about Christ's visit to the Nephites, and the Doctrine and Covenants are all wonderful places to "hear His voice."

DOING THE RIGHT THINGS FOR THE WRONG REASONS

As most of us know all too well, it is possible to consistently "say our prayers" and not connect with God. It is possible to spend much time "reading" the scriptures and not have them change our life. It is possible to "fast" and only be hungry. What is in our hearts—our motive—is so important in all we do! Examining and understanding our motives is essential to our recovery. Most of my life my reasons for serving in the Church or attending to personal religious practices (when I did) were mostly duty, custom, or a desire to receive blessings. Recently a friend said, "I am just now learning the difference between serving God and loving God." What a difference that is! The deeds we do out of love bless us much more than those done merely out of duty.

As I looked at my past motivation for praying, I found myself with yet another confession to make. Back then I didn't pray very well. Oh, I used all the "correct" words, but something deeper than the words was frequently missing. Through those years, the Lord answered my prayers, but only at the depth I was willing to bring to them. For example, when circumstances got tough or important decisions loomed and I finally started praying for direction, He gave it. When I prayed so many times for forgiveness, He granted it. You might be tempted to ask, "So, what was wrong with your prayers?" The answer is so simple by the light of today's revelations: *I didn't know the One who answered my prayers. I didn't know the dear Savior my Father in Heaven sent to me. I missed out on the single greatest Gift the Holy Ghost conveys—the companionship of the Lord Jesus Christ.* Thus, I was always "repenting" without coming to that *remission* of sin that only the Savior could administer to me.

My reasons for opening the scriptures weren't much better. I very seldom read for personal understanding. Instead, I was stingy with my time and defined reading the scriptures as getting through some minimal amount: a chapter a day or 15 minutes a day. I would read to prepare for a lesson or a talk, or to attempt to keep up in a Sunday School class. I would read a little every now and then, to be a "righteous parent" and set an example for my children. Unfortunately, none of those motives were enough to sustain my efforts. Sooner or later, I'd find some excuse to miss a day, and then another day, and then another… you know the rest of the story. Obviously, I did not *delight* in the scriptures. Again, thank God, that has changed.

DOING THE RIGHT THINGS FOR THE *RIGHT* REASONS

Admittedly, it has taken some time to become committed and thus consistent in praying and reading the scriptures. Today, if I go more than twenty-four hours without reading and rejoicing in the scriptures, something precious is missing—and I feel it. Today, these are not just so many inspiring stories of miracles I can't relate with or expect in my own life. Today, I read the scriptures so my heart can **"sing the song of redeeming love" (Alma 5:26)** along with the prophets. The scriptures and daily prayer are like oxygen to my soul—they are a real lifeline to me now, even as this testimony from recovering alcoholics in one of AA's basic texts tells us:

> Those of us who have come to make regular use of prayer
> would no more do without it than we would refuse air,
> food, or sunshine. (*Twelve Steps and Twelve Traditions*, 99)

What did those original recovering alcoholics know that I didn't understand at first? Surprisingly, they knew exactly the same thing the prophets knew and had been trying to convince me of for decades—that God's character was one of patience and love, and that I could talk with Him as one man does with another.

> These are incomprehensible ideas to some, but they are simple. *It is the first principle of the Gospel to know for a certainty the Character of God, and to know that we may converse with him as one man converses with another.* (*Teachings of the Prophet Joseph Smith*, 345, italics original)

Learning to live Step Eleven every day of my life has totally changed my attitude toward prayer and scripture study (or better said, scripture-guided meditation). I know, today, that neither of these activities is an end in itself. Both are means, or ways, by which I may draw closer to God and converse with Him through the gift and power of the Holy Ghost.

It was certainly an amazing thing to realize at fifty years old, after a lifetime of activity in the Church, that I was just learning the true meaning of prayer; that prayer can and, in fact, *must* become a mutual exchange, a two-way channel of communication. Of course, I had learned the mechanics of prayer in Primary, and as I mentioned earlier, I had received some truly miraculous answers to prayer—answers giving me major direction in my life. But the kind of prayer that turns inward and changes a person's heart was still beyond my grasp. I love how the SA White Book describes the contriteness and humanity of sincere prayer:

> Learning how to pray in sobriety is like learning how to walk or talk; no one can tell us how or do it for us. We learn by doing, like everything else in this program. *We just start talking to God.* (*Sexaholics Anonymous*, 138, emphasis added)

"We just start *talking* to God." What an important concept that was for me to grasp! It was an invitation to sit down, not just with my Father in Heaven, but also with my Savior, and just start pouring my heart out—and then letting my Lord pour His heart out to me! In talking to my Savior in this way—counseling with Him, wrestling with Him, conversing, reasoning together—I did not picture myself praying in the formal, proper sense of the word. I continued to address my official prayers to my Heavenly Father in ever-deepening awe and gratitude to Him for sending me His Only Begotten Son to be my best friend, dearer to me than any other living soul, save only the Father. When I began to come unto my Savior, in order to become as one with my Heavenly Father, my life began to change forever, and saving grace (power) beyond my wildest imagination began to flow into my soul.

A DAILY PRAYER HABIT THAT ISN'T ROUTINE

I know now how essential prayer is. I have finally started listening to the Spirit that teaches a man that he must pray, as Nephi said:

> **And now, my beloved brethren, I perceive that ye ponder still in your hearts; and it grieveth me that I must speak concerning this thing. For if ye would hearken unto the Spirit which teacheth a man to pray ye would know that ye must pray; for the evil spirit teacheth not a man to pray, but teacheth him that he must not pray. But behold, I say unto you that ye must pray always, and not faint; that ye must not perform any thing unto the Lord save in the first place ye shall pray unto the Father in the name of Christ, that he will consecrate thy performance unto thee, that thy performance may be for the welfare of thy soul. (2 Nephi 32:8–9)**

Today, my prayer life consists of many "prayers" or supplications to God throughout my day. Each new day begins with a formal "opening prayer" offered on my knees, addressed to my Heavenly Father. In this prayer, I am sure to express my greatest desire—that He will communicate His will for me, as I seek the words of Christ whispered to me through the Holy Ghost—and that through this channel of revelation I may know the truth of all things. I also ask my Father for the grace or power to carry out His will for me. Later, as the day goes on, I frequently reach heavenward to stay in touch. I plead for rescue when temptation arises, or when I am in a hard place and being tormented by the power of the Liar. Since **"Jesus Christ [is] the only name which shall be given under heaven, whereby salvation shall come unto the children of men" (Moses 6:52),** I have learned to call upon Him directly to save me in these moments of trial or temptation. *"Dear Savior, I can't handle this temptation. Will you please take it away for me?"* This plea, "spoken" silently in the depths of my heart, is like Alma's own, when he cried unto the Savior **(Alma 38:8).** I feel no offense or impatience from my Heavenly Father when I address my thoughts to the Savior in moments of temptation. I feel the witness, even as the Savior expressed in **3 Nephi 19:22,** that the Father hears my plea to His Son for salvation as a plea unto Him. Then, in addition to pleas for relief from temptation, there are the almost continuous "conversations" I have learned to address to the Lord as I seek understanding and guidance for my daily decisions and as I seek comfort when I am sad or lonely or otherwise in need. And above and through all of these interactions with my Father and His Son, there is the constant prayer of thanksgiving and praise for the miracle of my abstinence and recovery. And finally, there is the formal "closing prayer" of my day, offered again, on my knees and addressed unto my Father in Heaven.

Thus, throughout my day, from morning until night, I live my life "unto God." Though my conversation is often interrupted to interact with others in my day, I no longer "hang up" on God to do so. I pray you will understand the testimony I am trying to share. It is about coming to understand how it is possible to live according to the command to **"pray without ceasing" (Mosiah 26:39).**

> **Call upon his holy name, that he would have mercy upon you; Yea, cry unto him for mercy; for he is mighty to save. Yea, humble yourselves, and continue in prayer unto him. Cry unto him when ye are in your fields, yea, over all your flocks. Cry unto him in your houses, yea, over all your household, both morning, mid-day, and evening. Yea, cry unto him against the**

power of your enemies. Yea, cry unto him against the devil, who is an enemy to all righteousness. Cry unto him over the crops of your fields, that ye may prosper in them. Cry over the flocks of your fields, that they may increase. But this is not all; ye must pour out your souls in your closets, and your secret places, and in your wilderness. *Yea, and when you do not cry unto the Lord, let your hearts be full, drawn out in prayer unto him continually* for your welfare, and also for the welfare of those who are around you. (Alma 34:17–27, emphasis added)

By letting our hearts be **"drawn out in prayer unto him continually,"** we will find that temptations come to have very little power over us. Just picture how you would respond to a temptation if the Savior were walking by your side. His help can be that real.

REJOICING IN THE RECORDED WORDS OF GOD

As I have worked through the principles of the gospel represented in each of the Twelve Steps, I have been blessed with new ears to hear and a new heart to understand the scriptures. When I read and truly ponder them, the Holy Ghost brings them to my heart with an impact that cannot be matched by any other writing. Today, I see the scriptures as precious words, spoken by the Lord Himself and recorded by His servants. The Standard Works have become like code books that teach me how to set my heart and mind on the same wavelength as God, so I can receive my own personalized direction through the revelations they contain. We can gain so much from the scriptures, especially by likening them unto ourselves, capturing from them and using them as a springboard for further revelation (See Appendix A). Because I now understand the Lord's willingness to actually converse with each of us, I recognize the scriptures for what they are: preserved conversations with God. A beautiful example of this is given in **D&C 121.** Verse one begins: **"O God, where art thou? And where is the pavilion that covereth thy hiding place?"** In the first six verses, Joseph pours out his heart to God, asking how long it will be before He comes to the aid of the suffering saints. Starting with verse seven, we read the Lord's reply to Joseph, beginning with the words:

> **My son, peace be unto thy soul; thine adversity and thine afflictions shall be but a small moment; And then, if thou endure it well, God shall exalt thee on high; thou shalt triumph over all thy foes. (D&C 121:7–8)**

The rest of the section, through verse 46, is a continuation of the Lord's answer to Joseph, as perceived by the mind of the Prophet and written down for all of us to read. If we exercise our faith and accept the truth that the ideas and promptings we receive in response to our own prayers are indeed coming from the Lord, we, too, can record those in His voice, as if He is speaking directly to us. Nephi described this process of receiving the Lord's words spoken to us through the mediation of the Holy Ghost:

> **Do ye not remember that I said unto you that after ye had received the Holy Ghost ye could speak with the tongue of angels? And now, how could ye speak with the tongue of angels save it were by the Holy Ghost? Angels speak by the power of the Holy Ghost; wherefore, they speak the words of Christ. Wherefore, I said unto you, feast upon the words of Christ; for behold, the words of Christ will tell you all things what ye should do. (2 Nephi 32:2–3)**

It is my testimony that we can receive the voice of the Lord and record it for ourselves, because I have experienced it and cannot deny the power those communications have had in changing my heart and my life. It is the voice of gladness spoken of by the Prophet Joseph:

> **Now, what do we hear in the gospel which we have received? A voice of gladness! A voice of mercy from heaven; and a voice of truth out of the earth;…a voice of gladness for the living and the dead; glad tidings of great joy. How beautiful upon the mountains are the**

feet of those that bring glad tidings of good things, and
that say unto Zion: Behold, thy God reigneth! As the
dews of Carmel, so shall the knowledge of God
descend upon them! (D&C 128:19)

GROWING IN RECEIVING PERSONAL REVELATION

I have heard it said that there is no recovery without revelation.
That might shake you up a bit, but I hope you won't let it deter you from
your efforts to implement this mighty change. There is no need to feel
anxious about expecting and living a life based on personal revelation.
We are not talking about great panoramic visions like those Nephi,
Moses, and Isaiah had. We are simply talking about "conscious contact
with God," of being aware of His love and His presence, of living, as we
often refer to it in the Church, "by the Spirit." Such still, small doses of
revelation are more than adequate to lead us into the presence of the
Lord and out of the bondage of mortal fears and addictions. According
to Joseph Smith:

> A person may profit by noticing the first intimation of
> the spirit of revelation; for instance, when you feel pure
> intelligence flowing into you,…and thus by learning the
> Spirit of God and understanding it, you may grow into
> the principle of revelation, until you become perfect in
> Christ. (*History of the Church* 3:381)

Since Step Eleven is about improving our conscious contact with
God, I would like to offer a few suggestions that have helped me to grow
in the principle of personal revelation.

1. *Acknowledge the revelations of God that already bless your life.*

Brigham Young taught that even advances in technology are
revealed through the Holy Ghost. He said:

> There are men of talent, of thought, of reflection, and
> knowledge in all cunning mechanism; they are expert in
> that, though they do not know from whence they receive
> their intelligence. The Spirit of the Lord has not yet

entirely done striving with the people, offering them knowledge and intelligence; consequently, it reveals unto them, instructs them, teaches them, and guides them even in the way they like to travel. Men know how to construct railroads and all manner of machinery; they understand cunning workmanship, etc.; but that is all revealed to them by the Spirit of the Lord, though they know it not. (*Discourses of Brigham Young,* 33)

Understanding this truth opens the door for us to realize that God's revelations are responsible for all of the comforts and blessings we enjoy in our modern way of life. Even if we have not yet recognized much *personal* revelation, we must admit we are literally held in a cocoon of His blessings.

2. *Give the Lord credit for the intelligence and wisdom that come into your mind on a personal level.*

The Lord has said:

> **And in nothing doth man offend God, or against none is his wrath kindled, save those who confess not his hand in all things, and obey not his commandments. (D&C 59:21)**

In the spirit of recognizing that God's hand is in *all* things, I have decided to humble myself and admit that *any* good ideas that come into my mind are coming from Him. I have become converted to the truth that King Benjamin pronounced with such fervor:

> **Believe in God;...that he has all wisdom, and all power, both in heaven and in earth; believe that man doth not comprehend all the things which the Lord can comprehend. (Mosiah 4:9)**

God has *all* wisdom and *all* power, both in heaven and in earth! As I have often heard Colleen ask with a smile: What part of "all" don't we understand?

In the same spirit, I have chosen to acknowledge that it is God that does **"bring all things to [my] remembrance,"** even as **John 14:26** testifies. It may seem like a small thing, but I've stopped thinking in terms of, "I'm so glad I remembered that!" and have started thinking in terms of, "Thank you, Lord, for reminding me of that." Recognizing God in everything I once took credit for doesn't make me feel diminished in any way. Instead it fills me with awe to realize how intimately and lovingly He is involved in my life.

3. *Be willing to ask and believe that answers can, and will, come according to the Lord's timetable for us.*

Joseph Smith taught the importance of expanding our vision and exercising faith by being willing to ask:

> The things of God are of deep import; and time, and experience, and careful and ponderous and solemn thoughts can only find them out. Thy mind, O man! if thou wilt lead a soul unto salvation, must stretch as high as the utmost heavens, and search into and contemplate the darkest abyss, and the broad expanse of eternity— thou must commune with God. How much more dignified and noble are the thoughts of God, than the vain imaginations of the human heart! (*Teachings of the Prophet Joseph Smith,* 137)

We need to always avoid the cynicism and faithlessness expressed by Laman and Lemuel, who prejudged God and therefore refused Nephi's admonition to pray:

> **And I said unto them: Have ye inquired of the Lord? And they said unto me: We have not; for the Lord maketh no such thing known unto us. (1 Nephi 15:8–9)**

We can miss out on so many blessings by assuming the Lord will not give them to us, and therefore we don't even ask Him!

4. *Act on the promptings we receive.*

Why should the Lord continue to give us direction if we do not exercise enough faith to *act* on what we have already received? Joseph Smith captured this principle in a wonderful statement of obedience.

He said: "I made this my rule: When the Lord commands, do it" (*History of the Church*, 2:170). We grow in our ability to *hear* the Lord's voice as we *obey* the Lord's voice to us.

5. *Strive to live as worthily as we can.*

I can promise you, due to my own experience, that acting on even the smallest intimations of inspiration will lead you to live the commandments more fully. And living the commandments will result in an even clearer channel of revelation. The closer we follow the Lord and the more we surrender our will to His, the easier it will be for us to communicate with Him and for Him to reciprocate.

LIVING EACH DAY ACCORDING TO THE REVELATIONS OF CHRIST

Being aware of the Lord in our lives does not have to be only an occasional highlight or a rare spiritual experience. His presence is available to us constantly. Colleen shared this beautiful testimony about living from day to day in this spirit of continuing revelation:

> To be "highly favored of the Lord" means one thing and one thing only to Nephi and all others who have known the experience. It is to have the gift of personal revelation. It is to have the "lights on," so to speak, through the "night" of this life. It means to walk this mortal journey with a flashlight, and occasionally even a floodlight, illuminating our way. And since, as the saying goes, "It's always darkest before the dawn," we can be sure that no people have ever walked in greater darkness or have ever had more need of "further *light* and knowledge" than we do at this point in the earth's history. We are no longer simply in the Saturday evening of time; we are entering the darkest period known on earth—the dark before the dawn. We need not be in despair, however, if we walk in the light and with the light, even Christ.

Wouldn't you, after some honest thought, agree with this statement: I could get through *anything* if I just knew what God wanted of me, and that He was there for me. (*He Did Deliver Me from Bondage*, 148; italics original)

As we continue with our journey, may we make companionship with the Lord not just an occasional experience, but the very walk and talk in our inner life. The more time we spend with Him, the more precious He becomes to us. I love the sentiment expressed in the hymn, "Jesus the Very Thought of Thee":

> Jesus, the very thought of thee
> With sweetness fills my breast;
> But sweeter far thy face to see
> And in thy presence rest.
>
> Nor voice can sing, nor heart can frame,
> Nor can the mem'ry find
> A sweeter sound than thy blest name,
> O Savior of mankind!
>
> O hope of ev'ry contrite heart,
> O joy of all the meek,
> To those who fall, how kind thou art!
> How good to those who seek!
> (*Hymns*, no. 141)

Living by revelation is more than turning to the Lord only when we are in trouble, or only to free us from addictive behaviors. Living by revelation means having an ongoing relationship with the Lord because we want to be with Him—because we love Him, and He loves us. I leave my testimony with you, that I know these principles are true. They have helped me to come to know my Savior once again. He is now my closest and dearest Friend. I know He loves me and I have no fear of Him. I know I can have His help, His friendship, and His company whenever I need it—and I need it every hour, every moment. He said:

I will not leave you comfortless: I will come to you. (John 14:18)

And He meant it! My continuing abstinence is the fruit of this spiritual reality. I bear this testimony to you, dear friend, in the name of Jesus Christ, amen.

MAKING THE MOST OF THIS CHAPTER

Please take time to answer the following questions in your recovery journal.

1. What we believe has the power to open doors or close them, especially in our spiritual lives. Write a short "Step Eleven Inventory" of your beliefs about receiving personal revelation. Write another short inventory—this time about your experiences with reading the scriptures. Examine your belief in the experiences you've had, or others have had, of opening the scriptures and finding answers to their current challenges. Take one verse from the Book of Mormon and rewrite it as if it were being spoken directly to you by the Lord.

2. In admonishing the readers of the Book of Mormon to test its truthfulness by prayer, Moroni first asked us to remember the things the Lord had done for His children. **"Behold, I would exhort you that when ye shall read these things, if it be wisdom in God that ye should read them, that ye would remember how merciful the Lord hath been unto the children of men, from the creation of Adam even down until the time that ye shall receive these things, and ponder it in your hearts" (Moroni 10:3).** Write about some experiences in your life when you felt that you (or a loved one) were being mercifully helped or guided by the Lord.

3. Write about your prayer experiences. What has helped you the most to feel connected to God when you pray? Write about someone you know who prays "powerfully." In your opinion, what is it about them that allows their prayers to open such a powerful connection with God?

4. Copy the words of Hymn no. 277, "As I Search the Holy Scriptures," into your recovery journal and capture from them. What do they teach you about personal revelation?

5. Sometimes we fear asking the Lord for revelation because we are afraid He will tell us to do something we don't want to do. Write about why it is important that we surrender our will to God in order to fully open the channels of communication from Him.

Chapter

16 *Step Twelve*

Having had a spiritual awakening as the result of these
steps, we tried to carry this message to others still
suffering from the effects of compulsive behaviors and
to practice these principles in all our affairs.
(Heart t' Heart traditional version, adapted from A.A.)

*Having experienced a mighty change and having
awakened unto God as a result of our sincere repentance
demonstrated in taking these steps, we were willing to
become instruments in carrying this message to others
and to practice these principles in all our affairs.*
(Alma 5:7; Mosiah 27:36–37; Moroni 7:3)
(Heart t' Heart scriptural version)

Our first joy in participating in Twelve Step work is, of course, our
own deliverance from addiction. Most of us have spent years trying to
get free from its clutches. Relief, so long desired, is gladly welcomed. But
that joy seems, after a while, not to be enough. We want to see others
share in this blessing. The closer we come to God, the more we understand how joyful it is to see the spiritual progress of others. Indeed, the
Lord has told us: **"This is my work and my glory—to bring to pass the
immortality and eternal life of man" (Moses 1:39).** I think "glory"
must include a great deal of happiness, and He has made it possible for
us to share in that happiness. Think of the joy Ammon expressed when

he was reunited with his brothers after their fourteen years of missionary labors among the Lamanites:

> Yea, we have reason to praise him forever, for he is the Most High God, and has loosed our brethren from the chains of hell. Yea, they were encircled about with everlasting darkness and destruction; but behold, he has brought them into his everlasting light, yea, into everlasting salvation; and they are encircled about with the matchless bounty of his love; yea, *and we have been instruments in his hands of doing this great and marvelous work.* Therefore, let us glory, yea, we will glory in the Lord; yea, we will rejoice, for our joy is full; yea, we will praise our God forever. Behold, who can glory too much in the Lord? Yea, who can say too much of his great power, and of his mercy, and of his long-suffering towards the children of men? Behold, I say unto you, I cannot say the smallest part which I feel. (Alma 26:14–16, emphasis added)

The Lord has restated this joy in His own words in our dispensation:

> And if it so be that you should labor all your days in crying repentance unto this people, and bring, save it be one soul unto me, how great shall be your joy with him in the kingdom of my Father! And now, if your joy will be great with one soul that you have brought unto me into the kingdom of my Father, how great will be your joy if you should bring many souls unto me! (D&C 18: 15–16)

What a marvelous blessing—the Lord permits us to join Him in this work of bringing salvation to the souls of men! What a blessing to stand beside the Savior in extending these saving principles to our brothers and sisters! What joy to see others turn from despair to hope, to see lives changed, marriages saved, and families reunited! This is the spirit and the promise that these true principles represent!

HOW DO I START SHARING THE MESSAGE?

It is such a blessing to have the support of others as we try to become free from devastating addictive behaviors. The help I have received from others has been of vital importance to me.

> **Two are better than one; because they have a good reward for their labour. For if they fall, the one will lift up his fellow: but woe to him that is alone when he falleth; for he hath not another to help him up. (Ecclesiastes 4:9–10)**

Some imagine that they must make a grand, public effort in order to begin helping others. Not true. You start offering service to others the moment you begin participating in a fellowship of recovery. This can be as simple as talking one-on-one with another individual who is struggling, or it could be in an organized recovery group, such as the groups listed in Appendix C. When you participate in such a group, you admit by your mere presence that you are looking for help. Even that humble admission is a testimony which strengthens and encourages others. It embodies the hope that recovery is possible, and is worth seeking.

When you begin to share your own story with others, you might start by describing the devastation addiction has caused in your life. This, too, is comfort to others, for in hearing your story they understand they are not alone. As you begin to have success in allowing the Lord to rescue you from acting out, you have more to share, including the testimony that relief is possible, that a person can be tempted without having to give in to the temptation. Those first experiences of being saved from acting out eventually grow into consistent abstinence, which is what most of us were seeking when we first admitted we needed help. As you are able to bear testimony of continuing abstinence, you serve as a beacon of hope to those who are still struggling. None of this requires great understanding of philosophical or religious doctrines. It simply grows from telling your story as it unfolds and progresses. The stories of others who are recovering become our first lessons in recovery. They allow hope, which may have seriously dimmed, to be rekindled. In fact, our personal story is the most effective way to carry the message. One member of SA expressed it this way:

> The only thing I can bear witness to is the truth of my own experience. Because that's what I want to hear from others. I want to see and feel the real truth about someone's inner life and behavior that I can identify with. I don't want to be told or preached at. Knowing the truth about religion or the program didn't do it for me. Coming to see and acknowledge the truth about myself is what got me through the door into this new way of life. It's the truth about myself—the imperfect truth—that attracts others; not all the preaching in the world. (Sexaholics Anonymous, 144; italics original)

BEING SURE WE'RE "TWELVE–STEPPING"— NOT "TWO–STEPPING"

Often, upon finding the hope and promised relief in learning these true principles, many of us get very excited—for the "other guy's" sake. After all, we can immediately think of a dozen people who *really* need this! We have the reaction: "Wow, I've got to tell 'so-and-so' about this!" I admit, this may not be the first reaction of a sex addict as often as it is with other kinds of addicts because of the heightened level of shame we have to get over, but even among us it happens. Starting in AA long ago, this premature zeal—this sharing a message we haven't yet applied to ourselves—became known as "two-stepping." In other words, the new enthusiast reduces the twelve steps to two—hearing and then sharing—conveniently leap-frogging over the personal challenge represented in each of the ten intermediate steps. However, in the Savior's own words, preserved for us in **Luke 22:32,** we find His own counsel given to Peter, but perfectly fitting for us: **"When thou art converted, strengthen thy brethren."**

I have to admit I have been tempted myself to apply a new principle or practice I have learned to someone else before I embraced it and internalized it for my own sake. As soon as a new precept would dawn on me, I would immediately begin to hear the adversary's efforts to distract me from *my* own need for salvation by reminding me of someone else's need. I would read or hear some new principle and instantly think, "That's a really great thought. I should use that in a talk or a lesson," or even, "I should write a book about that!"

One thing the Twelve Steps inevitably teach us is the lesson of humility, which is essential to learning these principles for ourselves. I am humbled and grateful to say that as I continued to work the steps, I eventually realized I could only carry to others the portion of the message I had *lived.* I had to be able to say, unequivocally, that I was consistently practicing what I was recommending to others. Meanwhile, I needed to focus on the only salvation I could work out—my own.

> **O then despise not, and wonder not, but hearken unto the words of the Lord, and ask the Father in the name of Jesus for what things soever *ye* shall stand in need. Doubt not, but be believing, and begin as in times of old, and come unto the Lord with all *your* heart, and work out *your own* salvation with fear and trembling before him. (Mormon 9:27, emphasis added)**

Hyrum Smith, the Prophet's brother, may have had this same overly enthusiastic desire to prematurely share the message of the dawning restoration. In May, 1829, before the Church had been organized, before the translation of the Book of Mormon was finished, the Lord, through the Prophet Joseph, gave Hyrum this revelation:

> **Behold, I command you that you need not suppose that you are called to preach until you are called. Wait a little longer, until you shall have my word, my rock, my church, and my gospel, that you may know of a surety my doctrine...**
>
> *Behold, this is your work, to keep my commandments, yea, with all your might, mind and strength. Seek not to declare my word, but first seek to obtain my word,* and then shall your tongue be loosed; then, if you desire, you shall have my Spirit and my word, yea, the

> power of God unto the convincing of men. (D&C
> 11:15–16, 20–21, emphasis added)

Though it is humorous, the old adage is also true that "nobody has all the answers like an addict with two weeks of sobriety." It takes time for recovery to mature.

BECOMING READY TO CARRY THE MESSAGE

The effect of working the steps is simply the result of repenting at a heart-deep level. In admitting our powerlessness, our need for our Savior, and in deciding to trust Him, we began our journey of repentance. Admitting our actions and our faults and making what amends we could helped us "clear away the wreckage of the past." Continuing our inventory and increasing our constant contact with the Lord helps us prevent the smaller mistakes of today from growing into larger ones. If we have taken these steps in depth, we can expect the same miracle that blessed the lives of King Benjamin's people when they repented of their sins.

> **And they had viewed themselves in their own carnal
> state, even less than the dust of the earth. And they
> all cried aloud with one voice, saying: O have mercy,
> and apply the atoning blood of Christ that we may
> receive forgiveness of our sins, and our hearts may be
> purified; for we believe in Jesus Christ, the Son of
> God, who created heaven and earth, and all things;
> who shall come down among the children of men.**
>
> **And it came to pass that after they had spoken these
> words the Spirit of the Lord came upon them, and
> *they were filled with joy, having received a remission of
> their sins, and having peace of conscience,* because of
> the exceeding faith which they had in Jesus Christ
> who should come. (Mosiah 4:2–3, emphasis added)**

These principles apply in our day as much as at any time in the history of the earth. The Lord will reach out to heal each one of us in the same way He did the people of King Benjamin. Through applying the detailed repentance process outlined in the Twelve Steps, I have found the same joy Benjamin's people found. I have experienced that same peace of conscience. The feelings of shame that followed me through all the years of my enslavement in sexual addiction are washed away in the Savior's forgiveness. As a result, I not only have the desire to share this message with you, I find myself able to bare my soul in this open forum, knowing that even if some find reason to criticize me for it or for my past, I am all right, because I am right with God. **"If God be for us, who can be against us?" (Romans 8:31).**

This desire to share the glorious experience of redemption the Lord has wrought in our lives is the natural fruit of the healing process. When we are cleansed by the Spirit of the Lord, shame leaves us and we want to talk with others to share the miracle of our forgiveness with them. We also want to share the growth we have experienced, but most of all, we want to share the joy. We become like Alma, who shared so honestly about his past sins and his marvelous conversion.

> **And oh, what joy, and what marvelous light I did behold; yea, my soul was filled with joy as exceeding as was my pain! Yea, I say unto you, my son, that there could be nothing so exquisite and so bitter as were my pains. Yea, and again I say unto you, my son, that on the other hand, there can be nothing so exquisite and sweet as was my joy. (Alma 36:20–21)**

WHEN OUR ATTEMPTS TO HELP DON'T SEEM TO WORK

To face the whole truth, however, we must admit that wherever there is the potential for joy, there is also the potential for sorrow. These opposites must necessarily exist **(2 Nephi 2)**. Thus, when we seek to help others, we also risk experiencing sorrow and pain, because not all will hear the message, nor join us in rejoicing in recovery. One of my earliest attempts to carry the message comes to mind.

A few years ago, a man I knew got himself into trouble through sexual sin. He held a position of leadership in the Church and was quickly excommunicated. His transgression was also a violation of the law, and he had been arrested and charged with a crime. When I learned about his sad situation, I wanted to talk with him. He was still at home, waiting for his trial. I knew it was very unlikely that the act which had caught the public's attention was the first time he had given in to sexual temptation. There had to have been a series of lesser sexual sins paving the way for his ultimate downfall. It seemed obvious to me that this man was caught in sexual addiction. I thought perhaps I could help. I had read in *Alcoholics Anonymous* that the best time to approach someone is often when they have hit bottom, and this man had surely hit a terrible bottom.

When I telephoned him, he seemed nervous and reluctant to see me, but I reassured him my intent was friendly. He finally agreed, so I went to his home and expressed my love for him. I was slightly surprised to learn that several others had done the same. I then shared with him my story of sexual addiction and the recovery I was finding in attending Twelve Step meetings and studying the scriptures and the Twelve Step literature. I had taken with me a couple of books that had helped me a great deal, *He Did Deliver Me from Bondage* and the SA White Book, *Sexaholics Anonymous*. I was willing to give them to him for free, but he insisted on paying for them. I told him of the local Heart t' Heart support meetings, but he declined the invitation to attend, explaining that legal action against him was still pending, and he had to be careful about what he did in public that might influence that judgment (despite the fact that the identities of people who attend Heart t' Heart or any other Twelve Step meetings are kept strictly confidential). I encouraged him to read and study the materials I had brought, and then I left after expressing once more my love for him and my testimony that God could help him overcome his difficulties.

You can imagine my disappointment when, within a week, he called me back, saying he had to return the books. "I need the money more than I need the books," he claimed. He probably did need the money, since he had lost his job as a result of his actions, but in my mind I screamed, "No! There is nothing on earth you need more than *these* principles at *this* point in your life. They will help you find your Savior, who is your only hope!" But I said nothing; I simply returned his money and sadly took back the books. Shortly afterward I heard on the news that my friend had pleaded "not guilty" to the criminal charges against him. I suppose he was following what is the standard legal advice in situations like his, but I had to wonder if his plea also echoed an unreadiness to admit to himself, as well as to the court, the seriousness of his situation.

I said before that God allows us to share in His joy in bringing salvation to others. In a similar way, when we try to share this message with others, but the message is rejected, we partake of the sorrow He also feels. In an earlier chapter I quoted Enoch's experience of seeing God weep at the wickedness of His children. This passage touches me even more since I started doing Twelfth Step work.

> **And it came to pass that the God of heaven looked upon the residue of the people, and he wept...The Lord said unto Enoch: Behold these thy brethren; they are the workmanship of mine own hands... misery shall be their doom; and the whole heavens shall weep over them, even all the workmanship of mine hands; wherefore should not the heavens weep, seeing these shall suffer? (Moses 7:28, 32, 37)**

While we feel sorrow for those who do not accept the Savior's rescuing hand, this is a different sorrow from that which our own addiction caused. It is a purer sorrow, the sorrow of God, which causes us sadness but does not drag us down to despair. One fact that gives us hope is that hearing *our* testimony is probably not someone's last chance for repentance. Perhaps the person we seek to help is not ready to hear the message yet. That is okay. The Lord gives people more chances than one, and so must we. This may be true even of someone who begins the recovery process, even attends Twelve Step meetings with us for a while, but then "goes out there" again, surrendering once more to temptation. Our friend may want recovery, but may need to experience still more pain before he is willing to pay the required "price" of humility that opens the door to the Savior's grace. As Colleen has written:

No matter how afflicted I feel by sin, the greatest damage *any* sin or mistake can cause comes through resisting the lesson it could potentially teach me. When I do that, I remain in ignorance and can be sure that life (and God) will orchestrate another chance for me to learn it. In other words, I'll repeat the mistake. Learning good from evil is what this life is all about. It is one of God's main purposes in sending us here. (*He Did Deliver Me from Bondage*, 65, emphasis original)

When our friends slip or decline our offer of help, we can take comfort in knowing that we are not all God has to work with. Life will eventually teach what we could not. I believe the best motto pertaining to Twelfth Step work is, "Carry the message and let go of the results."

GIVE ALL CREDIT TO THE LORD

When someone with whom I have shared my story *does* take the message to heart and begins to make progress in breaking free from his addiction, I am faced with another temptation—pride! Pride is such a trap for me! It got me into addiction in the first place, it kept me from accepting the solution when I first heard it, and now, when I have begun sharing the blessings the Lord has given me in recovery, pride tempts me back into feelings of self-sufficiency or self-importance—and thus, alienation from God. I need to keep constantly before me the example of Ammon. He rejoiced in the success he and the other sons of Mosiah had in their missionary labors, but he quickly gave all the glory to God **(Alma 26)**. In doing Twelfth Step work, we must do the same. God is the *only* One who has the power to lift temptation or to change anyone's heart. As much as we desire to help, we can never fill the role of the Savior in our friends' recovery. This is the lesson of Step One: we must never forget our own powerlessness and God's omnipotence.

And in nothing doth man offend God, or against none is his wrath kindled, save those who confess not his hand in all things, and obey not his commandments. (D&C 59:21)

**He that receiveth of God, let him account it of God;
and let him rejoice that he is accounted of God
worthy to receive. (D&C 50:34)**

If I am blessed in any way, either in my own recovery or through
participating in someone else's recovery, it is vital that I give the credit
to God, knowing that all redemption comes only from Him. I am simply
grateful to God for letting me see it happen. I know I have no more
power to save anyone else than I had power to get myself out of my own
addiction in the first place.

HOW SHARING THE MESSAGE SUSTAINS
OUR OWN RECOVERY

I have many reasons for telling my story, and not all of them are
altruistic. Carrying this message does something for me. In bearing testimony of these principles, I am reminded of them myself. In bearing
witness of the change the Lord has brought about in my life, I am again
renewed and blessed in so many ways.

**And if thou draw out thy soul to the hungry, and
satisfy the afflicted soul; then shall thy light rise in
obscurity, and thy darkness be as the noonday: And
the Lord shall guide thee continually, and satisfy thy
soul in drought, and make fat thy bones: and thou
shalt be like a watered garden, and like a spring of
water, whose waters fail not. And they that shall be of
thee shall build the old waste places: thou shalt raise
up the foundations of many generations; and thou
shalt be called, The repairer of the breach, The
restorer of paths to dwell in. (Isaiah 58:10–12)**

Some have said that they have to give this message away in order to
keep it. I think that is probably true, but I also find deeper reasons. I
think of the story of the ten lepers Jesus healed. After they had shown
themselves to the priest, as their law required, only one returned to give
thanks, praising God for his healing. **"And Jesus answering said, Were
there not ten cleansed? but where are the nine?" (Luke 17:17).** I

cannot bear to be one of the nine. I must give thanks to God for His miracle in cleansing my life. I was unable to cleanse myself; it took the Lord's power. My recovery, therefore, is not my own, but His. Who am I, then, to hide it?

APPLYING THESE PRINCIPLES IN ALL OUR AFFAIRS

I have emphasized that the Lord wants to redesign our whole lives, not just our addiction. And as I have tried to live these principles, I have had to admit that my addiction was only a symptom of my disease. My attitudes toward life, others and God all needed to be transformed. That process continues in Step Twelve as we "practice these principles in all our affairs."

Some talk about people having an "addictive personality." I definitely fall into that category. I can see evidence for it even in my childhood. For example, as soon as I discovered sweets, I was hooked. I remember an occasion when I was in grade school when my father soundly reprimanded me for spending my whole allowance on candy. As soon as I was old enough to get a paper route, I routinely stopped at a little store to buy chocolate bars and orange sodas. One day the shopkeeper told me about a recent news report that said people could actually get addicted to chocolate. I must have already been adept at denial, for I quickly brushed aside his comment as irrelevant to myself.

I continued my love affair with junk food through my teens and twenties, blissfully free of any consequences (except for the deteriorating state of my teeth), because I seemed to be able to eat anything I wanted without gaining weight. Of course, my marvelous metabolism was a constant source of annoyance to my wife! But when I hit about thirty years of age, something changed, and I started to put on weight. Where my weight had stayed pretty close to 170 for years, now I began a gradual climb up the scale, until at age fifty, I weighed close to 235 pounds. I knew I should change my eating habits, but I was too used to finding comfort in the foods I loved. I stubbornly defended my right to eat whatever I wanted to, whenever I wanted to. After all, I wasn't *that* much overweight!

One day, after I had been working the Twelve Steps for about four years, something "clicked." An opportunity to try a new, healthier way of eating was presented to me, and while I had never in my life restricted what I ate, I somehow suddenly found myself willing to give it a try. I cut out cookies and cakes and ice cream and candy. I was amazed. I didn't even seem to mind doing without. This just wasn't like me; something was definitely different!

I think what I experienced was the fruit of those recent years of learning to surrender my will to the Lord in the area of sexual temptation. In surrendering sexual thoughts and desires, I was giving the Lord access to my heart, and He was changing it, bit by bit. I hadn't looked for anything but relief from the addiction to pornography that had made my life so miserable for so many years. But the truth is, my food addiction had also cost me. I was not as healthy as I could have been. My physical activities were limited by my weight. My self-esteem was definitely affected, even though I tried not to think about it. (Let's not even talk about my teeth!) The Lord knew the changes I needed, and once I gave Him permission to start on me, He just kept going!

This morning, as I write this, I weigh 195 pounds, down 35–40 pounds from my highest weight. It has been about twenty-five years since I passed this weight on the way up. That's a lot of years to spend with that much extra weight.

I don't mean to give the impression that I am now perfect. Far from it! I see the invitation of the Twelfth Step as a challenge to continue to turn my will over to the Lord in other ways. I don't have to look very hard to find areas where I am still reluctant to give Him full control over my life. Even with the eating, my surrender is better at some times than others. However, if I stay close to the Lord, day by day He continues to invite me to surrender my life to Him, and I am responding.

Perhaps the most important thing the Twelve Steps teach us is to be willing to examine our lives—our motives and our actions—with a willingness to hear the guidance of the Lord. It is my testimony that He cares for us more than we can comprehend, that He desperately desires our happiness, and that He will be there with each of us as we put ourselves in His care.

AND FINALLY WE ARE DONE—OR ARE WE?

Well, here we are at the end of Step Twelve. We have worked through our addiction, surrendered it to the Lord, and become free from its clutches. We have experienced a mighty change of heart and have become a new creature in Christ...or have we? If you are like me, maybe all these things haven't happened for you just because you've read this book all the way through. I know that my first reading of *He Did Deliver Me from Bondage* did not mark an instant end to my problem. I had to go back and read it again, and this second time, commit to doing all of the writing exercises I skipped over the first time through.

During my first exposure to the material, I was still so filled with shame and so unaware of the Savior's mercy and grace, that I couldn't even bear the thought of putting the word "pornography" down in black and white in my recovery journal. What if my children ever read it? Or my parents? What if I accidentally left my journal somewhere and someone—a colleague at work, a friend, or a member of my ward— found it and read it? After all, once it was written down, it was "out there" and I could no longer deny it or ignore it. But wait! That was the whole point of doing the writing, wasn't it, to get honest with myself? I had to get over that roadblock or I would never be able to do the writing that would help me examine the inner vessel of my heart and mind, and thereby begin to let the Lord cleanse it.

As I continued to wrestle with this predicament, I went ahead and kept reading the chapters on each of the steps. Somewhere along the path, as I began to understand the spiritual nature of addiction, my heart began to ache inside to do anything—*anything*—to be freed from my prison of shame. I finally allowed the Lord to whisper the solution to me, and it was so straightforward and simple, I should be embarrassed to admit how long it took me to face it. I'm not embarrassed, though, because I know each of you can empathize with my initial reluctance. Eventually, I accepted the promptings of the Spirit and prayerfully sought a time and situation where I could talk to each of my family members and even some of my closer friends. I told them of my years of imprisonment in the invisible clutches of addiction and my recent efforts to become free. To my surprise, they all reacted compassionately. No one gasped. None of them disowned me. I still continue to marvel in gratitude at their degree of patience and maturity.

Once I told my loved ones—especially my children—about my addiction, I felt free to begin writing my honest responses to the exercises provided in *He Did Deliver Me from Bondage*. Almost immediately, I began to experience the powerful tool that personal, heart-deep writing can be. Over the course of my recovery, it has become one of my surest channels of truth and personal revelation—so much so, I feel a need to conclude with a section on how I have learned to use writing in my recovery (see Appendix A). Believe me, I am very aware that I do not have any authority to tell you what you *have* to do to recover. All I can do is strongly suggest and plead with you: if you've read straight through *Clean Hands, Pure Heart* and have not done the writing exercises, *please* go back and start again. Please be willing to do the writing. It will open your heart and mind to receive the Lord's wisdom and the gift of a changed and blessed life.

I am amazed at how different I feel now than I did in the beginning, when I was so terrified of anyone learning about my secret life. Today I sit here, writing the final chapters of a book I actually hope and pray *everyone* will read and be blessed by. I have experienced a 180-degree turn from where I was before—a complete change of heart.

As I finish this effort to reach out to you, my beloved brothers and sisters, I feel the need to thank you for the joy it has brought to my heart to imagine your hope being rekindled by this message. If you were, or still are, like I was—convinced you are down for the count—may I hold out my lamp to light your path to reclaim your own innocence. I cannot loan you my oil, but I can hold my lamp high and invite you to come to Christ. The Lord has changed my life. He has given me back both clean hands and an ever-increasingly innocent and pure heart. He has restored my agency, restored me to sanity of the highest order, and given me a purpose—His own. The Prophet Joseph Smith said it so well:

Love is one of the chief characteristics of Deity, and ought to be manifested by those who aspire to be the sons of God. A man filled with the love of God [from Him and for Him]…ranges through the whole world, anxious to bless the whole human race. (*History of the Church*, 4:227)

I know He loves me, and I know He loves you. It is my constant prayer that you will seek Him, trust Him, and allow Him to recreate your life in His own image, beginning today and for the rest of your mortal life. I look forward to meeting you someday and rejoicing with you in the blessings the Lord has brought into our lives. I share all this with you in the sacred name of Jesus Christ, amen.

ONE FINAL INVITATION

I have placed in Appendix A the most important tools of recovery that have helped me in coming unto Christ. I have referred to most of them previously in this book. However, let me invite you to read through it as one final hug from me. May God bless you in your continuing journey of recovery.

MAKING THE MOST OF THIS CHAPTER

Please take time to answer the following questions in your recovery journal.

1. One description of the "mighty change of heart" is given in the following passage: **"Behold, he changed their hearts; yea, he awakened them out of a deep sleep, and they awoke unto God. Behold, they were in the midst of darkness; nevertheless, their souls were illuminated by the light of the everlasting word"** (Alma 5:7). Write about your own awakening "unto God." Has your soul been "illuminated by the light of the everlasting word?" What changes do you see in your life to this moment?

2. We can learn many wonderful recovery principles from our hymns. Contemplate the message of Hymn no. 219, and write in your journal how this hymn applies directly to you:

> *Because I have been given much, I too must give;*
> *Because of thy great bounty, Lord, each day I live*
> *I shall divide my gifts from thee with ev'ry brother that I see*
> *Who has the need of help from me.*

Write about your gratitude to the Lord and about your desire to share the gift of recovery with others.

3. In **Mosiah 27:36–37** we read, **"And thus they were instruments in the hands of God in bringing many to the knowledge of the truth, yea, to the knowledge of their Redeemer. And how blessed are they! For they did publish peace; they did publish good tidings of good; and they did declare unto the people that the Lord reigneth."** Copy this verse into your journal and capture from it. What does it mean to "publish peace?" What are the "good tidings of good?" What good tidings do you have to publish?

4. Sharing the message of your personal recovery from sexual addiction requires great sensitivity to the Spirit. Write about any experiences you have had in feeling prompted to share your story with others. Write about the importance of having the confirmation of the Spirit before sharing your experiences.

5. Most of us who have sought to reform some area of our lives have had the experience of taking a class or participating in a program that was helpful while we were involved in it, but which lost its effectiveness in our lives once the class was over. Write about your plans to retain the blessings you have experienced so far through participating in gospel principles represented in the Twelve Steps as you seek to "practice these principles in all [your] affairs."

Epilogue

There is no way I could begin to express the joy and peace God brought into my life when He gave me Phil Harrison as a companion. I was not around for those early, developmental years of his life, but I am assured Phil has not always been as spiritually mature (Christ-like) as he is now. Thus, it has been a great blessing to me to read his story and to observe the changing of his heart in *Clean Hands, Pure Heart.*

I didn't even know Philip Harrison existed until his wife, Kathy introduced us. I had only known her for about two weeks, when she brought Phil to a Heart t' Heart meeting at my home in Logan, Utah. I was up to my eyebrows in doctoral classes at Utah State University, still dealing with tidal waves of aftereffects from the tragic circumstances surrounding the demise of my first marriage, nine years before. Believe me, I had absolutely no inkling that I was meeting the two people who would do more to change my life for the better than anyone else I've ever known.

Over the next four months, Phil and Kathy would linger after every Heart t' Heart meeting, and the three of us would talk for hours about the Twelve Step program, the Gospel, our life stories, our children's unfolding lives, and a dozen peripheral subjects. Our hearts were singing in perfect harmony with each other. I knew I had found forever friends.

Kathy and Phil were so cute together. There was such an aura of unity and "perfect-fit" about them. Through all my years in the church, I have only met two or three other couples who radiated such a spirit of enjoyment and adoration of each other. I could tell that in the nearly thirty years these two people had been married, they had become truly married—truly one in heart. Everyone who attended our Heart t' Heart group felt the energy they shared and it blessed all of us with a resurgence of faith in the principle of marriage.

Then came the fateful day when, returning home from teaching summer classes at the university, I heard a very subdued message on my voice mail. The speaker was obviously in shock. "Colleen, I thought you'd want to know that Kathy collapsed at work yesterday. She's in intensive care, and the doctors aren't giving her much hope. Oh, this is Phil, Phil Harrison. I thought you might want to come see her soon."

Even as I write these words, tears well up in my eyes. I will never forget the power of the Lord that swept through me and carried me to the hospital that afternoon. That Divine influence never left me throughout the entire next week, during which Kathy left this life, but not before she appeared to both Phil and I in the eyes of our understanding—completely unbeknown to each other—to convey to each of us her wish that we remain together and marry as soon as possible

We were both stunned and maybe even a little terrified—well, maybe a lot terrified—by the social and emotional implications of our separate witnesses from Kathy. She seemed so adamant, so certain and even excited to leave the two of us together. It seemed to bring her great joy. Knowing Kathy and her generous heart, neither of us were surprised that even in death she would be thinking of others, wanting to give us both the gift of her blessing. And that is how our interpretation of her excitement and joy has continued for the six years since then—until now—until the publishing of *Clean Hands, Pure Heart*. As this book comes forth, bearing Phil's name, it represents not only his testimony and his recovery, but mine and Kathy's also. I know she had this hope in mind when she left us together. It wasn't just us she hoped to bless. It was each of you, as well, dear readers. We all have cause to call her name blessed. In her behalf, I take the liberty of signing this epilogue for both of us.

—Kathleen Francis Harrison

—Colleen C. Harrison

Appendix A

Some Important Tools

Contents of Appendix A

In this appendix I will describe some practices that have helped make recovery real in my life. I pray these practices and principles will help to awaken you to the goodness and grace of Christ and thus open the door to a personal relationship with God that will change your heart and life forever.

TOOL 1: CAPTURING—GETTING THE MOST FROM THE SCRIPTURES AND OTHER SOURCES

As I have said before, I spent most of my life reading the scriptures (if I read them at all) as if they were a dreaded school assignment. My goal was to get the job done, whether I internalized anything or not. Each day I'd fulfill my "assignment" to read a certain number of chapters or to read for a certain length of time. While I became acquainted with many of the stories and general teachings in the scriptures, I seldom related to them personally or saw how they applied in my day-to-day life. Reading them was all about doing my duty and appearing to myself and to others to be a faithful Latter-day Saint. Sadly, this way of approaching the scriptures didn't teach me to love them or to find joy and salvation through them.

The way I perceived the scriptures changed forever when I read *He Did Deliver Me from Bondage* and learned a method of studying called "capturing." Here is the explanation of capturing that Colleen provided her readers:

What Is Capturing?

What does "capture" mean? It means to get hold of something, really get hold of it, and make it your own. Here's how you capture thoughts from any source.

1. If your source is in the form of written material, underline the words or phrases that stand out to you. If it's in the form of a lecture, take notes as you listen. (Remember, taking notes is not the same as taking dictation. The goal is not to recreate every word the speaker says. The goal is to note those single thoughts that stand out to you.)

    Most people think that this is the entire procedure, that this constitutes "capturing." Sorry. This is only the step of identifying what it is that you want to capture. (If you were an old-time cowboy and were sitting up on a ridge watching a herd of wild mustangs below you, just picking out the ones that look good to you is not the same as making them your own.)

2. Get a notebook of some sort (maybe a journal) and a pen and then rewrite the words, phrases, sentences or whatever you underlined or noted into that notebook. When I copy quotes, I usually underline them as well as put quote marks around them so they stand out from the rest of what I write.

    Now are you done? After all, you have written the thought down in your own notebook or journal. Sorry, this still does not make it your own. There is a third and final step. Without this last step you are only a collector of thoughts, not a captor.

3. Now write all that comes into your mind about the thought or quote that you have previously copied into your notebook. Why was it important to you? How did it connect for you? What does it say to you? How do you see that it applies to your life? This is capturing.

    For me, this process of capturing thoughts, scriptures and quotes has also become a way of praying. I often find that I have just naturally entered into a prayer mode somewhere during this process, writing prayerful thoughts, expressing myself directly to God. And in just as easy and simple a manner I nearly always find myself realizing that what I am hearing in my thoughts is the voice of the Lord, through the Holy Spirit's mediation, speaking to my mind and heart. (Colleen C. Harrison, *He Did Deliver Me from Bondage*, A–3, 4)

At first I resisted Colleen's suggestion about capturing. It just seemed like too much effort. After all, it was taking me long enough to get through the scriptures as it was. If I stopped and wrote about everything I read, I would never get through them! What an amazing new perspective hit me, though, when I realized that maybe "getting through" the scriptures might not be the most important way to approach them.

When at last I agreed to **"experiment upon [the] word" (Alma 32:27)** and try capturing for myself, I was amazed with the results. While I had experienced *occasional* new insights into the scriptures before, now I began to see new applications and meanings in virtually every verse I captured! I found as I *prayerfully* wrote down the thoughts and impressions that came into my mind, I could not deny that a Power greater than my own was inspiring and teaching me.

Years have passed since my first attempt to believe in the tool of capturing. I have used it almost daily to allow the Spirit of the Lord to guide my thoughts and my life. In fact, it was while I was capturing **Psalm 24:3–8** that I was led to the title of this book. Since it is usually easier to grasp a concept if you can see an example of it, I would like to share that capturing with you. In this example, each phrase from the scriptures is in bold, followed by the thoughts that came to me as I opened my mind and heart to the Spirit of Truth.

Capturing on Psalm 24:3–8

Who shall ascend into the hill of the Lord? or who shall stand in his holy place? I love God. He represents my Home, and I desire to be with Him again in the eternities. Not all will receive that blessing, due to their choices in this life. How can I be sure to find myself among those who will go home to God and stand with Him in His holy place?

He that hath clean hands, Clean hands are a symbol of purity of action, of refraining from sin. However, since I, along with all of mankind, have sinned, clean hands must more accurately be a symbol of repentance, of willingness to have my hands cleansed of sin.

and a pure heart; My actions begin with my thoughts, and my thoughts spring from my innermost beliefs and desires—my "heart." I see the truth that if my desires are not pure, I have not fully repented, even if my actions are no longer sinful. Complete repentance will bring a remission of sin and a spiritual rebirth, with new thoughts and new desires—a new and pure heart.

who hath not lifted up his soul unto vanity, When I look at my years of addiction, vanity was at the root of it all. I have sought my own way and put my own opinion of happiness above God's infinite knowledge. If that is not vanity, what is?

nor sworn deceitfully. A person can't indulge in addictive behaviors and escape becoming a liar. I have to admit this was true for me. As I practiced my addiction, I lied constantly to myself. I minimized and excused my actions as not being *that bad.* I lied to others to keep them from finding out about my behavior. I also lied to myself about how much I was hurting myself and others.

He shall receive the blessing from the Lord, and righteousness from the God of his salvation. Recovery comes from the Lord. If there is any righteousness in my life, it is a gift from God. It is His power that enables me to abstain from my addictive behaviors. The Lord is the God of my salvation in every way. He not only forgives me when I repent, He also gives me the *power* to repent when I come to Him in humility.

This is the generation of them that seek him... How many in this generation are turning to Him, mainly because they find themselves trapped in the temptations of the world, and are coming to know that the only way out is through the Lord's grace (power)? They seek Him, as I have, first for their own healing, and then out of love for Him.

Lift up your heads, O ye gates; and be ye lift[ed] up, ye everlasting doors; and the King of glory shall come in. What are the gates and the doors that must be opened in order for the King of Glory to come in? They are the gates and doors of my heart! They are opened as I come unto Christ in deepest humility and surrender my bruised and broken will to Him.

Who is this King of glory? The Lord strong and mighty, the Lord mighty in battle. And what is the battle? The battle with Satan for my soul. The battle with addiction to reclaim my damaged agency. How can I serve God when my will is not my own—when I have surrendered it to my addiction (and thus to my adversary)? The Lord will restore me, and give me the victory, that I may in turn serve Him and my Father in Heaven in righteousness, all the days of my life, yea, even into Eternity.

How many times had I heard these beautiful words from **Psalm 24?** How many times had they been just that—beautiful—but not profound or life-changing? Capturing made them come alive and speak to my particular needs. By "pondering" the scriptures in this way, my study time has become a source of intimate one-on-one counseling with the Lord. Now, when the Spirit invites me to read in the scriptures, instead of responding, "No, I don't want to do that," I think "Yes. I would enjoy that. I love the scriptures." What a marvelous change!

TOOL 2: LIKENING THE SCRIPTURES UNTO OURSELVES

Another way I have learned to personalize the scriptures is to do what Nephi called "likening."

> **And I did read many things unto them which were written in the books of Moses; but that I might more fully persuade them to believe in the Lord their Redeemer I did read unto them that which was written by the prophet Isaiah;** *for I did liken all scriptures unto us, that it might be for our profit and learning.* **(1 Nephi 19:23, emphasis added)**

Nephi did not reserve this practice for himself only, as a prophet and teacher of his people. He pled with his people to liken the scriptures to themselves:

> **Hear ye the words of the prophet, which were written unto all the house of Israel, *and liken them unto yourselves*, that ye may have hope as well as your brethren from whom ye have been broken off; for after this manner has the prophet written. (1 Nephi 19:24, emphasis added)**

In other words, we will not get from the scriptures what *we* personally need if we read them merely as a historical record, or even as an account of how the Lord guided a people who lived and died ages ago. It is not only interesting to notice how their lives and experiences parallel our own, *it is essential.* The Lord Himself declared: **"What I say unto one, I say unto all" (D&C 93:49).**

Our modern leaders have taken up Nephi's plea. Consider the following suggestion from Elder Ronald E. Poelman of the Seventy:

> The prophet of this dispensation, Joseph Smith, and his companion Sidney Rigdon gave testimony of the gospel, as recorded in the 76th section of the Doctrine and Covenants. Each of us may receive *a similar* spiritual witness, and therefore I suggest that we may express their testimony as our own *in these words:*
>
> "And this is the gospel...That he came into the world, even Jesus, to be crucified for [me], and to bear [my] sins..., and to sanctify [me], and to cleanse [me] from all unrighteousness; That through him [I] might be saved" (D&C 76:40–42). (*Ensign*, Nov. 1993, 86; italics original)

When personalized, this single verse of scripture moves me to tears! Suddenly, it's not about someone else being loved by Jesus. It's about *me* and His willingness to rescue *me* from *my* sins! Looking back over my life, I can see the many times this message of personal redemption was presented to me, and I ignored it. Satan had me right where he wanted me, convinced that my sins were so bad I was beyond the Savior's atoning power. Likening the scriptures to myself turns the standard works into one-on-one counsel from the Lord to me. Using this tool has made the Savior's Atonement come alive *for me.*

Colleen expressed this personal approach to the Atonement as well. I could not deny the love of God I felt as I read the following example she gave of personalizing the scriptures:

> I began to understand that Christ doesn't atone for us all at once, *en masse.* He atones for us one person at a time; He cleanses us one heart at a time, and He loves us one at a time as choice and unique individuals...I still have a continuing struggle not to break into a rousing and unique version of Handel's "Messiah"...
>
> **For unto [*me*] a child is born, unto [*me*] a son is given; and the government [of my life] shall be upon his shoulder; and his name shall be called Wonderful, Counselor, The Mighty God, The Everlasting Father, The Prince of Peace. (2 Nephi 19:6; emphasis added)**
> (*He Did Deliver Me from Bondage,* 35–36)

I love these words—and I *know* they apply to me as well as they do to Colleen, Isaiah or anyone else.

TOOL 3: CONVERSING WITH THE LORD

As I took hold of these first two tools—capturing and likening the scriptures to myself—practicing them with faith in Christ and calling continually upon the Holy Ghost to guide my thoughts, I began to experience something I had never felt before in all my years as a member of God's true church. I felt encircled in God's *love.* I felt awakened to His perfect administration not only of justice, but also of mercy. I could feel myself being changed in this energy, this awakening. But what was I awakening to? Could this actually be the Lord "speaking" to me? Could this really be happening? I found my answer in the testimony of the Prophet Joseph Smith:

> It is the first principle of the Gospel to know for a certainty the Character of God, and to know that we may converse with him as one man converses with another. (*Teachings of the Prophet Joseph Smith*, 345)

But wait! Hadn't I read this quote before? Actually, I had read it many times through all the years I was struggling with my addiction. In the past, though, I had distanced myself from Joseph's testimony of the Lord's willingness to communicate so intimately—as one person would converse with another—assuming Joseph was referring only to prophets like himself. The famous promise of James led Joseph to the Sacred Grove. How did I miss its application to myself? After some experience with capturing and likening the scriptures to myself, I was ready to hear Joseph's words as they applied personally to me:

> **If...you lack wisdom, [Philip]...ask of God, that giveth to all men liberally, and upbraideth not [I won't scold you, Philip]; and it shall be given [you]. (James 1:5)**

Capturing and likening the scriptures to myself were teaching me the true character of God. They were teaching me that if I would come unto the Lord with faith that His ability to love and save me was greater than my ability to do wrong.

At these immensely important moments, these pivotal points in our progress, I am certain Satan senses what is about to happen, for he immediately tries to interfere. Thus he challenged me with the thought, *How can you expect the Lord of the Universe to pay attention to someone as lowly and broken as you are?!*

At first I found myself listening to those doubt-filled thoughts. How *could* I expect the Lord of the Universe...? But just as immediately, the Lord, through the Holy Ghost, whispered His own thoughts to me, reminding me of examples from the scriptures. During His mortal life, hadn't the Lord been willing to mingle and break bread with "publicans and sinners?" Wasn't He the Great Physician who sought out those who were sick, not those who were well **(Matthew 9:11–13)?** Instantly, I saw and I *knew* He felt the same compassion toward me as He had toward the sinners at the time of His mortal ministry! I saw that His mission was, and still remains, not to judge but to save us all—*including me!* Then came the remembrance of how He **"descended below all things" (D&C 88:6),** and I *knew,* by His own witness to my heart, that "all things" included *my* sins. As I turned to the scriptures, I was led to the following verse and felt it likened unto me in the most tender spirit:

> **He loveth [you, Philip], even that he layeth down his own life that he may draw [you] unto him. Wherefore, he commandeth none [not even you] that they shall not partake of his salvation. Behold, doth he cry unto any, saying: Depart from me? Behold, I say unto you, Nay; but he saith: Come unto me [Philip], buy milk and honey, without money and without price. (2 Nephi 26:24–25)**

With the promise of God's love for me burning in my heart, I decided to trust His promise and put it to the test. I decided to trust the Prophet Joseph's testimony and to attempt to "converse" with the Lord. This exercise of my faith has been deeply rewarded. I have learned for myself that He is, indeed, willing to talk with me. I have come to realize my lack of connection with Him all those years was because of my reluctance to approach Him, not because of any reluctance on His part.

Following the Prophets' Examples of Praying to the Father and Counseling with the Saviour

This idea of conversing or counseling directly with the Savior may seem as puzzling to you as it was to me at first. Like me, you may be wondering, *"I thought we were only supposed to pray to our Father in Heaven, not to the Savior."* That's true—the Lord Himself commands us to always pray to the Father in the name of Jesus Christ:

> **Behold, verily, verily, I say unto you, ye must watch and pray always lest ye enter into temptation; for Satan desireth to have you, that he may sift you as wheat. *Therefore ye must always pray unto the Father in my name;* And whatsoever ye shall *ask the Father in my name,* which is right, believing that ye shall**

receive, behold it shall be given unto you. *Pray in your families unto the Father, always in my name,* that your wives and your children may be blessed. (3 Nephi 18:18–21, emphasis added)

Nevertheless, at the same time, we are encouraged to develop a personal relationship with the Savior. Again, you may ask, as I did, *"How can I have a relationship with Jesus if I can't talk to Him?"* Indeed, how could we have a relationship with *anyone* we couldn't talk to? The truth is, we can talk with Him. We actually can! As we noted in studying Step Eleven, Brigham Young talked about our relationship with the Savior in very intimate terms, explaining our need to communicate *directly* with Him:

> The greatest and most important of all requirements of our Father in Heaven and of his Son Jesus Christ....is to believe in Jesus Christ, confess him, seek him, cling to him, make friends with him. Take a course to open a communication with your Elder Brother or file-leader— our Savior. (*Journal of Discourses,* vol. 8, 339)

Elder Bruce R. McConkie reserves the use of the word "prayer" to apply only to our communications with the Father, but it is clear from his own writing that he felt communication with the Son is an important part of the spiritual journey of the faithful:

> There is nothing clearer or plainer than this. We pray to the Father, not the Son; but according to the laws of intercession, advocacy, and mediation, our answers come from the Son...Righteous persons do have a close, personal relationship with their Savior. It is through him that forgiveness comes. Because of his atonement we may be free from sin. Salvation is in Christ. He pleads our cause. He is our Mediator and Intercessor. And we do and should sing praises to his holy name, as do the angels of God in heaven also...
>
> There is no language of worship and adoration that surpasses the language of prayer. What is more natural

than to use the noblest and most perfect expressions utterable by mortal tongues in addressing Him who sits upon the great white throne? It is no wonder, then, that in praising the Lord Jehovah we often do so as though we were addressing him in prayer, even as though we were pleading with him for eternal blessings. (*The Promised Messiah*, 335–6)

Nephi bore testimony of the sweet, tender relationship he had with Jesus and the marvelous communication he enjoyed with Him:

> **I glory in plainness; I glory in truth; I glory in my Jesus, for he hath redeemed my soul from hell...And if ye shall believe in Christ ye will believe in these words, for they are the words of Christ, and he hath given them unto me; and they teach all men that they should do good. (2 Nephi 33:6,10)**

Moroni's testimony is similarly plain and powerful. He further encouraged us to develop the same relationship with the Savior that he enjoyed.

> **And then shall ye know that I have seen Jesus, and that he hath talked with me face to face, and that he told me in plain humility, even as a man telleth another in mine own language, concerning these things...And now, I would commend you to seek this Jesus of whom the prophets and apostles have written, that the grace of God the Father, and also the Lord Jesus Christ, and the Holy Ghost, which beareth record of them, may be and abide in you forever. Amen. (Ether 12:39,41)**

Hearing these testimonies, how can we think that talking directly with the Savior would in any way offend Him or the Father? Don't the scriptures teach us they are one with each other in heart and mind? The Father is not jealous of any relationship we have with the Son, but is pleased when the Son is glorified **(Colossians 1:18–19)**. In modern times, Jesus has reaffirmed that the Father and He are one, and that we can also come to hear the Savior's voice:

> **And the Father and I are one. I am in the Father and the Father in me; and inasmuch as ye have received me, ye are in me and I in you. Wherefore, I am in your midst, and I am the good shepherd, and the stone of Israel. He that buildeth upon this rock shall never fall. And the day cometh that you shall hear my voice and see me, and know that I am. Watch, therefore, that ye may be ready. Even so. Amen. (D&C 50:43–46)**

I am truly amazed and humbled at the marvelous blessings that are open to us as soon as we are ready for them. It is also my witness that we don't have to wait for the day when we might be in the Savior's presence to "hear" His voice. It has been said that we *feel* the Lord's voice, more than literally *hear* it with our ears. Thus we can come to realize how the Holy Ghost whispers the Savior's own words into our mind and heart:

> **Yea, behold, I will tell you in your mind and in your heart, by the Holy Ghost, which shall come upon you and which shall dwell in your heart. Now, behold, this is the spirit of revelation. (D&C 8:2–3)**

I believe these promises. In fact, I have experimented upon the testimonies of the prophets and of the Lord Himself. I have found that being this close to the Savior in my mind (thoughts) and in my heart (feelings) is not only possible, but is the single most essential factor in my being able to stay sober from my addiction.

Of course, under the influence of the Savior's own example, as well as the prophets' admonition, I offer my formal prayers always to the Father. Following Elder McConkie's example, I have come to call the communication I hold with the Savior in my heart and mind "counseling with the Lord." As I counsel with Him, I "converse" and sometimes even "plead" or "cry out" unto Him in my heart, as Alma, the Younger did **(Alma 36:18)**. Validation for this direct, personal way of relating to the Savior is found in many scriptures of which the following are just a few:

> Teach them to withstand every temptation of the devil, with their faith on the Lord Jesus Christ...let all thy thoughts be directed unto the Lord; yea, let the affections of thy heart be placed upon the Lord forever. Counsel with the Lord in all thy doings, and he will direct thee for good. (Alma 37:33,36–37)

> Never, until I did cry out unto the Lord Jesus Christ for mercy, did I receive a remission of my sins. But behold, I did cry unto him and I did find peace to my soul. (Alma 38:8)

Another person who received "peace to his soul" through personal communication with the Savior was Oliver Cowdery, when he asked for a witness of the truth of the restored gospel. We don't have a record of Oliver's plea, but from the Savior's reply, it sounds as if Oliver addressed his original concerns directly to the Savior:

> Behold, thou art Oliver, and *I have spoken unto thee because of thy desires;* therefore treasure up these words in thy heart. Be faithful and diligent in keeping the commandments of God, and I will encircle thee in the arms of my love. *Behold, I am Jesus Christ, the Son of God*...Verily, verily, I say unto you, if you desire a further witness, cast your mind upon the night that *you cried unto me in your heart,* that you might know concerning the truth of these things. *Did I not speak peace to your mind concerning the matter?* What greater witness can you have than from God? (D&C 6:20–23, emphasis added)

Later in the same revelation, the Lord invited Oliver, as he invites us all, to "look unto me in every thought; doubt not, fear not" (D&C 6:36). What closer communication could we have with our Savior than to look unto Him in every one of our thoughts?

A particularly plain example of the interplay of prayer to the Father
and counseling with the Savior is seen in a letter Mormon wrote to his
son, Moroni. He first told Moroni of his constant prayers (to the Father)
for Moroni's welfare:

> **I am mindful of you always in my prayers, *continually***
> ***praying unto God the Father in the name of his Holy***
> ***Child, Jesus,* that he, through his infinite goodness**
> **and grace, will keep you through the endurance of**
> **faith on his name to the end. (Moroni 8:3, emphasis**
> **added)**

Mormon then said he had heard that Moroni's people were advo-
cating the baptism of little children. Mormon felt that this practice was
in error, so he counseled *with the Savior* about it:

> **For immediately after I had learned these things of**
> **you I inquired of the Lord concerning the matter. And**
> **the word of the Lord came to me by the power of the**
> **Holy Ghost, saying: Listen to the words of Christ,**
> **your Redeemer, your Lord and your God. Behold, I**
> **came into the world not to call the righteous but**
> **sinners to repentance; the whole need no physician,**
> **but they that are sick; wherefore, little children are**
> **whole, for they are not capable of committing sin.**
> **(Moroni 8:7–8)**

Mormon made a practice of praying to the Father, acknowledging
His supreme position as God over all, but when he needed specific
instruction on a point of doctrine, he went directly to the Savior for
advice. This is a perfect example of how both prayer to the Father and
counseling with the Lord Jesus Christ are appropriate spiritual
resources, available to us all. May these opportunities to commune with
heaven bless our individual lives as they have the lives of so many who
have gone before us.

TOOL 4: RECORDING THE WORD OF THE LORD IN OUR JOURNALS

Using our journals to record our lives is an admonition of the prophets that I, unfortunately, gave little heed to in my past. Once in a while I would take a stab at it, usually to record some momentous occasion like the birth of one of my children. But then, upon opening the nearly empty pages and seeing the years that had passed since the last entry, with all the catching up there was to do, I would become discouraged and overwhelmed again. Believe me, I could make a journal last for a *very long time.* My whole attitude about journal writing changed when I realized my journal was not just to be a diary of events, but the most significant part of my life. I needed to record my own *living* relationship with the Lord—even my own conversations with Him.

The Prophets' Witnesses About Writing

Writing is a powerful means of receiving revelation, one that has been used and recommended by men of God through the ages. The Lord has frequently instructed men to write the things which He has revealed to them.

> **The word that came to Jeremiah from the Lord, saying, Thus speaketh the Lord God of Israel, saying, Write thee all the words that I have spoken unto thee in a book. (Jeremiah 30:1–2)**

Elder Boyd K. Packer, in a suggestion to teachers in the Church, emphasized the importance of writing down inspiration in the moment it is given, before it can be forgotten. He testified that writing can even assist us during our prayers.

> The scriptural injunction to "treasure up in your minds continually the words of life, and it shall be given you in the very hour that portion that shall be meted unto every man" (D&C 84:85) has much significance for teachers of the gospel of Jesus Christ. Let your mind find constant employment in observation, in meditation, in prayer; then let your hand always be near a pencil and paper to

record the essentials of such preparation before they vanish as quickly and completely as time itself. (*Teach Ye Diligently*, 260–261)

Elder Richard G. Scott has taught the importance of learning to listen to the guidance from the Holy Ghost, and to record those promptings. He also emphasized that this is a learned skill that improves as we practice it.

> You can learn vitally important things by what you hear and see and especially by what you feel, as prompted by the Holy Ghost. Most individuals limit their learning primarily to what they hear or what they read. Be wise. Develop the skill of learning by what you see and particularly by what the Holy Ghost prompts you to feel. Consciously seek to learn by what you see and feel, and your capacity to do so will expand through consistent practice. Ask in faith for such help. Live to be worthy of it. Seek to recognize it. *Write down in a secure place the important things you learn from the Spirit. You will find that as you write down precious impressions, often more will come.* Also, the knowledge you gain will be available throughout your life....What you write down from the impressions you feel will be the most valuable help you can receive. (*To Acquire Knowledge and the Strength to Use It Wisely*, Brigham Young University, 23 January 2001, emphasis added.)

Hearing the Voice of the Lord Through the Holy Ghost

The way the Lord speaks to man is often described as a **"still small voice" (1 Kings 19:12, 1 Nephi 17:45, D&C 85:6).** Not only is His voice a quiet one, but it is usually communicated to us through impressions and thoughts rather than through our ears.

> **Yea, behold, I will tell you in your mind and in your heart, by the Holy Ghost, which shall come upon you**

and which shall dwell in your heart. Now, behold, this is the spirit of revelation. (D&C 8:2–3)

The Lord speaks to us through the ministrations of the Holy Ghost. It is an amazing arrangement that I did not previously understand. I always thought of any prompting I received as coming *from* the Holy Ghost, not *through* Him. I used the expressions we are all familiar with to refer to revelation: "I felt an impression from the Spirit that I should…" or even more plainly, "The Spirit told me…" Today, in humble awe, I appreciate the Holy Ghost's unique mission of complete "anonymity." When the Holy Ghost communicates with us, He does not speak for Himself, but rather conveys to us the words of Jesus Christ. The Lord testified of this when He told His apostles anciently:

Howbeit when he, the Spirit of truth, is come, he will guide you into all truth: for he shall not speak of himself; but whatsoever he shall hear, that shall he speak: and he will shew you things to come. He shall glorify me: for he shall receive of mine, and shall shew it unto you. (John 16:13–14)

Nephi also taught that the Holy Ghost conveys the words of Christ:

Do ye not remember that I said unto you that after ye had received the Holy Ghost ye could speak with the tongue of angels? And now, how could ye speak with the tongue of angels save it were by the Holy Ghost? Angels speak by the power of the Holy Ghost; wherefore, they speak the words of Christ. Wherefore, I said unto you, feast upon the words of Christ; for behold, the words of Christ will tell you all things what ye should do. (2 Nephi 32:2–3)

As I became aware of this reality about the relationship of the Holy Ghost and the Savior, I began to understand the promptings I felt as being **"the words of Christ"** (Alma 37:45, Moroni 8:7–8). Therefore, I began to record them in my journal in His voice. In this way, my written "meditation" has truly become a record of my two-way conversations with the Lord. In all humility, recognizing that this is truly "sacred ground" I am sharing, I feel led by the Spirit (that is, by the Lord) to include here a brief example of one of my "conversations" as I sought His help to overcome my addiction. I have written in italics what I perceived to be the Lord's words to me as they came into my mind.

November 12, Sunday, 7:20 a.m.

Good Morning, Dear Savior.

Yes, it is a good morning. It is always good when you counsel with me.

I had just the slightest bit of a hard time with my abstinence yesterday while I was in town. I was tempted to look at several women in a way I haven't done for a few weeks. Thank you for helping me to get out of that. I didn't realize I was in such danger of being tempted.

You will find that this gift of being able to withstand temptation will come and go as your contact with me increases and decreases. Stay close to me, and you will have the greatest protection.

I will try to do better. I see that I have let the rush of tasks over-whelm me again. I am so close to getting [a particular project] finished, and… I see, as I write this that none of my excuses for neglecting my time with you matter, do they?

I'm sure you've noticed that the adversary doesn't respect your excuses. In fact, he will use those situations to tempt you to think you don't have time for me. That is a very dangerous thought. Please don't let anything tempt you away from me for that is the temptation that leads to all others. It is, first of all, the time you spend with me that protects you. Then it is through remembering to call upon me throughout the day that you are protected in thought, and therefore, in action.

I see that the more time I spend with you, the greater my protec-tion. So if I, or any of my brethren, are having a hard time, the answer is to spend more time with you.

Yes, as long as it is really time with me. Time with the scriptures doesn't always represent time spent with me. Reading the scriptures can be just time spent, with no real benefit. Teach your brethren to make the scriptures come alive and be a bridge to me. That way, they can have access to my Spirit, which is the real source of power, instead of just going through the motions that make them feel they have done something "spiritual" without really being uplifted.

Using this most amazing gift has transformed my journals into "scripture" for myself—personal instruction as absolutely tailored to my personal daily needs as when the Lord told Lehi where they should hunt for food, or when He instructed Nephi how to build a ship to take them to the promised land. It is my testimony that the Lord does indeed speak to us when we give Him our full faith and attention. These writings are very sacred to me, and in a sense, have become my own personal extension of the scriptures, even in the same spirit as captured in this testimony:

> **And, behold, and lo, this is an ensample unto all those who were ordained unto this priesthood, whose mission is appointed unto them to go forth [and learn to live by every word that proceeds out of the mouth of God]—And this is the ensample unto them, that they shall speak [and write] as they are moved upon by the Holy Ghost. And whatsoever they shall speak [or write] when moved upon by the Holy Ghost shall be scripture, shall be the will of the Lord, shall be the mind of the Lord, shall be the word of the Lord, shall be the voice of the Lord, and the power of God unto salvation. Behold, this is the promise of the Lord unto you, O ye my servants. (D&C 68:2–5)**

Some of you may feel I am being too matter-of-fact or casual about conversing with the Creator of the Universe. Once again, may I assure you, I do not take these sacred things lightly or casually. Because of what I have experienced through these practices, I *know* God lives and He loves me, and the testimonies of the scriptures and of the modern prophets are true. I know He will turn away no one who hungers for His word, whether that word comes through the scriptures, through modern prophets, or through His own testimony whispered directly to one's heart and mind. I encourage you to use these principles of communion with the Lord for yourself, and I promise you that your walk with Him will become a *real and living* experience—not just a hope or a theory. You do not have to live on borrowed light.

Let me also emphasize that this was not a quick, nor an easy process for me. In addition to exercising faith in the Lord, I had to also believe in my own ability to hear the words of the Lord to me. At first I was full of doubt. I wondered if I was making all this up; after all, I hadn't heard any audible voice. All these "messages" from the Lord were merely in the form of "inspiration"—thoughts appearing in my mind. Often a thought would come that didn't have any specific words attached to it—I just had to express it the best I could in my own words. And sometimes the words I chose to express the Lord's thoughts didn't sound very much like the words I imagined the Lord would have chosen. Gradually, though—one conversation or dialogue at a time—I began to recognize this constant and ready flow of wisdom and counsel was not coming from within me. I could not deny that I was experiencing what the Prophet Joseph described as "pure intelligence flowing into [me]" (*Teachings of the Prophet Joseph Smith*, 151).

I want to bear my testimony that the Lord will guide each of us in this very personal way. He truly loves us enough to walk *and talk* with us every day through the Holy Spirit. His words to me have helped me immeasurably in the writing of this book as I have translated His counsel to me, a recovering sex addict, into my testimony to you. As individuals, we do not have the right to receive revelation for the Church as a whole or for other individuals, but we do have the right to be guided in our personal lives. It is my testimony that this guidance can be much more real than we have ever imagined.

Perhaps the greatest blessing of this kind of writing is coming to know, as I mentioned in the earliest chapters of this book, the *character* of God through personally experiencing His Spirit and His thoughts. In the words He whispers to my mind, I have felt a tenderness and a love I have longed for all my life, but never found in any other person—not my parents, not my best friends, not my wife. In His words to me, I have felt tremendous power, as well as tremendous love, compassion and patience. Those gifts of love have given me permission to have compassion and patience for myself. The negative, prodding, critical thoughts that tormented me for decades, that I mistakenly attributed to Him, have been washed away in the sweet, comforting reassurances of the love He has for me. My fear that I had a problem that would never be overcome has been washed away in the dawning awareness of His amazing, protecting power. I know without any doubt whatsoever, that my Lord, my Jesus, loves me enough to die for me. And the expression of this love is to me, **"most precious...sweet above all that is sweet, and...white above all that is white, yea, and pure above all that is pure" (Alma 32:42).** As Nephi said to the angel, **"The love of God... is the most desirable above all things."** And the angel replied, **"Yea, and the most joyous to the soul" (1 Nephi 11:22–23).** This has also become my witness. Through this marvelous gift—the feelings I have received through communing with the Lord in my journal—I have also come to *know* the profound and personal love that He has for me, He also has for you, my beloved friend.

I pray we may all come to know this love, for it is the most exalting experience I have ever had. I know that the Lord loves each and every one of us, and He will give to all of us these same blessings, as we apply the saving principles of the gospel in our lives and seek this same Jesus of whom the prophets have testified, and of whom I also testify, in the holy name of Jesus Christ, amen.

Thank you, my dear friend, for sharing this journey with me. It has truly been one of the greatest joys of my life. I look forward to meeting you one day, whether in this life or the next, and listening to you share with me the miracles the Savior has brought to pass in your life. Until then, may God be with us all.

MAKING THE MOST OF THIS APPENDIX

One last time, please write about the following questions in your recovery journal. I hope this journal has become a dear friend to you by now. I also hope that the practices of capturing from the scriptures and examining yourself through writing will continue with you throughout your life.

1. If you read the section on capturing when you were first referred to it in the assignment at the end of Chapter Two, you've known about this very helpful practice for some time now. I hope it has been a blessing in your life already. Whether you have already started using capturing or not, please turn to **2 Nephi 33** and use it as an exercise in capturing. It is only 15 verses long, but it is rich with insights and will give you much to think about.

2. Copy **2 Nephi 10:23–25** into your journal, likening each phrase to yourself. Read **2 Nephi 11:8,** then write about your feelings on applying the scriptures to yourself.

3. In the scriptures we read the Savior's invitation: **"Listen to him who is the advocate with the Father, who is pleading your cause before him—Saying: Father, behold the sufferings and death of him who did no sin, in whom thou wast well pleased; behold the blood of thy Son which was shed, the blood of him whom thou gavest that thyself might be glorified; Wherefore, Father, spare these my brethren that believe on my name, that they may come unto me and have everlasting life" (D&C 45: 3–5).** Jesus is our advocate with the Father, and as such, He prays for us. Write the words that you can imagine Jesus praying to the Father in your behalf. How do you feel about Him being a spokesman for you?

4. In Matthew, we read of Jesus' willingness to eat with "sinners and publicans." **"And it came to pass, as Jesus sat at meat in the house, behold, many publicans and sinners came and sat down with him and his disciples. And when the Pharisees saw it, they said unto his disciples, Why eateth your Master with publicans and sinners? But when Jesus heard that, he said unto them, They that be whole need not a physician, but they that are sick. But**

go ye and learn what that meaneth, I will have mercy, and not sacrifice: for I am not come to call the righteous, but sinners to repentance" (Matthew 9:10–13). Write about how willing you feel Jesus is to spend time personally with you. What do you picture He would talk with you about if you were eating a meal together? Can you picture Him talking with you about more than just your sins?

5. Write one more letter to Jesus, expressing your gratitude for what He has done for you. Talk to Him about your hopes and dreams. What impressions do you receive that you think could be from Him? You may want to practice recording those impressions in His "voice," spoken directly to you. (Review the model for this practice found in **D&C 121,** where Joseph prays and the Lord answers.)

Appendix B

Helps for a Personal Recovery Program

Contents of Appendix B

MAKING A STEP FOUR INVENTORY

Step 4: Made a searching and fearless moral inventory of ourselves.

Many people struggle with Step Four. Part of that struggle is the challenge of getting rigorously honest with one's self and facing the truth about the wrongs one has done. This is a scary proposition, hence the encouragement to be "fearless." Often, to avoid some of our fear, we are tempted to go a little too easy and minimize our wrongs, hence the word "searching." Here again, in Step Four, as in all the steps, it will take a super-human effort to face the job and get it done. We will have to pray for the grace (power) to keep plugging away at this "good work."

You may be willing to face the fear and do your inventory but are wondering about the simple "mechanics" of doing it. You are ready for some suggestions on just how to do it. Hopefully this article will provide you with some basic directions so you can get started and not become bogged down in the middle.

1. First of all, write your inventory as briefly as possible. Make it a list, not a story.

2. Don't include specific details that may trigger you. The purpose of this inventory is to haul the garbage out so we can take it to the dump, not so we can simply sort through and rearrange it.

3. It's not necessary to use complete sentences, or even complete words. If abbreviating or using "code words" helps you get the whole truth down on paper, use them. The purpose of your inventory is to put you (not anyone else) in conscious contact with the reality of your past, so do whatever works for you and makes it possible to accomplish this step.

The Time–Table Inventory Approach

What you are trying to discover in this process is not just the events of your lives that trouble you, but also why you did those things. If you are prayerful in writing this record, you will succeed in **"bringing to light all the hidden things of darkness" (D&C 123:13),** and discover the character faults that preceded your actions. It may help you remember them better if you divide your life up into time segments. I used a format like the one on the following page.

Of course, I'm just providing a brief example in each time period. I'm sure you will think of many more events to complete your inventory. Notice, however, these are not just sex-related offenses, although those are included. The patterns of deceit and disobedience show up in more areas of my life than just my sexual behavior. When I look at other events in my life, I see how I have rebelled against God and refused to take His counsel in my life, whether conveyed to me through my parents, Church leaders or through the Holy Ghost. This deeper exam- ination helps me to see what character traits were motivating my misdeeds and thus need to be surrendered in Steps Six and Seven.

If this format seems like it will be helpful to you, I have included a blank copy on page 280. You may want to photocopy and enlarge it to the size of your journal pages for easier writing or create a similar form of your own. If you write your inventory on a computer, you may want to secure the file with a password to protect your privacy. You may decide to destroy your list after you have finished working through Step Five, or you may want to keep it until you have finished working through Steps Eight and Nine, as it will help you in identifying people to make amends to.

May God bless you in this exercise. It may be challenging, but I promise you it will be worth it. Writing down a personal inventory and then using it as a guide in admitting our past to another living person is a very liberating experience. I wish you well with your own adventure.

Sample Personal Inventory		
Age	Event	Negative Character Trait(s)
0–5 years old	Ran away when it was time for chores	Laziness, self-will
Grade School	Played "doctor" with neighborhood children	Disobedience, enticed by curiosity
	Took lunch money to store instead of eating at school as instructed by Mom, then lied about it	Theft, sneaking, disobedience, lying
Junior High	Began masturbating	Disobedience, secrecy, drawing into myself (self-pity)
	First exposure to pornography	More secrecy, hiding from parents, seeking the "forbidden" (self-will)
High School	Tried to date as many girls as possible	Used girls to bolster ego (pride) Began to see women as objects to be used for my purposes (insensitivity)
	Inappropriate behavior on dates	Used girls for my own thrills (pride), ignoring their feelings (insensitivity)
Early College	Dating behavior continued	Saw girls as conquests, victories (insensitivity)
Mission	Stayed out past curfew to attend ward party	Disobedience of mission rules (self-will); thinking I knew better than the mission president what was best (pride)
22–30 years	Started using pornography again	Disobedience—knew much more clearly that it was wrong— rebellion against God
		Continued to objectify women
and so on...		

Personal Inventory Form		
Age	Event	Negative Character Trait(s)

STEP SIX INVENTORY OF CHARACTER DEFECTS

We inventory our character flaws in Step Six so we can surrender them to the Lord in Step Seven. President Benson said pride was at the root of all other sins, so we can expect to see pride show up on our list with some regularity. Pride can take many disguises, and part of our task is to discover those disguises. Self-will, self-pity, and self-rightness (self-righteousness) are all expressions of pride. When faced with a challenge, self-will says, "I don't want this," self-pity says, "I don't like this," and self-rightness says, "I don't need this." Inventorying these feelings can help us identify how our wants and feelings dominate our thinking. In the example in the previous section on Step Four, I demonstrated identifying some of these "self"-absorbed attitudes in my own inventory.

Here are some further questions to help you identify patterns in your character. These traits usually fall into either an "aggressive" pattern or a "fearful" pattern. Aggressive traits often express themselves in controlling, dominating behavior, while fearful traits manifest as expressions of codependency—intimidation by others, feelings of self-pity and efforts to manipulate others by playing the needy person or victim.

Questions That Relate to Aggressive Traits
- Do I always have to be right?
- Do I have to win every argument?
- Do I manage things so I always get my way?
- Do I frequently play the hero?

Questions That Relate to Fearful/Codependent Traits
- Do I think things are usually my fault?
- Do I give in against my better judgment?
- Do I always put my desires last?
- Do I frequently play the martyr?
- Do I frequently play the victim, blaming others for my actions?

CODEPENDENCY

SUGGESTIONS FOR THE ADDICT AND HIS OR HER FAMILY

Early in the study of alcoholism it was discovered that family members of alcoholics often manifest a number of dysfunctional characteristics of their own, usually as a result of living with addiction. Their fear *for* the addict or *of* the addict can twist and distort a loved one's thinking and cause a ripple effect throughout the entire family system. While the addict is "hung up" on drugs or alcohol, loved ones can become "hung up" on the addict. Many people refer to this phenomenon as codependency.

Even after the addict becomes sober, loved ones may still be trying to deal with their own reactions to the trauma they experienced during the fearful years. Thus loved ones often need to do some recovery work of their own. The following thoughts might prove helpful to those who have lived or still live with addiction.

Many of us deal with feelings of unworthiness and emptiness that began in a difficult or abusive relationship with a practicing addict. Some of us were raised in families where addictive compulsive behaviors were manifest in alcoholism, drug addiction, workaholism or perfectionism. In some families the addiction was compulsive spending, gambling or raging. Some of us experienced sexual abuse, the result of another's most hideous compulsion. Others of us were subjected to the effects of these same addictive compulsive behaviors during our adulthood by either a spouse or a child.

In reaction to these circumstances we have learned to *endure* life rather than to *live* life. We have developed personality characteristics which act as coping mechanisms. These mechanisms, while at one time protective, prove to be detrimental to forming healthy relationships. Some of these characteristics are:

1. We assume responsibility for other's feelings and/or choices.

2. We have difficulty identifying our own feelings: happiness, pain, anger, joy, sadness, loneliness, etc.

3. We have difficulty expressing our feelings in healthy ways.

4. We tend to fear that our feelings or needs will be belittled or rejected by others.

5. We tend to minimize, alter or even deny the truth about our feelings or needs.

6. We tend to put other's feelings and needs ahead of our own, not allowing there to be a healthy balance with our feelings and needs.

7. Our fear of other's feelings (especially anger) determines what we say and do.

8. Our serenity and attention is determined by how others are feeling or by what they're doing.

9. We do not realize that feelings are not good or bad, that they just are.

10. We question or ignore our own conscience, our own values, in order to connect with significant others—trusting and obeying their feelings or opinions more than our own.

11. Other people's actions or desires tend to determine how we respond or react.

12. Our sense of self-worth is based on other/outer influences instead of on our personal witness of God's love and esteem for us.

13. We have difficulty making decisions and are frightened of being wrong or making a mistake.

14. We are perfectionistic and place too many expectations on ourselves and others.

15. We are not comfortable acknowledging good things about ourselves and tend to judge everything we do, think, or say as not being good enough.

16. We do not know that it is okay to be vulnerable and find it difficult, almost impossible, to ask for help.

17. We do not see that it is okay to talk about problems outside the family, thus we leave ourselves and our families stranded in the troubles they are experiencing.

18. We are steadfastly loyal—even when that loyalty is unjustified and often personally harmful to us.

19. We have to be needed in order to have a relationship with others.

Applying the principles found in the Twelve Steps to our daily lives and relationships can bring us a sense of balance and sanity and free us from these destructive characteristics. Each of us is growing at our own individual rate as we learn to relate correctly with our Heavenly Father and our Savior. In recovery, we have come to realize that our relationship with God is the most important one of all and must be functioning well before any other relationship will function.

No matter how traumatic your past or how despairing your present may feel, there is hope in these principles for a new way of life. Through living these principles and concepts, we guarantee you will find the strength within to be what God intended you to be—precious and free.

"Fearing [Others] More Than God"
An Ancient Problem

"Fearing man more than God" is a universal malady. Many people who are successfully recovering from addiction have discovered that this tendency to depend on other fallible mortals—parents, spouses, children—for validation and comfort was actually the root of their need to practice their addiction.

Down through the ages the prophets have counseled us repeatedly to "fear"—respect, need, or rely on—God before anyone else. President Ezra Taft Benson stated this concept very clearly:

> We should put God ahead of *everyone else* in our lives."
> (*Ensign*, May 1988, p. 4; italics original)

Three years later, Elder L. Tom Perry made another plain statement of this true principle:

> If we increase our dependence on anything or *anyone* except the Lord, we will find an immediate decrease in our freedom to act. (*Ensign,* November 1991, p. 65; emphasis added)

Scripture study shows that reliance on man rather than God is actually a confusion of agency, or as some people say, "boundaries." Where does our stewardship or responsibility for another person end and their stewardship or responsibility begin? Just whose salvation do we have the power or ability to "work out?"

The following is a partial list of scriptures which examine these issues and support this concept:

Fearing Man More Than God:

Psalms 3:1–3	Psalms 27: 1,3	Jeremiah 1:8
2 Nephi 8:7	D&C 3:7	D&C 5:21

Confusion of Boundaries:

Matthew 13:21	Gal. 6:4–5	Alma 29:4
Helaman 14:30–31	Ether 12:37	D & C 1:11

Traditions of Our Parents:

Psalms 27:10	Matthew 19:29	Alma 30:25
Helaman 16:20	D & C 123:7	Moses 6:54

Excerpted from the pamphlet, "Speaking Heart t' Heart on Codependency." Reprinted with permission from Heart t' Heart General Service Board.

SEX, LOVE AND LUST IN MARRIAGE

If we have become entrapped in addiction to pornography or other forms of sexual acting out, we shouldn't be surprised if intimate relations in our marriage have also been affected. It is impossible to listen to and follow the lies about sexuality that have led us into addiction, and not have *all* areas of sexual activity contaminated by those lies. While a whole book would be required to properly address this sensitive topic, I hope to give a few thoughts that you may find helpful in examining this important part of your life.

I don't think I have talked with a single addict who didn't think getting married would solve his sexual addiction. After battling with the temptation to use sex in unsanctioned ways, the addict sees marriage as a "legal" outlet for his desires and urges. The truth is, marriage does not give us a *carte blanche* sexual arrangement with our spouse. We must be constantly on our guard against the temptation to think of sex primarily as a means of having our own personal needs met. That is merely a continuation of the selfishness that is the hallmark of addiction.

A healthy sexual relationship must be approached from the perspective of a union between two people, each with their own feelings, needs and background. The feelings of the spouse must never, never be overlooked, discounted or minimized in any way. President David O. McKay expressed this concern for women in marriage when he counseled the brethren to avoid the "breaking of women's hearts." He said:

> Let us instruct…young men throughout the Church, to know that a woman should be queen of her own body. The marriage covenant does not give the man the right to enslave her, or to abuse her, or to use her merely for the gratification of his passion. Your marriage ceremony does not give you that right.
>
> Second, let them remember that gentleness and consideration after the ceremony is just as appropriate and necessary and beautiful as gentleness and consideration before the wedding.
>
> Third, let us realize that manhood is not undermined by the practicing of continence, notwithstanding what some psychiatrists claim. Chastity is the crown of beautiful womanhood, and self-control is the source of true manhood, if you will

know it, not indulgence. Sexual indulgence whets the passion, and creates morbid desire.

Let us teach our young men to enter into matrimony with the idea that each will be just as courteous and considerate of a wife after the ceremony as during courtship. (Conference Report, April, 1952, 86–87)

Brethren, it is clear that we have been admonished not to force or coerce a spouse into sex. I think we need to look at our actions very closely. Are there ever times when we push the issue, even if our spouse has expressed a desire not to have sex? That expression of reluctance may be more forceful or less so, but we must always listen. A small "no" is still a "no," and we must respect it.

In examining our attitudes toward sex and our spouse, let me share with you some thoughts a friend shared with me, addressing the existence of lust within the bounds of the marriage relationship:

From the viewpoint of an addict, the need for arousal, desire, and passion, and their expression in the way we want to express them, makes it nearly impossible to see what God wants, what His limits are on sexual desire; or even that it is possible to meet such strict limits.

As I have been willing to accept God's will for me, He has asked me to identify a lot of things as lust that I would have thought were crazy before. I am learning that lust covers a great deal of ground. Though I thought I was okay in my desire and passions, they really were not okay. They were only lustful to a lesser degree than what I thought was over the line.

This is how it works for me:

- Arousal, desire, or passion caused by anyone or anything other than a *love* and *appreciation* for my wife is lustful.

- Arousal, desire, or passion that is purely physical, even if it is centered on my wife, is lustful.

- Arousal, desire, or passion that is *mostly* physical, even if it is centered on my wife, is lustful.

- Arousal, desire, or passion that is focused on me, on fulfilling my desires, is lustful.

- Arousal, desire, or passion that cannot be given up without resentment when it is right for me to give it up, is lustful.
- Arousal, desire, or passion that seeks after fireworks is lustful.
- Arousal, desire, or passion that cannot be satisfied with anything less than climax is lustful.
- Arousal, desire, and passion themselves are not lustful, but they must be rooted in charity and gratitude to be free from lust.
- Arousal, desire, or passion that seeks after emotional and spiritual union and enhancement of love is not lustful.
- Arousal, desire, or passion that can be satisfied by a loving look or word or non-sexual touch is not lustful.
- Arousal, desire, or passion are to be kept within the bounds the Lord has set, which are surprisingly strict, from the perspective of a hopeless addict like me.
- The bounds the Lord has set around arousal, desire, or passion are merciful in their strictness, from the perspective of having lived within them, for only within these bounds can I find complete intimate union with my precious wife, where God blesses and magnifies that union.
- Arousal, desire, or passion that is hyper, impatient, or superficially intense is lustful; whereas arousal, desire, or passion that is calm, patient, and intense in profound immersion in love and gratitude is not.

None of this means that there can be no excitement, and that there can be no intensity, but only that I do not direct the flow of arousal, desire, or passion; but that I give the direction and expression of that flow entirely to God.

This is how one sex addict found balance in addressing the issue of lust in marriage. Each person or couple will have to evaluate these thoughts for themselves. Prayerful counsel with our Heavenly Father will help each of us to develop appropriate sexual attitudes and behaviors.

USING OUTSIDE SUPPORTS

From the beginning, when God provided Adam with a companion, it has been one of the basic realities of human life: **"it is not good [to] be alone" (paraphrasing Genesis 2:18).** We all need help and support to get through the trials life presents us. Nowhere is this more true than in the daunting task of overcoming addiction. As the scripture says:

> **Two are better than one; because they have a good reward for their labour. For if they fall, the one will lift up his fellow: but woe to him that is alone when he falleth; for he hath not another to help him up. (Ecclesiastes 4:9–10)**

Throughout this book, I have tried to stress with all the energy of my soul that we each must come directly to Heavenly Father and to the Savior for the ultimate degree of support and fellowship we can ever hope to receive. Nevertheless, I am still very aware that the most significant and powerful way that God works in our lives, after personal revelation given directly and individually to each of us, is through the support and fellowship of other God-centered, believing mortals. Since, as we seek direction from the Lord, He often guides us to other resources, I would like to share a few thoughts along these lines.

BE SURE EXTERNAL SUPPORTS ARE GOD–CENTERED

We need to be prayerful and seek His guidance to know what external aids to our recovery will be best for us. We need to think of Him as our "Primary Physician"—the one who oversees our recovery and who also refers us to other resources. We can be sure that whatever aids we find, whether they include friends, Twelve Step meetings, Internet filters, reporting software, professional counselors or priesthood leaders—they will only be lastingly helpful if they encourage us to seek divine guidance and empowerment in overcoming our addiction.

> **Wherefore, all things which are good cometh of God; and that which is evil cometh of the devil; for the devil is an enemy unto God, and fighteth against him continually, and inviteth and enticeth to sin, and to do that which is evil continually.**

> But behold, that which is of God inviteth and enticeth to
> do good continually; wherefore, every thing which inviteth
> and enticeth to do good, and to love God, and to serve him,
> is inspired of God. (Moroni 7:12–13)

I would like to share some thoughts concerning the advantages of several of these resources, as well as some cautions for each one.

TWELVE STEP RECOVERY GROUPS AND SPONSORS

Advantages: We often hear the expression "support" groups, but I feel that when a Twelve Step group functions as it is meant to—directing its participants to seek healing power from God—it becomes far more than a "support" group. It becomes a "recovery" group. While support groups can put us in touch with others dealing with a problem similar to our own, so we don't feel so alone, recovery doesn't come from such social support. In Twelve Step recovery groups, we will find not only others with whom we can relate, but also others who are progressing in recovery and can show us the path they have taken that has led them to abstinence. Group members with more experience can point out the pitfalls we're likely to face in our early (and usually half-hearted) efforts at recovery. As we progress in recovery and gain sobriety, Twelve Step groups offer us a place where we, in turn, can help others who are new and struggling.

Cautions: Some have raised the concern that support groups only help us feel better, in that we are no longer alone, but do not require us to progress beyond that point. The addict may allow himself to be content, now that the pain of isolation has lessened. He may not feel the need to progress all the way to total abstinence. This depends on the group and on the desires of the individual. In choosing a group to attend, look for members who have an intense desire to be clean and who are actively working toward it.

Even in a well-functioning group, there is the danger of allowing the group to become the primary focus of one's recovery—taking the place that only the Lord can truly fill. Remember, all supports are only that—supports. Christ is the True Healer.

INTERNET FILTERS

Much attention has been given to the use of Internet filters, and much energy is sometimes focused on finding a filter that will block out all the undesirable sites, while allowing access to wholesome sites.

Advantages: Filters are an especially good idea in homes with children, to protect them from accidental exposure to harmful materials. In addition, a filter can be a helpful tool for the individual trying to overcome addiction, so long as it is not used in place of reliance on God. If the filter is used "unto God," it can be an excellent support to a recovery program.

Cautions: No filter program is perfect. A knowledgeable computer user can find ways around most filters. Indeed, the presence of a filter may only present a challenge to outsmart the program or the person who holds the password. If the addict has not truly surrendered his heart to the Lord in an honest attempt to become clean, he may very likely see the filter or the administrator as just another source of "drama" and adrenaline rush.

Relying on a filter to keep one sober also breaks down when one suddenly finds himself with unfiltered access to the Internet, such as at a public library, a university, at work, at a friend's home, or when someone forgot to turn on the filter at home. *A filter is only as good as the intentions of the addict.* In truth, the only sure filter is the one the Lord places in our heart when we surrender it to Him.

REPORTING SOFTWARE

Another approach similar to using a filter is to install software that sends an e-mail to some other person reporting all the Internet websites one has visited.

Advantages: Use of this software allows others to "look over your shoulder" while you are on your computer. It takes away the anonymity that makes surfing for pornography so inviting, allowing the addict to feel he has "gotten away with it." The software thus provides an avenue for the user to be accountable to someone else for his Internet use.

Cautions: While this approach may provide some temporary local support, it is borrowing strength from others instead of turning to the Lord for relief. In addition, it reinforces one's fear of man rather than fear of God. Since most addicts have a problem with codependency, this approach may be more harmful than helpful.

The same concerns expressed in regard to Internet filters apply here as well. The "protection" offered by the reporting software is limited to the computer on which it is installed.

PROFESSIONAL COUNSELORS OR THERAPISTS

Advantages: Addicts have a hard time seeing themselves accurately. They both minimize and exaggerate. They have often blinded themselves to the choices they make in the process of acting out, including the thoughts and attitudes they harbor. A counselor, who is trained to be an objective observer, can show the addict where they are making choices, and where they do indeed have agency when they think they do not. He or she can help a person recognize emotions and work though them, instead of turning to addiction.

In addition, counselors may also help people work through issues from other areas of their lives, such as marriage and family of origin issues. Many addicts share the heritage of a dysfunctional home life; help with these issues can be particularly needed. Since addiction warps our sense of intimacy, a good counselor can also help us gain an understanding of true intimacy.

In my opinion, the most helpful counselor is one who can help you apply the principles of the gospel, especially the Atonement of Jesus Christ, to the challenge of recovering from addiction and building a healthier life.

Cautions: In our culture, we are inclined to pay a lot of respect to authority figures and people with professional training and credentials. It may be of value to remember that counselors, like other mortals, have the potential to make mistakes. As a consumer of the counselor's professional services, you should ask yourself, "Does this counselor share, or at least respect, my religious beliefs and values? Does he or she strengthen or weaken my desire and ability to obey God's commandments? Does he or she look to God for guidance and encourage me to do the same?"

These are important issues, and if the first counselor you see does not share these values, you have a right (and an obligation to yourself) to look for one that does. **"Trust no one to be your teacher nor your minister, except he be a man of God, walking in his ways and keeping his commandments"** (Mosiah 23:14).

In addition, always remember that the Lord will confirm to you by His Spirit what is good counsel and what is not. Do not hesitate to pray about any counsel you receive that does not sound right to you. On the other hand, be careful about rejecting out-of-hand the counsel you receive just because it makes you uncomfortable. Many things we need to do in the process of recovery are uncomfortable. It is in trying to avoid legitimate pain that we have turned to addictive behaviors. With the reassurance of the Spirit, we can face any difficult task the Lord, through an inspired counselor, may put before us.

PRIESTHOOD RESOURCES

Advantages: There are two main reasons for turning to a bishop or stake president. The first is they are the "common judges in Israel," and as such, have the stewardship to vouch before the Lord that we are worthy to receive certain blessings in the Church, such as the privilege of attending the temple. We cannot completely repent of serious sins without confessing them to our bishop. Most sexual sins are in this category.

The second reason for consulting with the bishop is to receive help, counsel, support, teaching, comfort and encouragement. The bishop may also give priesthood blessings as part of his ministrations in our behalf.

Cautions: While all the ways a priesthood leader can help us are appropriate and God-given, *we cannot expect the bishop to be responsible in any way for our recovery.* We always retain our agency, and continue to have the responsibility to acknowledge the Lord in any healing we experience at anyone's hand. While the bishop can give inspired counsel and comfort, and even extend forgiveness on behalf of the Church, he, of himself, cannot heal. That is solely the mission of our Savior. The bishop helps us most when he helps us develop our relationship with our Lord, so we can find true healing from Him.

SUMMARY

The Lord has provided many ways to help us with our struggles. Some people tend to reject these helps, saying they are crutches. That's true, they *are* crutches. But the other half of the *whole* truth is that when you have a broken leg, you *need* crutches. Of course, we would be foolish to begin to believe that the crutches are what would heal our broken leg. They do not accomplish our recovery, but they give support while we are healing through the miraculous process the Lord has built into our bodies. The same principle applies to supports we may use in recovering from addiction. The Lord has provided these supports, and as long as we put our faith in Him first of all, and look to Him for "referrals," we have no need to feel reluctant or ashamed to use them. Still we must always remember Elder Richard G. Scott's testimony:

> Yet no matter what the source of difficulty and no matter how you begin to obtain relief—through a qualified professional therapist, doctor, priesthood leader, friend, concerned parent, or loved one—no matter how you begin, those solutions will never provide a complete answer. The final healing comes through faith in Jesus Christ and His teachings, with a broken heart and a contrite spirit and obedience to His commandments. (*Ensign*, May 1994, 9)

Appendix C

Helps for Holding Twelve Step Recovery Meetings

Contents of Appendix C

TWELVE STEP MEETING FORMAT

Each Twelve Step organization has its own meeting format, but here is a sample format that could be used or adapted by an unaffiliated group using the Twelve Steps. Before the meeting starts, members arrive and greet each other. Chairs are often arranged in a circle so members can more easily see each other during sharing.

1. Welcome.

2. Opening prayer. (Ask for volunteers since some members may not be comfortable offering public prayers.)

3. Introductions by first name only. Members may mention the addiction or challenge that brought them to the meeting, plus their length of abstinence. Avoid details, especially of sexual behavior.

4. Read the Twelve Steps. Two versions of the Twelve Steps of Heart t' Heart are included (p. 298): the bold type version, which is very close to AA's original steps; and the italicized version, which uses language from Book of Mormon verses. Heart t' Heart uses both versions, although the italicized version is used more frequently.

5. Read the Twelve Traditions, if your group uses them (p. 301).

6. Collect voluntary donations to cover cost of building or literature (if your group does this).

7. Sharing on the Tools of Recovery (p. 304).

8. Reading from scriptures or Twelve Step literature, such as this book, *Clean Hands, Pure Heart*, or *He Did Deliver Me from Bondage*.

9. Sharing. This can be done volunteer style, as in testimony meeting, or by going around the room, allowing each person to share or pass.

10. Reminder of anonymity. At close of each meeting, a simple reminder to keep everything that has been said confidential, thus preserving everyone's anonymity.

11. Closing prayer.

THE TWELVE STEPS OF HEART T' HEART

1. We admitted we were powerless over compulsive addictive behaviors*—that our lives had become unmanageable. *Admitted that we of ourselves are powerless, nothing without God. (Mosiah 4:5; Alma 26:12)*

2. Came to believe that a Power greater than ourselves could restore us to sanity. *Came to believe that God has all power and all wisdom and that in His strength we can do all things. (Mosiah 4:9; Alma 26:12)*

3. Made a decision to turn our will and our lives over to the care of God as we understood Him. *Made the decision to reconcile ourselves to the will of God, offer our whole souls as an offering unto Him, and trust Him in all things forever. (2 Nephi 10:24; Omni 1:26; Mosiah 3:19; 2 Nephi 4:34)*

4. Made a searching and fearless moral inventory of ourselves. *Made a searching and fearless written inventory of our past in order to thoroughly examine ourselves as to our pride and other weaknesses with the intent of recognizing our own carnal state and our need for Christ's Atonement. (Alma 15:17; Mosiah 4:2; Jacob 4:6–7; Ether 12:27)*

5. Admitted to God, to ourselves, and to another human being the exact nature of our wrongs. *Honestly shared this inventory with God and with another person, thus demonstrating the sincerity of our repentance, and our willingness to give away all our sins that we might know Him. (Mosiah 26:29; Alma 22:18)*

6. Were entirely ready to have God remove all these defects of character. *Became humble enough to yield our hearts and our lives to Christ for His sanctification and purification, relying wholly upon His merits, acknowledging even our own best efforts as unprofitable. (Helaman 3:35; 2 Nephi 31:19; Mosiah 2:20–21)*

7. Humbly asked Him to remove our shortcomings. *Humbly cried unto the Lord Jesus Christ in our hearts for a remission of sins that through His mercy and His grace we might experience a mighty change of heart, lose all disposition to do evil, and thus be encircled about in the arms of safety because of His great and last sacrifice. (Alma 36:18; Alma 38:8; Moroni 10:32; Mosiah 5:2; Alma 34:15–16)*

8. **Made a list of all persons we had harmed and became willing to make amends to them all.** *Made a list of all persons we had harmed and became willing to make restitution to all of them (even those we had harmed in what we might have considered righteous anger), desiring instead to be peacemakers and to do all that we could to come unto God by being first reconciled to others. (3 Nephi 12:9; 3 Nephi 12:24; 3 Nephi 12:44–45)*

9. **Made direct amends to such people wherever possible except when to do so would injure them or others.** *Made restitution directly to those we had harmed, confessing our own wrongdoing in each instance except when to do so would further injure them or others. (Mosiah 27:35; 3 Nephi 12:25; Mosiah 26:30)*

10. **Continued to take personal inventory and when we were wrong promptly admitted it.** *Realizing that the weakness to be tempted and to sin is a part of the mortal experience, we continued to take personal inventory and when we were wrong promptly admitted it, being willing to repent as often as needed. (2 Nephi 4:18; 2 Nephi 10:20; Mosiah 26:30)*

11. **Sought through prayer and meditation to improve our conscious contact with God as we understood Him, praying only for knowledge of His will for us and the power to carry that out.** *Sought through prayer and meditation to improve our conscious contact with God, seeking the words of Christ through the power of the Holy Ghost that they might tell us all things that we should do, praying only for a knowledge of His will for us and the power to carry that out. (2 Nephi 32:3; Alma 37:37; Helaman 10:4)*

12. **Having had a spiritual awakening as the result of these steps, we tried to carry this message to others still suffering from the effects of compulsive behaviors and to practice these principles in all our affairs.** *Having experienced a mighty change and having awakened unto God as a result of our sincere repentance demonstrated in taking these steps, we were willing to become instruments in carrying this message to others and to practice these principles in all our affairs. (Alma 5:7; Mosiah 27:36–37; Moroni 7:3)*

*Any problem may be inserted here, in place of "compulsive addictive behaviors."

Permission to use the Twelve Steps of Alcoholics Anonymous for adaptation granted by A.A. World Services, Inc.

Excerpted from the pamphlet, "The Twelve Steps of Heart t' Heart." Reprinted with permission from Heart t' Heart General Service Board.

THE TWELVE STEPS
OF ALCOHOLICS ANONYMOUS

1. We admitted we were powerless over alcohol—that our lives had become unmanageable.

2. Came to believe that a Power greater than ourselves could restore us to sanity.

3. Made a decision to turn our will and our lives over to the care of God as we understood Him.

4. Made a searching and fearless moral inventory of ourselves.

5. Admitted to God, to ourselves and to another human being the exact nature of our wrongs.

6. Were entirely ready to have God remove all these defects of character.

7. Humbly asked Him to remove our shortcomings.

8. Made a list of all persons we had harmed, and became willing to make amends to them all.

9. Made direct amends to such people wherever possible, except when to do so would injure them or others.

10. Continued to take personal inventory and when we were wrong promptly admitted it.

11. Sought through prayer and meditation to improve our conscious contact with God as we understood Him, praying only for knowledge of His will for us and the power to carry that out.

12. Having had a spiritual awakening as the result of these steps, we tried to carry this message to alcoholics, and to practice these principles in all our affairs.

THE TWELVE TRADITIONS OF HEART T' HEART

1. In Heart t' Heart individual recovery depends on the loving, supportive fellowship of the group. Without acceptance and unity there can be no fellowship and thus no recovery.

2. In Heart t' Heart there is only one ultimate authority—a loving God who manifests His will for each group in our prayerful group conscience. Our Heart t' Heart leaders are but trusted servants, they do not govern.

3. The only requirement for Heart t' Heart membership is a desire to stop participating in compulsive addictive behaviors.

4. Each Heart t' Heart group is autonomous within the guidelines of the steps and the traditions, encouraged only to practice these principles in all its decisions.

5. Each Heart t' Heart group has but one primary purpose—to carry its message of recovery from compulsive addictive behavior to those who still suffer.

6. A Heart t' Heart group ought never endorse, finance or lend the Heart t' Heart name to any outside publication or enterprise, lest problems of copyrights, money, property or prestige divert us from our primary purpose.

7. Every Heart t' Heart group ought to be fully self-supporting through voluntary donations from members only.

8. Heart t' Heart should remain forever non-professional, but our world service center may employ special workers.

9. Heart t' Heart, as such, ought never be organized. We may, however, create service boards or committees directly responsible to those they serve.

10. Heart t' Heart has no official opinion on any outside issue. Neither is its intent to promote any doctrine or policy contrary to the Church of Jesus Christ of Latter-day Saints. Hence, the Heart t' Heart name ought never be drawn into any controversy, the opinions expressed being simply those of the individuals who share them.

11. Our public relations policy is based on attraction, rather than promotion. We need always maintain the spiritual foundation of personal anonymity, acknowledging that all recovery comes through dedication to the principles of the program.

12. Personal anonymity is the spiritual foundation of all our traditions—ever reminding us that this program is focused on principles and not personalities.

The Heart t' Heart Traditions are included for the convenience of Heart t' Heart and other Twelve Step groups that choose to use them. Excerpted from the pamphlet, "The Twelve Traditions of Heart t' Heart." Reprinted with permission from Heart t' Heart General Service Board.

Permission to use the Twelve Traditions of Alcoholics Anonymous for adaptation granted by A.A. World Services, Inc.

THE TWELVE TRADITIONS
OF ALCOHOLICS ANONYMOUS

1. Our common welfare should come first; personal recovery depends upon A.A. unity.

2. For our group purpose, there is but one ultimate authority—a loving God as He may express Himself in our group conscience. Our leaders are but trusted servants; they do not govern.

3. The only requirement for A.A. membership is a desire to stop drinking.

4. Each group should be autonomous except in matters affecting other groups or A.A. as a whole.

5. Each group has but one primary purpose—to carry its message to the alcoholic who still suffers.

6. An A.A. group ought never endorse, finance, or lend the A.A. name to any related facility or outside enterprise, lest problems of money, property and prestige divert us from our primary purpose.

7. Every A.A. group ought to be fully self-supporting, declining outside contributions.

8. Alcoholics Anonymous should remain forever non-professional, but our service centers may employ special workers.

9. A.A., as such, ought never be organized; but we may create service boards or committees directly responsible to those they serve.

10. Alcoholics Anonymous has no opinion on outside issues; hence, the A.A. name ought never be drawn into public controversy.

11. Our public relations policy is based on attraction, rather than promotion; we need always maintain personal anonymity at the level of press, radio and film.

12. Anonymity is the spiritual foundation of all our traditions, ever reminding us to place principles before personalities.

GUIDELINES FOR TWELVE STEP MEETINGS

ANONYMITY is absolutely vital to the survival of a group. This concept should constantly remind us that we are not in these meetings to learn "juicy" facts about others. There must be absolutely no gossip in this fellowship. We come together to help bear one another's burdens, not to increase them with judgment or backbiting.

Often in sharing we feel a need to express the hurts and fears we keep inside, to free ourselves from the blame and shame that are often carry-overs from the past. Anonymity gives us the freedom to do that.

CROSS TALK/SIDE TALK is discouraged in group meetings. This means we neither interrupt nor engage in dialogue with another speaker. Twelve Step meetings are not designed to be encounter groups or advice giving sessions of any sort. Commenting or giving advice discourages the individual's own ability to hear the Truth as spoken to their hearts directly by the Spirit **(2 Nephi 32:3).**

SEVENTH TRADITION COLLECTIONS are the sole support of most Twelve Step groups. Traditionally a cup or basket is passed at every meeting, inviting but not requiring donations.

PRAYER IN MEETINGS has been a tradition since the beginning of A.A. Twelve Step meetings generally use set memorized prayers, such as the Serenity Prayer. These prayers were chosen because of their acceptability to the general public. In our group meetings we are free to open and close our meetings in the manner we are familiar with—personal, spontaneous prayer guided by the Spirit.

Excerpted from the pamphlet, "The Twelve Traditions of Heart t' Heart." Reprinted with permission from Heart t' Heart General Service Board.

SUGGESTED TOOLS FOR RECOVERY

As a help in working the Twelve Steps and Twelve Traditions, participants in other Twelve Step groups have found the following tools to be of great assistance in their recovery. To be useful, a tool must be picked up and used. Not every recovering person uses every tool listed below. Those who do use them, do not always use each of the tools every day. However, we have found that the more tools we can use on a consistent, daily basis, the greater our potential for staying in recovery. Remember, the tools are not a replacement for the principles found in the Twelve Steps.

ABSTINENCE

Abstinence, simply defined, is the action of refraining from our compulsive behaviors, whatever they may be. Abstinence is a personal matter between ourselves and God. It will differ from person to person, even if their compulsions are the same.

Abstinence has been said to be both a tool of the program and a result. To be "physically" abstinent, to abstain from our compulsive behavior, is a tool because it helps us to honestly face our feelings, rather than resort to our compulsion to distract or comfort us.

There is also a dimension of abstinence that goes far beyond the physical realm. This is the spiritual gift of a complete loss of our desire to do our compulsive behavior. This gift comes as a result of applying the steps and their underlying principles in our lives. For some of us this gift comes quickly, and for others, it comes more slowly, but it does come to all.

ANONYMITY (CONFIDENTIALITY)

In many Twelve Step programs, anonymity (or confidentiality) is called the spiritual foundation of a recovery program. This tool reminds us that the focus in our recovery is on the principles and NOT the people in the group.

Anonymity assures us safety in the freedom of expression of our innermost thoughts and feelings without the worry of gossip or retaliation. We come together in our support groups to bear one another's burdens, not to increase them with judgement or backbiting. Our sharing must be received with respect and kept in confidence.

Anonymity does not mean we cannot share ideas and principles discussed in the meetings, only that identities not be attached to them.

Anonymity also reminds us that all are equal in these groups. There are no prescribed leaders or "gurus" within the group and outside status makes no difference. We all gather here to acknowledge our common humanity.

LITERATURE AND MUSIC

Literature is used to help us more fully understand our path to recovery and to reinforce the use of the Twelve Steps. It gives us the ability to have a meeting with just ourselves when we are not able to reach out and connect with others in recovery. We especially recommend the daily use of the scriptures, as demonstrated in this workbook. Some people have also found other Twelve Step program literature helpful.

It has been said that music is a powerful way to speak God's language, to praise Him and to express our deepest feelings to God and to others. It can be felt inside our hearts or performed aloud for others to enjoy. Listening to inspired music is both comforting and healing to our souls.

Hymns can be particularly healing. According to the 1985 LDS Church hymn book, "hymns invite the Spirit of the Lord... move us to repentance and good works, build testimony and faith, comfort the weary, console the mourning, and inspire us to endure to the end" (p.ix). These attributes correlate directly to Twelve Step principles.

MEETINGS

Meetings are an opportunity to come together to share our experience, strength, and hope. They are a way of providing ourselves with the fellowship of others who have finally decided to acknowledge personal powerlessness over one or more compulsive addictive behaviors in their own life or the life of a loved one, and who are seeking a God-centered solution.

PRAYER AND MEDITATION

Prayer and meditation are two sides of the same coin and are probably the most vital to recovery of all the tools. The whole focus and purpose of the Twelve Steps is to bring us closer to God. Communication between parties is critical to establishing a two-way relationship, and no relationship is more important than the one we have with our Savior, Jesus Christ. In honest prayer we share the intimacies of our heart. In quiet, sincere meditation He shares His will for us.

SERVICE

Service is a way of getting out of our compulsive behavior and into recovery. Sharing the message of recovery through faith in Jesus Christ and the application of the Twelve Steps is the most obvious form of service we can perform. However, any act of service will move us further into recovery. Going to meetings, sharing, listening to others share, talking to newcomers, and telephoning others between meetings are all acts of service that will enhance our recovery.

SPONSORING

When a person goes to a foreign country, they will often be met by a sponsor someone who knows the customs and practices of the country and will assist the new person in getting oriented. Sponsoring in Heart t' Heart works the same way. A sponsor is someone who is living the Twelve Steps to the best of his or her ability. Sponsors generally have more experience in the program and have maintained some level of recovery.

It is recommended that we ask someone to be our sponsor soon after coming into the program. We listen to the sharing and to the Spirit and then choose someone with whom we feel we share a common bond. Or we take down the name and phone number of someone who has checked the sponsor column on the "We Care" list. Sponsoring may develop into a long term friendship or it may be temporary. It is perfectly acceptable to have more than one sponsor at the same time so that we can be sure of reaching someone when we are in need.

TELEPHONING

In other Twelve Step groups, we are encouraged to use the telephone as a means of breaking through our isolation and getting back on the road to recovery. Using the telephone to call others has been compared to having a meeting between meetings. It's a tool we can use any time we need to talk about our feelings and experiences, whether it be before, during, or after engaging in our compulsive behavior.

We encourage you to begin building a personal phone list that you can keep in a convenient place and use to reach out to others. A page has been provided for that purpose. (308)

WRITING

Those who are most successful in recovery use the tool of writing frequently. Unspoken, unacknowledged feelings, whether positive or negative, are often the source of our need to "use" the reason we begin our compulsive addictive behaviors. Writing is a way of bringing our feelings to the surface and exploring them. Many people find that they do not realize what their true feelings really are until they see them in front of them in black and white. Once on paper, these thoughts and feelings can be acknowledged, and a solution to the problem can be found.

Writing can also be used as a means of communicating with God, as we write the prayers of our hearts and then record what we feel the Spirit reveal to us.

Excerpted and adapted from the pamphlet, "The Nine Tools of Heart t' Heart." Reprinted with permission of Heart t' Heart General Service Board. These tools are included in this book for the convenience of Heart t' Heart and other Twelve Step groups who choose to use them.

"WE CARE" LIST

Using the telephone or e-mail to contact others is a means of breaking through our isolation and getting back on the road to recovery. It has been compared to having a meeting between meetings. I encourage you to use this page to begin building a personal phone list that you can use to reach out to others.

Name	Phone	E-mail

Appendix D

Resources for Recovery

None of us travels the road to recovery without a lot of help. There are many books, articles and organizations available, and a complete list would simply be overwhelming. I have listed a few here to help you continue your study.

BOOKS

He Did Deliver Me from Bondage by Colleen C. Harrison. Revised edition. Pleasant Grove: Windhaven Recovery, Inc. dba Windhaven Publishing and Productions (www.windhavenpublishing.com), 2002. *In-depth examination of the Twelve Steps from the perspective of the Book of Mormon. This landmark book has been the springboard for the LDS Twelve Step movement. Distributed by Rosehaven Publishing, 888-790-7040, website: www.rosehavenpublishing.com.*

Patterns of Light by Colleen C. Harrison. Pleasant Grove: Windhaven Recovery, Inc. dba Windhaven Publishing and Productions (www.windhavenpublishing.com), 2002. *Individual booklets on each of the Twelve Steps, relating them to passages from the Book of Mormon and original literature of Alcoholics Anonymous. Distributed by Rosehaven Publishing, 888-790-7040, website: www.rosehavenpublishing.com.*

Sexaholics Anonymous (The SA White Book). Nashville: SA Literature, 1989. Also available through Heart t' Heart, www.heart-t-heart.org.

Recovery Continues. Nashville: SA Literature, 1990. Also available through Heart t' Heart, www.heart-t-heart.org.

Alcoholics Anonymous (AA Big Book). Fourth Edition, New and Revised. New York: Alcoholics Anonymous, 2001. Also available through Heart t' Heart, www.heart-t-heart.org.

Twelve Steps and Twelve Traditions. New York: The A.A. Grapevine, Inc. and Alcoholics Anonymous, 1981. Also available through Heart t' Heart, www.heart-t-heart.org.

Willpower Is Not Enough: Why We Don't Succeed at Change by A. Dean Boyd and Mark D. Chamberlain. Salt Lake City: Deseret Book Co., 1995.

Wanting More: The Challenge of Enjoyment in the Age of Addiction by Mark D. Chamberlain. Salt Lake City: Deseret Book Co., 2000.

The Worth of a Soul by Steven A. Cramer (Gerald Curtis). Cedar Fort: Cedar Fort Inc., 1983.

The Worth of Every Soul by Gerald and LoAnne Curtis. Cedar Fort: Cedar Fort Inc., 2004.

Conquering Your Own Goliaths by Steven A. Cramer. Salt Lake City: Deseret Book Co., 1988.

Sacred Intimacy by Brenton and Margaret Yorgason. Cedar Fort: Cedar Fort Inc., 2004.

Codependents' Guide to the Twelve Steps by Melody Beattie. New York: Prentice Hall/Parkside Recovery, 1990.

GENERAL CONFERENCE TALKS/ *ENSIGN* ARTICLES

There are so many wonderful talks given in General Conference. Each time conference is held, I marvel at how many talks address the principles of recovery. Here are only a sampling of some of the talks that have helped me:

Ezra Taft Benson, "Cleansing the Inner Vessel," *Ensign*, May 1986, 4

Ezra Taft Benson, "Beware of Pride," *Ensign*, May 1989, 4

Ezra Taft Benson, "Born of God," *Ensign*, July 1989, 2

James E. Faust, "That We Might Know Thee," *Ensign*, Jan. 1999, 2

James E. Faust, "It Can't Happen to Me," *Ensign*, May 2002, 46

Robert D. Hales, "Out of Darkness into His Marvelous Light," *Ensign*, May 2002, 69

Gordon B. Hinckley, "Our Mission of Saving," *Ensign*, Nov. 1991, 52

Jeffrey R. Holland, "Sanctify Yourselves," *Ensign*, Nov. 2000, 38

Neal A. Maxwell, "Apply the Atoning Blood of Christ," *Ensign*, Nov. 1997, 22

Neal A. Maxwell, "Notwithstanding My Weakness," *Ensign*, Nov. 1976, 12

Neal A. Maxwell, "Swallowed Up in the Will of the Father," *Ensign*, Nov. 1995, 22

Boyd K. Packer, "The Brilliant Morning of Forgiveness," *Ensign*, Nov. 1995, 18

Boyd K. Packer, "Washed Clean," *Ensign*, May 1997, 9

Boyd K. Packer, "The Touch of the Master's Hand," *Ensign*, May 2001, 22

Richard G. Scott, "To Be Free of Heavy Burdens," *Ensign*, Nov. 2002, 86

Richard G. Scott, "To Be Healed," *Ensign*, May 1994, 7

Richard G. Scott, "Learning to Recognize Answers to Prayer," *Ensign*, Nov. 1989, 30

Robert L. Simpson, "Pollution of the Mind," *Ensign*, Jan. 1973, 112

ORGANIZATIONS

There are Twelve Step groups designed specifically for LDS people, such as Heart t' Heart, as well as groups organized by LDS Family Services or by local priesthood leaders. In some areas, chapters of Sexaholics Anonymous have been specially organized for LDS people.

LDS–ORIENTED ORGANIZATIONS

Heart t' Heart, P.O. Box 247, Pleasant Grove, UT, 84062; website: www.heart-t-heart.org

LDS Family Services Addiction Recovery Program. For information on these groups, contact your local LDS Family Services agency. Some groups are listed at www.ldsmentalhealth.org.

Evergreen International Inc. (support group for those struggling with same sex attraction), 211 East 300 South, Suite 206, Salt Lake City, UT 84111 website: www.evergreen-intl.org

NON–LDS ORGANIZATIONS

Sexaholics Anonymous, (615) 370-6062, P.O. Box 3565 Brentwood, TN 37024, website: www.sa.org

Alcoholics Anonymous, Grand Central Station, P.O. Box 459, New York, N.Y. 10163, website: www.aa.org

INDEX

—NOTES—

ABOUT THE AUTHOR

Philip A. Harrison was raised in Provo, Utah. He was married to Kathy Francis for almost 29 years before she passed away from heart disease. Phil and Kathy are the parents of 5 children. In keeping with family academic traditions, Phil graduated from BYU with bachelor's and master's degrees in botany, then from the University of Georgia in Athens with a Ph.D., also in botany, with an emphasis in plant physiology. He currently conducts research on plant storage carbohydrates.

Following graduate school, Phil and Kathy lived in upstate New York and California before returning to Utah, where for 15 years they led workshops in the "Inner Peace Through Self-Mastery" program (an LDS-oriented adaptation of Recovery Inc., a cognitive therapy approach to emotional health). Kathy had 25 years of experience in Twelve Step work, and passed away only 5 months after discovering the LDS-oriented Twelve Step program, Heart t' Heart. Following Kathy's passing, Phil married Colleen, Heart t' Heart's founder and author of *He Did Deliver Me from Bondage,* herself a mother of 12 children.

A life-long member of the Church of Jesus Christ of Latter-day Saints, Phil served a mission to Germany and has taught priesthood classes, Gospel Doctrine, Family Relations and teen classes in Sunday School. He served as Elder's Quorum president in Georgia, New York and California, and has directed ward and stake choirs. He is currently the high priest group leader in his ward. Phil and Colleen live with their (Colleen's) youngest daughter, two cats and four horses in Hyrum, Utah. You may write to Phil at: Philip A. Harrison, c/o Windhaven Publishing and Productions, P. O. Box 31, Hyrum, UT 84319

Order Form

To order additional copies of *Clean Hands, Pure Heart* and other Windhaven products, send this order form along with check or money order in US dollars to:

Rosehaven, P.O. Box 247, Pleasant Grove, UT 84062

OR order online at www.rosehavenpublishing.com

ITEM	PRICE	X	QTY.	=	TOTAL
Clean Hands, Pure Heart, Philip A. Harrison	$17.95*	X	_____	=	_____
He Did Deliver Me from Bondage, Colleen C. Harrison	$14.95*	X	_____	=	_____
A Voice from the Fire, Colleen C. Harrison	$11.95*	X	_____	=	_____
Patterns of Light: Step 1, Colleen C. Harrison	$3.50*	X	_____	=	_____
Patterns of Light: Step 2, Colleen C. Harrison	$3.50*	X	_____	=	_____
Patterns of Light: Step 3, Colleen C. Harrison	$3.50*	X	_____	=	_____
Patterns of Light: Steps 4&5, Colleen C. Harrison	$3.50*	X	_____	=	_____

Subtotal _____

Sales Tax: Add 6.25% for books shipped to Utah address _____

Shipping: 15% of Subtotal, minimum $3.00 in U.S. only
Canada/Overseas, call for rates. _____

Total Enclosed _____

Please Print:

Date: _____ Phone: (_____) _____

Name: _____

Address: _____

City, ST, ZIP _____

Copy this page as needed for orders. If Ship-To address is different than above, please note on back. Credit card orders may be placed online at www.rosehavenpublishing.com or by phone at 888.790.7040 or by fax at 801.796.0923

* Prices subject to change without notice.